Tepoztlán and the Transformation of the Mexican State

Tepoztlán and the Transformation of the Mexican State

The Politics of Loose Connections

JoAnn Martin

The University of Arizona Press

Tucson

The University of Arizona Press
© 2005 The Arizona Board of Regents
♾ This book is printed on acid-free, archival-quality paper.
Manufactured in the United States of America
10 09 08 07 06 05   6 5 4 3 2 1

Library of Congress Cataloging-in-Publication Data
Martin, JoAnn, 1955–
Tepoztlán and the transformation of the Mexican state :
the politics of loose connections / JoAnn Martin.
p. cm.
Includes bibliographical references and index.
ISBN-13: 978-0-8165-2443-3 (hardcover : alk. paper)
ISBN 10: 0-8165-2443-2 (hardcover: alk. paper)
1. Ethnology—Mexico—Tepoztlán. 2. Political anthro-
pology—Mexico—Tepoztlán. 3. Land reform—Mexico
—Tepoztlán. 4. Tepoztlán (Mexico)—Politics and
government. 5. Tepoztlán (Mexico)—History. 6. Tepoztlán
(Mexico)—Social life and customs. I. Title.
GN560.M6M37 2005
306.2′0972′49—dc22
2005005385

Publication of this book is made possible in part by the
proceeds of a permanent endowment created with
the assistance of a Challenge Grant from the National
Endowment for the Humanities, a federal agency.

In memory of my father,
Charles Martin

Contents

Preface

This book has been ten years in the writing and even longer in the research. One clear consequence of extending the process so long is that it is not easy to give up this book, for it has been a constant companion, providing a safe haven from the stresses of academic employment, the pain of losing a beloved parent, and the joys of having and raising a child. In writing this book, my own thinking has undergone a number of changes that are themselves reflective of the movement of social thought. My early work on it theorized the obstacles to organizing social movements by examining the power, both real and imagined, of the Mexican state. At that time, I was influenced by the writings of Althusser and Gramsci. Later, I became enamored with the possibility of accounting for Tepoztecan politics as situationally shaped, almost without the weight of any historical antecedents. Suspicious that concepts of totality led to static understandings of social movements, I tried to highlight the possibilities for change that emerge when political actors creatively seize opportunities. The present version of the book has been shaped by Judith Butler's criticisms of identity politics and unity in *Gender Trouble* (1999) and by Julie Stephens's writings on antidisciplinary protest. Both authors helped me to think differently about the kind of "trouble" presented by those who remain on the margins of Tepoztecan social movements. Butler's observation that if making trouble is inevitable, the task is to determine "how best to make it" (Butler 1999:xxvii) captures my own sense of reading the politics of loose connections. As I argue in this text, scholars of social movements need to attend to those on the periphery of social movements who participate while holding back, troubling the calls for unity that shape social movements. At the same time, this book seeks to do justice to calls for unity, recognizing that those who make trouble for unity may also be drawn to the seductive power of discourses of unity.

The fact that this book has been rewritten so many times testifies to the impossibility of ever arriving at closure in ethnographic analysis. It also points to the healthy dialogue between theory and the constructions we call ethnographic data. When theory is appropriated in an act of cultural translation, it becomes enlivened with possibilities that never emerge in the pure space of theory (Butler 1999:ix). At the same time, the transformations in social thought reveal continually changing possibilities for translation. Indeed, I can envision further versions of this book. Were I to rewrite it now, I would deploy a writing style that would enable the reader to experience for herself or himself the passionate pull of visions of unity in Tepoztlán. Such an approach might better serve the demand to reenchant the world once it has been deconstructed, something I think Piya Chatterjee does quite well in her book *A Time for Tea* (2001). Also, I would attend more closely to the persons, events, and performances in Tepoztlán that provided their own deconstruction of categories of gender, race, class, age, and residency, which appear only sporadically throughout this book. Mary Weismantel's *Cholas and Pishtacos* (2001) provides numerous examples of the way deconstruction can be accomplished in clothing styles, language use, and the performances of everyday life.

After returning to Tepoztlán in the summer of 2002, I made a change in this text that is in many ways the most fundamental. I had originally chosen to do my research in Tepoztlán to take advantage of the works of Robert Redfield, Oscar Lewis, and Claudio Lomnitz to bring a deep historical perspective to my analysis. Soon after my arrival in Tepoztlán in 1984, however, I became concerned about the political implications of my research and promised those with whom I worked in the field that I would not use their names or the town's name. This decision, more than any others, has been responsible for the delay in publication of this book. It is almost impossible to write a description that does justice to a place while disguising its location when it is as well known as Tepoztlán. Moreover, as Tepoztecan organizing became more successful, my efforts to disguise the name of the town ran into several problems. Because of my concerns not to place any of my informants in jeopardy, I found that I could not speak out publicly on issues that affected the town. Thus, in

1992 and later in 1995, when Tepoztecans engaged in political struggles that garnered international media attention, I remained silent, refraining from helping in an effort to do no harm—despite the fact that several Tepoztecans assumed that I should be able to assist them in some way. Then, in 1998, Gerardo Demesa Padilla, with whom I had worked closely during my fieldwork, published his own book after serving more than two years in prison on trumped-up charges of homicide. His arrest and the charges were connected to Tepoztlán's fight against a multi-billion-dollar golf course to be constructed on land that had been in dispute since the 1960s. In addition, several other residents of Tepoztlán, with whom I had not worked, published books on the town's battle over the golf course.

These books placed me in an awkward position. I had to ignore the writings of those from Tepoztlán or reveal the name of the place where I had done my research. In the summer of 2002, I traveled to Tepoztlán both to do more research and to talk with those most likely to be affected were I to use the town's name. Many of my informants from the 1980s had died or moved, but I did talk with those who continued to live in the town and to remain politically active. With their help and encouragement, I decided to publish the book using the community's name. I have continued to use pseudonyms for individuals, but by using the town's name, I have been able to incorporate more of the town's history as well as others' work on Tepoztlán.

When I first went to Tepoztlán in 1984, the ghost of Oscar Lewis followed me throughout my research. I talked with people who remembered him and was continually confronted by the specter of his work. He had, I was told, deceived the town by writing about their gossip and presenting the community in a bad light. In addition, he is said to have shown the children inappropriate pictures (his Rorschach tests were understood as pornographic pictures), and he had never given anything back to the town. I mention this not to impugn Oscar Lewis's name, but to outline some of the tensions I felt at the time about using Tepoztlán's name and now feel about revealing where I did my research. As the reader will note, gossip plays a central role in the politics of loose connections, and my stay in Tepoztlán did not convince me that Oscar Lewis had done a disservice to the town in his representation of it. At the same time, however, I think my interpretation puts that gossip in a different light than did Oscar Lewis's analysis. Moreover, it makes sense of the discrepancies between Lewis's and Redfield's interpretations of the town. In this work, Tepoztecan gossip emerges as the underbelly of the high value placed on unity, something Redfield underscored, and those who gossip are shown to have played a pivotal role in defending the town from the state. In short, rather than viewing gossip as a social pathology, I view it as a creative act of resistance nurtured in encounters with the structures of the Mexican state that have shaped a kind of *habitus* of political participation. I hope Tepoztecans who read this book recognize that I have found in their own political practices something of a model for contemporary social movements.

It would be impossible to thank all the Tepoztecans who in one way or another contributed to this research and who have since become close friends. Members of the Comité para la Defensa de Tierra (Committee to Defend Communal Land) tolerated my presence even when it made them uneasy. I hope that they can pardon my intrusive presence. Women in the Mujeres Tepoztecanas inspired me with their bravery and never hesitated to impart their wisdom about marriage, childbirth, and family relations. The families of don Estanislau Ayala and don José Flores provided me not only with a place to live and delicious meals, but hours of warm and jovial conversation.

My read of Tepoztecan politics owes a great debt to Laura Nader, who was my advisor while I was a graduate student at the University of California, Berkeley. She challenges all her students to be attentive to the kind of practical knowledge that one encounters in the field and has little patience for theoretical abstractions that speak more to trends in thought than they do to the field reality. Given as I am to theoretical abstractions, she was for me the perfect intellectual interlocutor, allowing me to venture as far afield from ethnography as I wanted while challenging me to remain grounded in the tradition of anthropology. Her writings on her own fieldwork in Mexico alerted me to key ideas that inform my own work, such as the idea of politics having a style and the deployment of strategies to resist state control. Most important, Laura Nader recognizes the theoretical voice not merely as the property of intellectuals, but as something that shapes the way her informants in the field think about the world. Indeed, her suggestion that trends in anthropological thought have been shaped in part by how the subjects of ethnography try to represent themselves to the outside world locates ethnographic projects squarely within the domain of the politics of representation, a concern that has also shaped this text.

In addition to Laura Nader, I worked with Stanley Brandes on anthropology and Richard Salvucci on history. Stanley Brandes's influence in this text is reflected in my ability to find in Tepoztecan politics a performance in which ironic humor figures prominently. I took politics very seriously then, but Stanley's attention to the lighter, although no less serious, side of life shaped my thinking about my data. Richard Salvucci, although never completely happy with my theoretical approaches to history, enlivened my interest in Mexican history and challenged my often far too facile interpretations of Mexican history. And I would never have found my way to anthropology were it not for Phil Parnell's encouragement and support.

Graduate school is fortunately not the end of one's intellectual life. At the University of the Pacific, my colleague Longina Jakubowska helped me to see that the focus on anthropology's role in colonialism has erased another history of anthropology: that of its place in the construction of nationalism. Her ideas helped shape my thinking about Manuel Gamio's place in the construction of Mexican nationalism, which is discussed in chapter 2. At Earlham College (Richmond, Indiana), Jonathan Diskin challenged me to think a kind of postmodern Marxism, and he read and commented on earlier versions of the manuscript. Ferit Güven has become an intellectual soul mate over the past few years; hours of challenging intellectual discussion with him lay behind many of the ideas in this book. I thank Earlham College for nurturing the kinds of collegial relations that cross disciplinary boundaries so that an economist, a philosopher, and an anthropologist can enter into intellectual dialogues. My colleague Debra Jackson read and commented on the introduction and did not spare her editor's insights in the process. This book surely would not have been completed without Elizabeth Kesling's hard work and Annie Barva's remarkable editing. Allyson Carter of the University of Arizona Press has been a patient yet persistent acquiring editor. I thank her for all her support. At Earlham, Cheri Gaddis and Patty Ferriel helped to get the manuscript out on time and organized me in the process.

Money for research and for writing this book came from a Kellogg Institute Fellowship and from travel and research grants from the University of the Pacific and Earlham College.

My mother, Mabel Martin, provided hours of childcare so that I could work on this book. Without her stubborn support of my intellectual abilities, I undoubtedly would not have found my way to an academic career. I attribute to my father, Charles Martin, my interest in anthropology, for he had a great curiosity about the world and a knack for transcending the often divisive lines of class, race, age, education, and gender.

My husband, Wenyi Wu, has encouraged me in this project. His cheerful, friendly demeanor and his appreciation for architecture introduced me to a completely different dimension of Tepoztlán. Stories still circulate there about his failed attempts to make tortillas and his good humor and charm at finding that he could not do so. I am sure many Tepoztecans are now even more convinced that such skills are genetic. Most important, he softened the blow of so many hours of work on this book by being there for our son, Kailin. I thank Kailin for his wonderful companionship when we traveled to Tepoztlán in 2002.

Tepoztlán and the Transformation of
the Mexican State

Chapter 1

The Politics of Loose Connections

Despite the clearly democratizing impulse that motivates coalition building, the coalitional theorist can inadvertently reinsert herself as sovereign of the process by trying to assert an ideal form for coalitional structures *in advance,* one that will effectively guarantee unity as the outcome.
—Judith Butler, *Gender Trouble*

In the 1980s, Mexico experienced an economic crisis that doubled prices in the market places, devalued the currency, and produced cuts in social spending that affected the poorest of the poor. Popular movements emerged to protest a government that under the tutelage of the World Bank and International Monetary Fund (IMF) doggedly pursued privatization and ended government subsidies. The historic pact that had ensured the nation's stability seemed to be crumbling. The *políticos* of the ruling Partido Revolucionario Institucional (PRI, Institutional Revolutionary Party) who had effectively contained popular movements since the 1930s were being replaced by "technocrats" with economic policies seemingly better suited to an advanced industrialized nation.

This book examines how popular movements found fresh footing in this new political-economic landscape. In 1984, I traveled to Tepoztlán, Morelos, made famous in anthropology by the studies of Oscar Lewis (1951) and Robert Redfield (1930). I had learned that Tepoztlán was reclaiming its communal land and that members of this movement were well organized. I wondered what a study of such a movement might reveal about the Mexican state's handling of opposition movements. Would I find yet another case of the state's amply documented ability to co-opt opposition movements, or might I find that in the context of

Mexico's economic crisis, the state's ability to respond to such movements was weakened? Might the existence of this movement and others like it portend the development of a larger, more unified struggle to challenge the state and the PRI? What ties if any might the movement form with left-leaning parties? As often happens with such research, the answers to these questions turned out to be less clear-cut than I had hoped, and my research took me in directions that I could not have anticipated at the time.

Since 1984, I have returned to Tepoztlán several times: in 1988, again in 1991, in 1999, and most recently for a brief visit in 2002 to follow up on Tepoztecans' fight against a multi-million-dollar tourist project. Over the more than fifteen years covered by this research, I observed a metamorphosis of a movement modeled initially on a conception of revolutionary popular struggle into what I term a *politics of loose connections.* Temporary alliances, flexibly chosen identities, and shifting political rhetoric seemed to be opportunistically yet passionately adapted to the demands of the moment. This politics of loose connections proved well suited to participation in global social movements when Tepoztecans discovered the value of allies at the global level. From then on, their movement remained rooted in local conditions while leaping "immediately to the global level" in order to wage struggles that were "biopolitical" in the sense of being focused on the "form of life" (Hardt and Negri 2000:56).

The Politics of Loose Connections

The term *politics of loose connections* describes a style of political engagement that resonates with scholarly descriptions of what have been termed *new social movements.*[1] However, the term *loose connections* draws attention to questions overshadowed by attempts to distinguish between different types of movements. Indeed, many movements that might violate the "new" social movement paradigm may also deploy the practices of loose connections.[2] The questions that I ask of the politics of loose connections ultimately have to do with the nature of the social field in which such a politics develops and with the institutional and cultural outcomes of political practices built around fragile and temporary unities.

My own first insights into the politics of loose connections came when I read Arturo Warman's (1980) depiction of the Mexican Revolution in the state of Morelos in his book *We Come to Object*. Warman describes revolutionary fighters taking up arms against an *hacendado*, but then returning to work for the same hacendado the next day, switching generals because of personal antagonisms or giving up the struggle altogether.[3] I was struck at the time by how different Warman's depiction of the revolution was from theories of revolution. Yet the revolution persisted, leaving behind, if not the society envisioned by Emiliano Zapata, the constitutional guarantees of land that enlivened the next seventy years of land conflicts in Mexico. The roots of a politics of loose connection also lay outside of Mexico's geographic boundaries, however. The contemporary global world, characterized by the unprecedented impacts of media and migration, fosters the rapid adoption of identities and the fragility of connections (Appadurai 1996). Moreover, as neophyte global political actors attempt to find their footing in global movements, strategies of loose connections emerge in response to mistrust fostered by the history of enforced colonialism and so-called modernization that have shaped the experiences of all concerned. Unity is surely a goal—or, perhaps more accurately, a desire—of contemporary movements, but so too is the need to make connections with exits clearly marked.[4]

In drawing attention to the politics of loose connections, this book rescues the question of a political project from the ashes of modernist conceptions of social movements. It is concerned with political connections as an element of style: their fleeting nature, their relation to structures of power and domination, and their relationship to other kinds of connections. Contemporary scholars view style as a semiotic system that consciously or unconsciously expresses relations to structures of domination and power (Hebdige 1997) A politics of loose connections clearly expresses relations to structures of domination, but my interest in style revolves as well around two other related dimensions of style: homology and historicity. *Homology* refers to the orderliness that underlies even the most seemingly chaotic forms of style (Hebdige 1997:137). It is the property that makes a style recognizable and distinguishable from other styles. *Historicity* refers to the way styles change through time and in relationship to larger processes of social transformation (Mercer 1997). Taken together, these two dimensions of style enable an analysis of the subtle shifts in political practices that have taken place as Mexico has been incorporated into a global political world. What possibilities emerge through a politics of loose connections, and how are these possibilities related to a political world in transformation? Can it be that the politics of loose connections enjoys advantages foreclosed by more demanding styles of political participation? Even if we grant that a unitary capitalist project has given birth to contemporary fragmentation (see Benería and Roldan 1987; D. Harvey 1990), we gain little if we confine ourselves to endless repetitions of that thesis without raising questions concerning how movements manage to organize themselves within this new terrain.

Although the concept of style is most often used in relation to cultural products such as fashion, music, and art, my extension of the concept to political practices is inspired in part by Laura Nader's work on dispute resolution. Drawing on the writings of Alfred Kroeber, Nader defined style as the "continuous features that permeate court activities and constitute the form and manner of the court" (1969:70). She found style in the details of court proceedings, including the timing of responses, the use of physical mannerisms, the length of proceedings, and the manner of invoking authority. She argues that these details cohered around a theme of "balance" that could be related to underlying values. In later work, she notes that the style of conflict resolution that she had earlier analyzed as an expression of values can also be viewed as a tactical response to experiences of domination during the colonial period (Nader 1990).

The politics of loose connections is above all else a *style* of political participation that has proved adaptive in the contemporary political landscape, which includes media and migration as twin forces of globalization (Appadurai 1996). "Loose connections" are not failed alliances, but a set of strategies for maintaining connections that speak to discursive demands for integrity in the political process. To keep one's alliances loose means to be ready at any moment to sacrifice those alliances in the name of other commitments, such as those to community, family, or self, or to abstract moral principles such as honesty. At the same time, "loose connections" speaks to an ability to connect with other movements, viewed not so much as a folding into but as a form of "playful world travel" (Lugones 1997:149) in which political struggles emerge through a kaleidoscope of possibilities. In this process of connecting, the dense social significance of any given issue—or, in Althusser's term (1970), its "overdetermined" quality—emerges. For example, in political struggles, land can be evoked simultaneously as a means of production, a locus of community control, an ecological resource, and a fount of cultural and ethnic identity. The "looseness" of contemporary politics thus does not take shape around the instability of issues, as some critics of contemporary politics contend. Just as looking through a kaleidoscope creates the effect of difference as an object comes into view through an array of lenses, the politics of loose connections enables its participants to see the richness of issues and therefore to build coalitions. These coalitions, in turn, shape identity with passions drawn from novel renditions of familiar stories.

In describing the politics of loose connections as an emergent style of political participation, I have been influenced as well by Julie Stephens's book *Anti-disciplinary Protest: Sixties Radicalism and Postmodernism* (1998). Stephens directs our attention to the impact of the forms of 1960s protest that are most often dismissed as irrelevant by interpreters of the 1960s. She focuses on what she calls "a language of protest which rejected hierarchy and leadership, strategy and planning, bureaucratic organization, and political commitment, sacrifice, seriousness and coherence" (1998:4). She concludes that groups such as the Diggers and Yippies contributed a protest style on which contemporary political groups from AIDS activists to environmentalists and feminists have drawn (1998:120–27). I do not mean to suggest that the politics of loose connections has a descriptive affinity with Stephens's concept of "antidisciplinary" protest. But her book does suggest that new forms of political engagement emerge at particular historical junctures and cohere around a set of responses to a prevailing and perhaps hegemonic mode of political participation. Moreover, as her book emphasizes, scholars often reject these emergent styles of participation because such styles challenge prevailing senses of the political. Yet these styles of participation can inform subsequent generations of political actors in ways not anticipated by their contemporary interpreters. For example, Stephens maintains that theorists have denigrated the role of countercultural groups in the 1960s in favor of the more conformist politics of the new left.

An ethnography that embraces the personal narratives of those engaged in political organizing, captures the subtle details of the timing of human interactions, and documents the challenges faced by contemporary popular movements may be the best approach to understanding the politics of loose connections. Ethnography does not provide access to a reality obscured by theoretical discourse, but it does challenge the tidiness of theory with the instability of everyday life. For example, ethnography must embrace the fragility of contemporary coalition building along with the continual coalition building that travels along the same surface. Moreover, if the grand narrative of overthrowing capitalism now seems permanently condemned in the world of academia, it occasionally resurfaces as people gaze through the kaleidoscope of loose connections with a passionate commitment to finding their footing in a world transformed by globalization.

Contemporary theorists have illuminated globalization's impacts on the institutions and practice of specific places, but they have done so at the expense of questions dealing with the nature and quality of connections in the global world.[5] Whether we view globalization as producing García Canclini's (1995) hybrid cultures or Arce and Long's (2000) mutant forms, we need to attend to the connections themselves if we are to understand globalization's impacts. For example, if people enter into global social movements with an eye toward a possible exit, does it change the way they refashion their identities? Might it be more appropriate to talk of performance of identity in some circumstances rather than a reshaping of subjectivity, depending on the nature of the links formed? What kinds of work and counterwork do participants in coalitions do to maintain loose connections in the face of concerns about power inequalities, and how might such counterwork produce hybrid or mutant forms (Parkin 1995)?

The Mexican State and Popular Movements

During the period covered in this book (1984–2002), Mexico experienced large-scale and broad-reaching changes in its political and economic structure. In the 1980s, the country found itself in the clutches of an economic crisis. Banking on continual growth in the oil industry, Mexico had borrowed heavily from world capital markets and had expanded government expenditures. With the collapse of oil prices, the state found itself unable to meet its debts. Rampant inflation, capital flight, and instability in foreign-exchange markets generated widespread mistrust of the economy (Lustig 1992:2). The IMF and the World Bank imposed austerity measures that required the Mexican government to cut back on spending programs that had long guaranteed both economic and political security.

The economic crises of the 1980s affected the state expenditures that the government had relied on to ensure political stability (Collier

1992:76). The government reduced spending on public services and relaxed regulations on industry and trade (Lustig 1992). The historic alliances that the PRI had sustained with peasants, labor, and popular sectors were strained by economic restructuring and agreements with the IMF to continue debt restructuring and interest payments (Collier 1992:71–117). At the same time, political discourse shifted as party officials began to emphasize the PRI's role in assuring modernization and democracy rather than care and protection of the nation. By the late 1980s, the party seemed internally divided between technocratic modernizers as represented by President Miguel de la Madrid (1982–88) and the so-called políticos represented by Cuauhtémoc Cárdenas and Porfirio Muñoz Ledo. The políticos' personal and political ambitions had been shaped by the rhetoric of a revolutionary government and a protectionist state. Fearing the effects of the fiscal responsibility that modernizers threatened to introduce, políticos sought to maintain a stable state structure with government expenditures in social services.

Events at the national level transformed the terrain of politics as well. On September 19, 1985, Mexico City shook in one of the world's most devastating earthquakes. Alongside the tragic story of lives lost, disease, and homelessness, reporters and scholars saw something unexpected. Ordinary citizens of Mexico City pulled themselves together to rescue each other, to build temporary shelters, and to provide health care. Many spoke of their inability to depend on the government while boasting of their own resourceful communities, which were helping themselves (Tavera-Fenollosa 1999). Media coverage of the earthquake juxtaposed the organized, responsible citizens of Mexico City with the corrupt government that had allowed code violations in buildings and had tortured political dissidents (Tavera-Fenollosa 1999:122). It seemed that the earthquake had unearthed a dormant power within civil society. In a moment of crisis, the residents of Mexico City had captured the future in the image of citizens organizing independently of the structures of state power.

Although the mobilization of citizens around earthquake relief surprised even popular movements, the earthquake made visible forms of popular political participation that had up until 1985 remained hidden. These movements had formed out of the dissatisfaction felt by students, liberation theologians, peasants, and the indigenous population. The massacre at Tlatelolco had convinced students of the futility of direct confrontation with the state, so they turned to mass organizing of the poor in urban and rural areas as a strategy for more long-term change (Stephen 1991:28–249, 1997; Rubin 1997:108; Díaz-Barriga 1998:255). Moguel, calling the years between 1968 and 1988 the "second golden era of the Mexican left," points out that all the political organizations that were to dominate social struggles appeared in the years between 1970 and 1976.[6] These organizations represented a communist-socialist current, a Cárdenista-Lombardista current, a radical Marxist current with Leninist or pro-Cuban sympathies, and a radical Marxist current with Maoist origins (1994:170). Long-standing conflicts over power and authority within specific regions may well have fueled the student activists' work, but the students contributed a decidedly radical interpretation of these conflicts to challenge more reformist perspectives (Rubin 1997:102–49).

Although students may have radicalized urban and rural movements, they did so alongside other forces that encouraged listening to and incorporating ideas generated outside of their own radical paradigms. Neil Harvey (1990, 1999) underscores the role played by liberation theology, the mobilization of indigenous populations based on promises for land redistribution made by President Luis Echeverría (1970–76), and the failure of the Confederación Nacional Campesina (CNC, Confederation of Mexican Peasants) to represent its members at the state level as a catalyst for the 1970 organizing. He traces the emergence of the Ejército Zapatista de Liberación Nacional (EZLN, Zapatista Army of National Liberation) in Chiapas in 1983 to a new language of struggle that defied the old categories of the left by incorporating indigenous conceptions of knowledge (1999:164–68). Similarly, Rubin stresses the importance of indigenous beliefs and knowledge in the formation of Coalición Obreros, Campesinos y Estudiantes de Oaxaca (COCEI, Coalition of Workers, Peasants, and Students of Oaxaca) in Juchitán, Oaxaca, after 1974 (1997:167).

These post-1978 movements challenged the structures of PRI power that I described earlier as authoritarian and corporatist. In rural areas, activists confronted rule by local political bosses who used their control of resources and ties to the PRI in exchanges of favors (*caciquismo*), and in urban areas they organized against syndical *charrismo* (the use of PRI politicians as union officers) (Pérez Arce 1990:109; Rubin 1997). Urban activists' demands reflected the need for social services such as water, sewage, and housing. As primary organizers of the use of these resources, women emerged as central political actors in many of these grassroots movements (Bennett 1992:240–44; Martin 1992; Stephen 1997:111–206). For the most part, these movements shunned participation in the electoral process, focusing instead on mass mobilizations that emphasized independence from the state and political parties while asserting the people's rights to resources controlled by the state. Electoral participation, when it did occur, emphasized local control of associations such as ejidal and grazing collectives at the time controlled by the PRI. In an exception to this tendency, COCEI decided to field candidates for municipal offices in 1974 (Rubin 1997:132)

The economic crisis of 1982 marks yet another watershed in the development of Mexican social movements. By the early 1980s, social movements had proliferated around categories of identity not so easily incorporated into the PRI's corporatist structures: urban squatters, debtors, indigenous people, and so on. Scholars of social movements coined the term *popular* to distinguish these movements from class-based categories of identity and to highlight the *political* importance of the issues and practices that popular movements place on the national agenda. Foweraker explains:

> although it is impossible to deny the insertion of the movements in historically specific social structures they are primarily *popular* and not social—mainly because they comprise a struggle to constitute the "people" as political actors. In other words, popular movements are defined not by the interests they represent (such interests living a sort of "prepolitical life" in the economy or society) but by the demands they make, and the demands emerge through the process of popular organization and strategic choice. (1990:5, emphasis in original)

As I noted earlier, government spending on social services contracted sharply in the 1980s, in essence producing a shift in the pact that linked many sectors of the population to the state.[7] In what might have seemed a defense of the PRI's corporatist structure, popular movements responded with a range of strategies, including attempts to forge links with state institutions, but without charrismo and caciquismo (Foweraker 1990:16).

These movements defended the pact between the state and citizens, but under the banner of legal rights, in opposition to personal ties with bureaucrats (N. Harvey 1999:24); as we shall see, the transformation was not as easy or as complete as one might like. As Díaz-Barriga points out, and as my own research supports, organizing under the banner of need sometimes resulted in co-optation of movements (1996:291). In short, it is difficult to separate the historic relations that the state has maintained with the poor from the pernicious effects of that relationship. Although ridding the relationship of charrismo and caciquismo may have been important to some sectors, fulfillment of needs at any cost may have remained more important for others. Movements in the 1980s seemed to have remained wary of party absorption, but they entered coalitions with parties on the left in a manner that echoes my description of "loose connections" (Foweraker 1990:6). Struggles to maintain those coalitions in the context of conflicts over participation in electoral politics shaped social movements of the 1980s in many parts of the country (N. Harvey 1990:192, 1999; Ramírez Saiz 1990:234; Stephen 1991:228–49, 1997:111–57). Nonetheless, these coalitions created the impetus for movements in the 1980s to take on broader agendas, including housing, health care, food supply, labor exchanges, legal assistance, and so on. The first indication that these social movements might have broader impacts on the institutionalized power at the national level in Mexico came with the 1988 presidential election in which Cuauhtémoc Cárdenas, son of Lazaro Cárdenas (1934–40), campaigned against the PRI and many say defeated Carlos Salinas de Gortari (1988–94).

What role did the popular movements of the 1980s play in Cárdenas's electoral success in 1988? As this book illustrates and as Bruhn emphasizes, popular movements challenged loyalty to the PRI. In so doing, they paved the way for a Cárdenas near victory, although paradoxically they may also have enabled Vicente Fox's later successful conservative challenge to PRI hegemony. Many popular organizations shunned direct organizing for Cárdenas, however, concerned that electoral politics might distract them from their agendas and perhaps also from maintaining relations with PRI bureaucratic structures. As Bruhn suggests, "In many cases the participation of popular movements in the Cárdenas campaign resulted more from the initiative of their bases than from a deliberate decision on the part of their leaders to mobilize electorally" (1997:114). In Tepoztlán, popular movements, although stopping short of a formal endorsement of Cárdenas, reminded members repeatedly that the vote was secret and that they could attend PRI rallies and still vote for Cárdenas when they cast their ballot. Tamayo argues that, in the end, not only did popular movements benefit the Cárdenas campaign, but they themselves also benefited organizationally from its existence: "Syndicalists from different tendencies and sectors, urban popular movements, peasants and indigenous groups, ecologists, and student leaders passed through convergence in their support for Cárdenas and moved on to dialogue and unity in their sectoral struggles and linkage with the ensemble of social movements" (1990:131). These linkages proved critical in the post-1988 period.

The Programa Nacional de Solidaridad (National Solidarity Program) became the new president's (Salinas de Gortari's) vehicle for introducing novel forms of social welfare that promised to restructure the relationship between the state and civil society while repairing the damage left from the economic crisis. Financed in part with money from the privatization of national industries, tax revenues, World Bank funds, and even contributions from Mexican citizens living abroad, the program served as an umbrella organization for a range of social services, including infrastructure development, schools, health care, and agricultural credit (Cornelius, Craig, and Fox 1994:11; Lustig 1994:83). Special programs were designed to support indigenous populations, women, agricultural workers, and municipalities (*municipios*). As a share of total programmable public spending, spending on Solidaridad went from 2.63 percent in 1989 to 5.95 percent in 1992 and from 0.32 percent of gross domestic product (GDP) in 1989 to 0.68 percent in 1992 (Lustig 1994:89). The magnitude of these increases needs to be viewed against the precipitous drop in public spending in the early 1980s, which would have made any increase in social spending popular among the poor and middle classes.

Solidaridad seemed aimed at restoring the power of the president in a manner that echoed the strategies of Lázaro Cárdenas, with Salinas de Gortari traveling the country to take personal responsibility for introducing the program (Knight 1994:42). In states where the governor had fallen out of favor with Salinas de Gortari, Solidaridad funds traveled directly to municipalities or through other coordinating bodies, thereby establishing a more direct relationship between the president and grassroots organizations (Bailey 1994; Haber 1994). In some cases, the direct supply of funds to the grass roots reversed the long-standing policies where municipalities had little or no money at their disposal (Casanova 1970). In other cases, governors were given more discretion in the allocation of Solidaridad monies, and they used these monies politically (N. Harvey 1999:185–86). More important, evidence suggests that where PRI control seemed in jeopardy at the state or congressional level in 1991, Solidaridad spending levels increased (Molinar Horcasitas and Weldon 1994).

Did the money spent on Solidaridad programs hamper left opposition parties in the post-1988 period? Solidaridad called for the establishment of local committees to determine funding priorities and to develop and carry out projects, just the kind of organizational strategy that popular movements had already endorsed. The structure led many left groups to believe that Solidaridad differed from earlier social programs. Although many left-leaning popular organizations suspected that participation in the Partido de la Revolución Democrática (PRD, Democratic Revolutionary Party) might limit their access to Solidaridad funds, they drew on the funds as a way of establishing the kinds of institutional linkages discussed by Foweraker (Bruhn 1997:220). In addition, funds from Solidaridad enabled popular organizations to provide goods and services to the poor and reinforced their own legitimacy (Haber 1994; Moguel 1994). Finally, it helped that Salinas de Gortari appointed key members of the social left to administer Solidarity, thus using the program to bring new progressive talent into the administration (Knight 1994:39; Moguel 1994:173).

Knight argues that Solidaridad drew on deep traditions within Mexico that had long served to stabilize the system (1994:45), but there are numerous examples of Solidaridad money used effectively to enhance larger democratic processes even in the face of restrictions on styles of leadership and alliances with the PRD (Haber 1994:278; Bruhn 1997:221). Rubin notes that COCEI's decision to accept Solidaridad in Juchitán moved the organization more toward the center, but it did not signal the end of mass mobilizations. Nonetheless, COCEI's relations with Salinas de Gortari helped to solidify power among a small group of leaders who eventually were criticized for corruption (Rubin 1997:192). Haber's study of the Comité para la Defensa Popular (CDP, Committee for Popular Defense) in the state of Durango suggests, however, that involvement in electoral politics and use of Solidaridad funds pressured the CDP's highly centralized decision-making structure to democratize (Haber 1994:271). Neil Harvey notes that Solidaridad monies were used in Chiapas to isolate independent organizations and to reward municipalities that supported the PRI (1999:186). Clearly, generalizations about Solidaridad's impact are difficult.

Owing to Solidaridad's perceived novelty and the seemingly stable economy that reigned during his administration, Salinas de Gortari won many scholars' praise in the 1990s and seemed to enjoy considerable popularity within Mexico. Numerous PRD defeats in 1991 elections suggested that Salinas de Gortari had overcome the legitimacy problems facing the PRI. Indeed, he was proving to be a technocrat with a politician's acumen. In December 1994, however, the peso suffered a 50 percent devaluation, and a precipitous decline in the stock market caused investors to pull their money out of Mexico. The United States, Canada, and other nations came together to bail out a Mexican economy suffering from a 50 percent rate of inflation (Stephen 1997:115). New movements emerged, this time of debtors who had borrowed extensively to start new businesses or to improve agriculture or simply to purchase consumer goods during the economic crises (Torres 1999). Groups of debtors banned together to stop bank foreclosures on property and to demand better repayment terms from banks.

Assessment of these movements' impact has proved exceptionally difficult. Early on, when the movements apparently rejected the traditional avenues of social movement participation—that is, class and left-wing parties—or when scholars presented them as doing so, they seemed doomed to impotence (Eckstein 1989; Hellman 1992). The literature has more recently suggested a more complex relationship between popular movements and more traditional avenues of political participation. As I mentioned earlier, Cárdenas's successes in the 1988 presidential election and his eventual election as mayor of Mexico City seem in part attributable to popular movements (Tavera-Fenollosa 1999:126–28). Nonetheless, because such movements, unlike unions and political parties, tend to avoid clearly defined agendas such as getting candidates elected or even changing specific policies, it is difficult to enumerate their successes and failures and thus to assess their overall impact. When mass mobilizations arise in response to specific threats such as stopping unwanted government projects, however, they have proved resourceful in making alliances and manipulating identities to achieve their goals (Martin 1995; Hindley 1999). Additional interpretive problems emerge when popular movements take the form of multiclass alliances, raising questions as to whose interests might be served by the movement. For example, Torres notes in his discussion of the debtors movement that "well-known entrepreneurs . . . bought bankrupt businesses at bargain prices and then declared a moratorium on their loan payments and joined the debtors' movement" (1999:148). Few popular movements have the power to restrict this kind of exploitation of their demands.

The difficulties of interpreting the institutional impacts of popular movements have encouraged scholars to embrace broader understandings of social transformation. For example, the edited volume *Cultures of Politics: Politics of Cultures* argues for greater attention to popular movements' cultural impacts, suggesting that popular movements challenge or unsettle "dominant political cultures" (Alvarez, Dagnino, and Escobar 1998:8). These challenges to dominant political culture may occasion changes in institutional structures, as when the citizens of Mexico City demonstrated their ability to work together in the aftermath of the earthquake, thereby challenging stereotypes of individualism and apathy that had supported the state's arguments against the formation of accountable local political structures (Tavera-Fenollosa 1999). Popular movements may also serve to politicize new spaces and to transform the meanings of language and ethnic identity, or, as I have argued elsewhere, they may change the way people imagine what is politically possible and how they participate in a global environment (Martin 1995; Rubin 1997:141–64).

Although movements in the 1980s clearly built on structural foundations established in the 1970s (as demonstrated in Tepoztlán), the 1980s brought "cultural issues" to the fore in a faint echo of the kind of conscious self and societal production discussed by the theorists of new social movements (Touraine 1981; Melucci 1996). The difference seems to be that in Mexico, as in other parts of Latin America, "self-making" took the form of what Mignolo describes as border gnosis. Border gnosis, or gnoseology, places the battlefield of colonialism in the terrain of knowledge, arguing that one of the main struggles of colonialism took place when colonial powers "subalternized other kinds of knowledge" (Mignolo 2000:13). By returning to the colonial battlefield, social movements displace the frontiers established between the colonialists' knowledge and knowledges rendered subaltern in the process of building the modern-colonial world system. Subcomandante Marcos, leader of the Zapatista struggle in Chiapas, suggests a form of border gnosis in his description of the formation of the Zapatistas:

> We [non-indigenous leaders] had a very fixed notion of reality, but when we ran up against it, our ideas were turned over. It is like that wheel over there, which rolls over the ground and becomes smoother as it rolls, as it comes into contact with the people of the villages. It no longer has any connections to its origins. So, when they ask me: "What are you people? Marxists, Leninists, Castroites, Maoists, or what?" I answer that I don't know. I really do not know. We are the product of a hybrid, of a confrontation, of a collision in which, luckily I believe, we lost. (Quoted in N. Harvey 1999:167)

Border gnosis emerged as a critical mark of struggles in the 1980s and 1990s in Mexico and in the rest of Latin America. These struggles were in no small measure encouraged by official organizing for the Quincentennial, the five-hundred-year anniversary of Columbus's "discovery" of the New World (for Guatemala, see Nelson 1999). Many social movements drew on the Quincentennial to focus environmental and land struggles within the terrain of indigenous rights, as did people in Tepoztlán who participated in the Five Hundred Years of Resistance, an organization that brought together indigenous groups from the Americas. Indeed, the anniversary to celebrate the "discovery" of America was transformed into a contemporary battlefield in which the struggles over systems of knowledge and basic rights took a central position.

Tracing the history of a social movement along the path of its loose connections places in a new light many of the questions scholars have debated about contemporary movements. Loose connections evade dichotomous readings of history that have inspired endless debates about the "newness" of contemporary politics. Dichotomies between continuity and change can have little significance in a place where history matters on multiple levels. Attention to loose connections enables a reading of globalization that does not imply homogenization or simplistic notions of resistance. It speaks to a world in which fragility of connections becomes omnipresent, highlighting the fact that loose connections are not the same as an absence or failure of connections. Indeed, an important point of this book is that understandings of politics have been dogged by a conception of connections that may well be obsolete in the contemporary world. In the final analysis, this book is about how politics succeeds through loose connections.

Research and Writing Strategies

Tepoztlán's activism mirrors wider social movements in Mexico, although the town has benefited from its place in the history of anthropology and from its ability to attract prominent residents. In 1984, ideas of revolutionary social transformation brought about by movements of peasants and labor nurtured the imagination of activists whose political ideals had been shaped in the 1970s. Tepoztecans later began rediscovering their indigenous roots. In 1999, when I innocently inquired about Halloween, something Tepoztecans had marked with trick or treat alongside the Day

of the Dead celebrations, a friend informed me, "They tell us that Halloween is not our celebration, so we no longer do trick or treat."[8] In 1988, Tepoztecans debated how to relate to the Cárdenas campaign and in the end
voted in large numbers for the PRD. They also participated in the Five
Hundred Years of Resistance movement, the indigenous response to the
Quincentennial, and with that organization attended the nongovernmental
organization (NGO) preparatory conference for the Rio Summit on the
global environment. Although unique aspects of the local and regional
economy have shaped Tepoztlán's relationship to all of these movements,
the community provides a window on the politics of loose connections in
Mexico.

Tepoztlán is the name of both the district and the district seat. As a
district seat, Tepoztlán houses the municipal-level offices and hosts a
twice weekly market frequented by members of the seven surrounding
communities (*comunidades*) belonging to the district. The district seat's
prosperity relative to the surrounding communities' economic poverty is
striking and a source of tension between the district seat and its subject
communities. The picturesque community and temperate climate of
Tepoztlán attract tourists and foreign residents, who provide jobs for
district seat residents and revenue for businesses located in the district
seat. In contrast, the surrounding subject communities weave together
seasonal agricultural employment, factory work, migration to the United
States, and employment in the homes of wealthy residents of Tepoztlán
to generate a meager income. Of course, there are those within Tepoztlán, the district seat, who also engage in these income-generating
activities, but on balance those who live in the district seat have greater
access to wealth than those in the surrounding communities. Of the
surrounding communities, those lucky enough to have better agricultural
land and access to water do much better than those who have only meager
sources of income.

I had established myself as a resident of the district seat and began
participating in the Comité para la Defensa de Tierra (Committee to
Defend Communal Land; "the committee" for short) before understanding the full impact of the conflicts between the district seat and the
surrounding communities. The committee had formed in 1983 to do
something about the loss of communal land in Tepoztlán. Most members
of the committee were also residents of the district seat, and although
they did not welcome my presence, they soon came to tolerate me. However, my acceptance in the committee strained my relations with resi-

dents of the surrounding communities, who fit me into long-standing tensions between the district seat and its subject communities. Many of the cases that the committee handled and the requests for land came to the committee from the subject communities. My perspectives were clearly nurtured by residents of the district seat, whose relative economic security bolstered a form of community bravado that supported negative responses to "economic-development" projects. Although many residents of the subject communities agreed with the committee's perspectives on development, they mistrusted its leaders. Other communities embraced any plans for economic development that promised to relieve their poverty. Had I studied in one of these communities, my read of the relationship between the community and the state might have been very different. Nonetheless, my residence in the district seat placed me in a position to observe strategies used by both subject communities and the district seat to evade, negotiate, appropriate, and resist dominance. Indeed, my sense of the politics of loose connections comes from the gradual appreciation I developed for the perspectives of those who resided in the subject communities.

My first visit to Tepoztlán, in 1984, took place during Miguel de la Madrid's presidency. Having inherited a financial crisis from former president José López Portillo (1976–82), de la Madrid was in the process of implementing measures, described earlier, that he hoped would stabilize the economy. Tepoztecans complained about the increases in prices of foods in the market and about de la Madrid's commitment to repaying the nation's debts even as the country suffered. They sought U.S. dollars by sending their children to work in the United States and by seeking jobs among foreign residents—myself included—where they could be paid in dollars. Many women began businesses grinding corn for tortillas, opening roadside restaurants, or setting up stores in their homes to sell products that spouses and children working in the United States had brought back to Mexico with them. Those who could amass the capital to do so quickly built homes that could be rented out to summer vacationers who often paid in U.S. dollars. As Lustig has noted for the nation as a whole, such nonwage measures for capturing income may have cushioned the fall in wage income even among the poorest sectors of the population (1992:73).

Tepoztecans' resourceful response to the economic crises had repercussions for the political process as well. Although political groups often protested government policies, the burgeoning membership in political organizations in 1984 came about largely as people sought strategies to capture income in the context of the economic crises. As this book argues, many people who joined political groups in 1984 did so in the hopes of making connections that would help them weather the economic crises. Women hoped that their friends in the Mujeres Tepoztecanas (Tepoztecan Women) would help them get jobs for themselves or their daughters, and men and female heads of households usually began participating in communal land movements in the hopes that they might get a plot of land for housing or farming. Once businesses were started, jobs found, or land for housing or farming obtained, state regulations or the need to deal with local authorities, or both, encouraged further political engagement. But these economic incentives for political engagement are only part of the story, for although individual interests may have provided the initial impulse for political engagements, they were eventually reshaped into collective and social demands through the political process.

I arrived in Tepoztlán with the idea of studying challenges to state power rather than the intricate networks of co-optation and cooperation that so clearly characterized the Mexican state. But it became clear that the story of challenges needed to be told in tandem with that of co-optation and cooperation. Communal land imposed itself on my research agenda when María, a friend of my advisor, Laura Nader, told me of the struggle to defend communal land in Tepoztlán. Her description enlivened the practices of state power in day-to-day life and the people's attempts to resist the impact of neoliberal state policies on community power and control.

The day I arrived in Tepoztlán María's husband offered to take me to a meeting of the Comité para la Defensa de Tierra. I followed very little in that first meeting. An elderly campesino (peasant) and a younger man whom people referred to as the "Maestro" (the Teacher)—or Jorge, as he is commonly called—did most of the talking. The rest remained silent. María's husband introduced me, explaining that I was a graduate student from the United States here to work on issues of communal land. He tried to vouch for me. "I know her advisor in the United States, and she is a very good and trustworthy person," he explained. He added that I was staying with his family, kindly taking some responsibility for my behavior. He motioned to me that I should say something. Realizing that they would be foolish to trust me, I feebly explained that I wanted to learn about their land problems and hoped that I could help them in their struggle in some way. The Maestro invited me to come to the office on Saturday—he would tell me anything I wanted to know about communal land. I thanked him and left the meeting with María's husband.

I remember feeling uneasy with the outcome of my first meeting. Nothing horrible had happened, but my first encounter had felt strange. When I think back on that first meeting, I chuckle at my naïveté. The office must have come to life after I left the room as committee members wove a multitextured tale about my presence in the community. Surely the Maestro, voice lowered, would have warned people against becoming too close to me: one cannot know what my true intentions might be. Later I would observe other would-be researchers trying to make their way into the committee.

Weeks later a wife of one of the campesinos told me the tale that had been composed about me that night: I was without a doubt an agent of the U.S. Central Intelligence Agency. Why else would I be interested in this small group? Unbeknownst to me, everything I did confirmed their suspicions. I went to speak with the Maestro, and he gave me a two-hour interview, but I continued to attend meetings. If I merely needed to write a thesis, had not he given me all the information I needed? I participated with the committee in inspections of communal land, leaving the center of town at 5:30 a.m. and walking until late afternoon up and down the mountains, often in places where there were no paths—clear evidence that I had military training.

It is customary in anthropology to tell such tales as an example of a rite of passage that culminates, if the anthropologist is successful, in the establishment of rapport. In many tales of anthropological fieldwork, initial suspicions give way to acceptance into the community. The anthropologist has won her informants' trust, and we, the readers, can rest assured that her information is accurate.

I never received that ultimate victory of unqualified trust, nor did I remain a constant source of suspicion. The committee's trust of me remained relative to what I could be expected to know, something that was constantly negotiated and renegotiated. Toward the end of my first stint of fieldwork (March to November 1984), the rumors most damaging to my relations with the committee began. An elder committee member, a close friend and valuable informant, confided in me that another committee member was spreading rumors that I had been in the home of a wealthy foreigner against whom the committee was pursuing a case of illegal takeover of communal land. I did not even know the wealthy foreigner, but I had rejected the advances of the committee member who was spreading the rumor. My elderly friend suspected that the latter was the reason behind the rumor, but he warned me that I would be asked never to attend another meeting.

I did go to the meeting that night, and no one asked me to leave. However, with little time left in the field, I tired of imposing my presence on committee meetings, but continued to collect data on land cases through interviews with committee members and with those involved in land cases. I looked forward to my return to the United States, where the rumors about me seemed more manageable and where association with me did not usually inspire fear.

The constant need to negotiate trust and mistrust while carrying out research on sensitive political topics underlies all the data I present in this book. After several months of fieldwork, I began to understand that many Tepoztecans had continually to negotiate the degree of trust in social relations. More important, I came to appreciate the politics of loose connections as a product of the challenges to trust produced by the Mexican state's history of dealing with opposition movements, and later I began to observe how these same dynamics were played out on the global political scene.

I had initially conceptualized my research strategy as a blend of formal and informal techniques, with an emphasis on the kind of participant observation that would maintain a modicum of intellectual distance. Such intellectual distance may have served as a continual reminder to my informants to monitor the information they provided to me, but committee members would not tolerate such distance. Once the Maestro realized that I had not happily returned to the United States after his two-hour interview, he insisted that I had to be "really with the committee." I could not move freely from group to group during the course of my research, nor could I be seen with the wealthy foreigners who lived in the valley. The Maestro also placed restrictions on my participation in the committee, refusing my offers to contribute financially to the organization lest I be seen by the poorer committee members as yet another generous foreign patron. The Maestro was not alone in setting the terms on which I carried out my research. Many people were willing to talk with me, but not if I took notes or used a tape recorder. Close to the end of my research, I became disheartened by what I perceived as the lack of rigor in my field notes and tried to engage my closest friends in what Agar (1980:139–49) describes as "frame elicitation." Armed with a pile of index cards, each with a sentence taken from my notes that seemed to describe a key cognitive orientation in Tepoztlán, such as "In Tepoztlán the rich —————," I approached a good friend, explained what I was trying to do, and asked if she would complete the sentences while I listened. She leafed through the cards, examined several sentences, and suggested that I leave the pack with her. I never saw my cards again. In retrospect, it is embarrassing to think that I even attempted such an approach. Early on in my research, Tepoztecans reminded me that Oscar Lewis had shown dirty pictures to children, a reference I believe to his use of Rorschach tests in 1943–44 (Lewis [1951] 1972:306–18), and my frame analysis must have been viewed with similar suspicion. In a place where battles with words are integral to political struggles, putting words in people's mouth must have seemed the ultimate act of symbolic violence (Rabinow 1977).

Abandoning any hopes of professional distance and accepting the limited power my informants were willing to grant me, I found myself adopting a stereotypical female role in the committee. I made *tortas* (sandwiches) to bring along on committee inspections of land boundaries and endured the gentle teasing that characterized male/female interactions within the committee. I was always around. I attended almost every committee meeting (three per week), went on most inspections, and traveled with the committee to visit government offices in Cuernavaca. Committee members became my closest friends, and on a regular basis I enjoyed the company of their families, in those circumstances often finding myself privy to their doubts and anxieties about participating in the committee's work. During those family visits, informants revealed politically sensitive information about the committee—information that many may have later regretted sharing with me. These shared confidences now place me in the awkward position of adjudicating what should and should not be shared with readers.

My style of fieldwork changed considerably over the years since I first went to Tepoztlán. I returned to Tepoztlán in 1988, spending about four months in the community, then again about one month in 1991, for the summer of 1992, and again in 1999 for a brief visit. After my 1984 research, the line between friends and informants became increasingly blurred and talk about community politics became seasoned with gossip about families and news about the health of aging members of the community and of my own family in the United States. I became trustworthy, although still within ever-shifting boundaries. Between visits, letters and phone calls kept me informed of the latest political intrigues and family celebrations and tragedies. Tepoztlán is increasingly less a source of field data and more a place where I have some very good friends. The shifting nature of this relationship may help to explain my commitment to deploying a blend of theory, anecdote, case study, and life histories in the writing of this book.

Whenever I introduced myself in the Maestro's presence as an *antropólogo* (anthropologist), he would joke, "Antropólogo, antropófono" (anthropologist, cannibal). Echoes of critiques of anthropology resounded in my brain. He was right. Anthropologists consume lives, not totally different than consuming bodies, and, as with cannibals, they are most likely to consume the "other." And, of course, calling the anthropologist a "cannibal" cleverly inverts evolutionary theory, labeling the anthropologist the most primitive of primitives. At any rate, having so endured the label of *antropófono*, I, like many other anthropologists, am mindful of the dangers of representing the people whose passions are laid bare in this book as dehumanized cultural artifacts awaiting our consumptive interpretations.

Moved by the desire to challenge the "us/them" divide, many anthropologists have resorted to narrative forms to "write against culture" (Abu-Lughod 1993; Behar 1993). But the narrative form often entails a betrayal of confidences that might embarrass the people who have unwittingly shared the details of their lives with an anthropologist. Abu-Lughod finds this betrayal a necessary component of a tactical humanism, whose value far outweighs the costs of an embarrassment that her informants will probably never experience (1993:36–39). In the abstract, I can agree with Abu-Lughod's decision to betray details of her informants' lives and have used her book with much success in my classes, but I remain uncomfortable with the role of the anthropologist as "global gossip" (Trinh 1989:67–70; Lancaster 1992:72–74). Although I do "betray" a great deal in this book, I have chosen to hold back many details that might make the people I write about seem more human or, as mentioned earlier, details that might expose my informants to danger (for a discussion of "betrayal" as an allegory of ethnographic practice, see Viswesweswaran 1994:40–59). Moreover, we can no longer speak of "betrayal" as revelations about "them," conceptualized as nonreaders, given to "us," the world of readers. Most Tepoztecans do read, and many have looked forward to the publication of this book, promising to have it translated into Spanish.

Anthropologists commonly use pseudonyms for the communities in which they carry out research, sacrificing depth descriptions of place for pseudonymical descriptions, as in what one of my thesis readers called the "palm trees blowing in the wind" chapter. There is far more to a pseudonym than a response to the ethical injunction to do no harm to one's informants. Pseudonyms speak to the tensions between ethnography and fiction and to processes of betrayal and acts of symbolic violence that occur as part of fieldwork (Rabinow 1977; Visweswaran 1994). Ethnographers, by distancing themselves from a specific named site for their acts of symbolic violence, create a "no-person's-land" in which, one hopes, those represented do not have to defend themselves from the ethnographer's representations of their lives. In a political world in which representations really matter, pseudonyms protect our informants from having to answer to our representations of their lives, particularly if we are going to draw on our own imaginative processes to lay bare theirs.

It was with the idea of protecting Tepoztecans from my representations that I decided early on in my research to use the rather awkward pseudonym Buena Vista for their town. Tepoztecans alerted me to their concerns about representation when they complained that they continued to live with the effects of Oscar Lewis's characterization of them as mistrustful. They looked to me to set the record straight. I soon found, however, that although I could render Lewis's characterization more complex, I could not depict Tepoztlán as the peaceful, happy, united community that Robert Redfield had described in the years following the Mexican Revolution. Yet I knew that in many Tepoztecans' eyes, my account for why mistrust was so prevalent and how they managed to engage in politics despite that mistrust would seem a form of betrayal. In contrast, Tepoztecan political activists would feel betrayed if I did not use my book to expose their political enemies' misdeeds.

As someone whose thinking about social movements had been nurtured not only in the anthropology classroom, but also in the Central American solidarity activism of the 1980s, I felt the costs of these betrayals weighed heavily on me. Although I appreciate Nelson's insights into the furtive desires of the *gringa* solidarity activist who needs to carve the world into dichotomies so that she can fashion herself as a defender of the good brown people from lesser brown people (1999:41–73), my own activism alerted me to the power of dichotomies in a political world constrained by sound bites. I feared that the "loose connections" of Tepoztecan politics, the flimsy nature of the alliances formed, and the rapidity with which identities were seized upon and abandoned could be used to discredit their social movements. Taking refuge in a pseudonym, although inhibiting my ability to speak publicly in favor of Tepoztecan battles, seemed a small price to pay so that Tepoztecan activists would not have to confront my representations of their politics in their political activism. But my use of a pseudonym for Tepoztlán became increasingly complex after Tepoztlán's defeat of a mega–tourist project in 1995, which I describe in the epilogue to this book. One of my key informants published his own book on Tepoztecan politics, as did many others in Mexico. It seemed impossible to write about the same events without being in dialogue with these other works, and yet I could not cite the works without abandoning the pseudonym. In 2002, I met with the people with whom I had worked most closely and received their permission to use the town's real name in my book. Thus, the current book has been revised considerably to take into account their own work and to do justice to earlier studies of Tepoztlán that I originally dealt with only in passing.

In my first attempts to account for the mistrust and lack of unity within Tepoztecan social movements (Martin 1987), I resorted to notions of process in anthropology. It seemed that Tepoztecans experienced oscillations between periods of intense mobilization and demobilizations that in the end reinforced the PRI's hegemonic power. That explanation, now, seems flawed. Although there clearly are contradictions within the Mexican state, it seems difficult to envision any state that is not equally marked with contradictions. To treat the contradictory structure of the Mexican state as exceptional is to make those contradictions pathological. Likewise, to view oscillations in political structures as a "problem to be explained" is to suggest that the closure of identity, the fixing of political allegiances, and the unfolding of a logic of organization are the normal state of affairs. Probably the only place that politics unfolds in accordance with a preordained logic and with fixed paths of alliance is in the texts of social theory.

This book raises very different questions from the one that concerned me in my earlier analysis. Accepting political movements' continual "failure" to establish stable political identities, either at the level of groups or at the level of individuals, I now ask if it is possible to sustain political activity through a structure of loose connections. The question emerges from my observations over the extended period in which I have followed Tepoztecan politics. Tepoztecans have continued to engage in a wide variety of political activities in spite of the fact that no single group has gained hegemony in local politics and no group has disappeared altogether from the political scene. New groups constantly emerge, although occasionally with old faces as founders. Moreover, Tepoztecan politics has been effective. Various groups have won support from the state for development plans, and other groups have organized successfully against unwanted development projects. In the case of the committee, a new crop of young people—many educated to secondary school level—have emerged to defend the town's communal land, but the group has also added to its list of concerns. By 1988, the committee had changed its name to the Coordinadora Democrática to mark the fact that it had been transformed into an umbrella organization that included subgroups dealing with health, education, the rights of students, and so on. As someone whose initial reaction was an overwhelming sense of the "failure" of Tepoztecan politics, I now find myself challenged to rethink the meanings of success and failure in the realm of politics.

In writing this book, I found myself drawn to the different ways that history figures into an account of Morelos politics. The past is continuously evoked in everyday life through the telling of tales of the past and celebrations of past events. Therefore, to isolate history in an opening chapter only to leave it behind when exploring the contemporary period would be misleading (Martin 1992). Such an approach would objectify history as though it were a separate domain of analysis and, more important, treat it as though it can be disentangled from those who tell history. But Tepoztecans also draw on written histories when they tell tales of the past. Chapter 2, therefore, weaves past and present together by examining the case for the existence of communal land in Tepoztlán, drawing on a variety of differently positioned sources: the work of colonial scholars of jurisprudence on indigenous land tenure arrangements; the postrevolutionary reconstruction of colonial writing in the scholarship of Mexican historians and anthropologists; contemporary ethnohistorical work on communal land tenure; and Tepoztecans' own reflections on the place of communal land in their past. The dialogue that emerges when these time periods are brought into conversation with one another reveals Tepoztecan subjectivity as an imaginative project shaped by and through images of the nation's history. The point of the chapter is to help the reader appreciate the semiotic load placed on communal land. In the language of Althusserian Marxism, communal land is overdetermined.

Chapter 3 focuses more specifically on the translation of indigenous landholding patterns, as represented in the colonial literature, into Mexico's postrevolutionary agrarian reform law. Here my purpose is to highlight the productive nature of agrarian reform law by illustrating its incorporation of particular notions of community in the form of land law. In so doing, I am suggesting the need to examine the constructed and politically invested nature of community. This chapter contests the notion—common in historical and ethnographic writings as well as in Tepoztecan conceptions—that the Mexican state has polluted and deformed ties of community that existed sui generis. Rather, I argue that the state has *mandated* the existence of community-level organization, thereby creating an intractable problem for those who attempt to use "community" as a foundation for opposition to the state.

Chapter 4 takes up these problems with an examination of the Comité para la Defensa de Tierra and of its attempts to construct an imaginary for contemporary politics in the discourse of tradition. This chapter captures the passions associated with the past, particularly for the *ancianos* (elders) who obtained positions of power in the committee because of their ability to represent and invent the past. Although the ancianos deployed the idiom of tradition strategically, those who emerged as powerful leaders in the committee also lived a distinctive lifestyle that contested practices associated with capitalist agriculture. Thus, to say that the discourse of tradition supported a hierarchical arrangement of power is not to say that the arrangement was fundamentally the same as that which characterized other forms of relationship. Establishing a boundary between a counterhegemonic deployment of "tradition" and the "hegemonic" practices of the state is impossible, however, because the two are constantly interwoven through their common involvement in bureaucratic state institutions whose own foundation lies in the activist state.

Chapter 5 explores the legitimacy problems created by the interweaving of tradition, contemporary agrarian law, and the committee's political practices. It introduces the notion of the politics of loose connections as a response to an unruly collage of images (tradition, legality, community) that engendered concerns about corruption and abuse of powers within the committee. Leaders in the committee expected political participation to follow a more traditional notion of politics, with members achieving "higher" levels of consciousness, making stronger political commitments, and dedicating more time to the committee. But peripheral members participated in the committee while keeping their exits clearly in view. Chapters 4 and 5 taken together represent one period of mobilization and demobilization in Tepoztlán, that which I observed during my research in 1984.

Chapter 6 covers 1988, when Mexico experienced its first seriously contested presidential election since the PRI consolidated its control in the 1920s. With the hope of democracy, a younger generation of men and women schooled in liberation theology displaced the ancianos' authority and introduced shifts in the style and form of committee meetings. In this chapter, the semiotic richness of *democracy* is exposed as a way of talking about class relations in Tepoztlán, the oppressive role of the state in Tepoztecans' lives, and the power of *el pueblo* (the people). The concept of the "local" community emerges here as a site where "knowledge" insulates against the corrupting influences of politics at higher levels. This notion of knowledge informs the Tepoztecan deployment of the politics of loose connections in response to Cárdenas's challenge to PRI power.

Chapter 7, covering 1991, examines a critical shift in the history of the committee, now the Coordinadora Democrática, as the group joined the coalition of indigenous groups marking the five-hundred-year anniversary of Columbus's "discovery" of America and participated at the global level in international environmental NGOs. The chapter traces the Coordinadora's attempts to find a language that could translate the passions of place into a global political world informed by a rational ordering of spatial domination. This process of globalizing the local was accompanied by a limited resurgence of anciano authority, now as part of a claim to ethnic identity, and the incorporation of female political actors as the Coordinadora tried to reshape itself into the kind of movement that would have global appeal. The chapter focuses on the mistrust, grounded in the history of colonial and neocolonial domination, that characterized relations between indigenous groups and U.S. and western European environmental organizations. It shows how the politics of loose connections enabled political participation of indigenous groups in global movements even in the face of that mistrust.

Chapter 8, the conclusion, examines the privileged position given to notions of unity within social theory and argues that an appreciation of the politics of loose connections requires attention to the negation of unity by practices associated with a politics shaped by mistrust and suspicion. I argue that theorists of social movements often adapt the posture of leaders of social movements, believing that a fundamental task of any movement is to achieve higher and higher levels of unity and deeper senses of consciousness. In short, theorists begin with the question of how unity can be achieved and not with the question of what benefits might come from a more flexible, loosely structured political movement. If we look at social movements from the perspectives of those who position themselves on the margins rather than from the perspectives of those who position themselves as leaders, we derive a different understanding of the requirements for social transformation. I maintain that many members of social movements covet a position on the margin as a space from which they can monitor the behavior of would-be leaders and protect the community against those who seek personal benefit from political activism. The position of those on the margins of social movements turns out to be critical in shaping the movement's direction and requires the deployment of practices that entail monitoring community responses to political leaders and knowing how and when to insert political gossip into the play of community opinion and when to withdraw from the movement. In short, writing a history of a social movement from the margins affords a new vantage point on social movements.

In organizing the material in this book, I have been mindful of the need to theorize not only the continuities in Tepoztecan politics—the persistence of a politics of loose connections—but also the discontinuities. This book bears witness to a period in which one of the world's longest, single party–dominated governments came to relinquish power at the national level. Many factors clearly contributed to that historic transformation. Alongside the analysis of political parties' actions and of institutional changes in this period, which are often easier to trace, scholars need to attend to the more nebulous role played by people who at various points found themselves in confrontation with the then-existing

Mexican government. How did fleeting moments of political engagement result in such a momentous change in Mexican politics? At the same time, how might the continued existence of a politics of loose connections shape the long-term impact of changes in power at the national level? These are questions I address throughout this book.

My hope is that in a globally interconnected political world, a style of loose connections may be instructive for those seeking to traverse the local and the global and to survive in coalitions that cross-cut divisions shaped by race, gender, class, sexual orientation, geographic location, age, citizenship, and so on. I am convinced that the Tepoztecan political praxis can be instructive for contemporary global movements whose political participants may not be able to trust one another even as they find themselves united in "common" struggles.

Chapter 2

The Place of the Communal in
the Geography of Time

> In Mexico, as in many countries, the recreation of agrarian history is an essential
> ingredient in any characterization of national culture; it is, I believe, the keystone
> without which the coherency of the cultural edifice would tumble down.
> —Roger Bartra, *The Imaginary Networks of Political Power*

This chapter examines the creation of the local through nationalist representations of history that shaped the emergence of the contemporary Mexican state. Producing the local has been a project of nation building in Mexico. Rather than homogenize space and time, Mexico, early on in its history, sought to celebrate and contain diversity by mapping its geographical coordinates around a theme of historical development of the nation. But the sense of the local is constantly in flux as the state draws on nationalism to underwrite structural shifts such as those taking place today with the Mexican state's embrace of neoliberalism. That embrace has occasioned shifts in the regional accents that shape Mexican nationalism. As northern Mexico has come to dominate the nation's imagination, other regional sensibilities have been dislocated. This was especially true during the decade leading up to the signing of the North American Free Trade Agreement (NAFTA) in 1994, when I carried out the bulk of the research for this book. At that time, the importance of the center of the country as the cradle of *mestizaje* was displaced by the north of the country, which now figured as the cradle of modernity.

The sun filtered through the window, accentuating the deep wrinkles on the face of the tiny woman with the big smile sitting before me. Her face, her tiny physique, and her delightful manner of talk-stories drew foreigners to her. When she spoke, she often held your hand or caressed your face. While seeming to embody "tradition," Rosa was an apt business-woman. When Tepoztecan women turned to hospitals to deliver their babies, Rosa, a *partura* (midwife) found new customers among the foreign tourists for whom the pain of childbirth was lessened as much by the aura of "authenticity" that she contributed to the event as by her skillful massages. Like everything else in Tepoztlán, Rosa's prices rose to meet the capacity of foreigners to pay for her services. Insiders complained that they could not even afford her services and that she extracted equally high prices from the poor as from the rich.

As we sat in the kitchen, a space that is outside the main house with an open hearth for cooking, Rosa reflected on the past. In the past, she explained, the community took care of its poor, and if someone had neither land nor money, the town would give him or her a plot of commu-nal land. Now, she said, those in charge of communal land will tell a poor person that there is no land, but if a rich person offers them money, he or she will get a plot of land. The past was much better. Now, there is much hunger and poverty.

Many Tepoztecans saw communal land as an insurance policy for the poor, but they debated who should have access to communal land. Should it be for all the poor of Mexico or only those of the district seat? If only for those in the district seat, how long should one have lived in Tepoztlán to be considered a resident? If communal land was held by the whole district, shouldn't it be for those from the whole district? These questions emerged repeatedly in my discussions with Tepoztecans.

Demands on communal land came not only from Tepoztecans, but also from immigrants to Tepoztlán from Guerrero, Michoacán, and Oa-xaca, but those born and raised in Tepoztlán felt that their own needs for communal land took precedent over these outsiders' needs. "With the little land [communal land] Tepoztlán has, it should be given only to Tepoztecans," a twenty-four-year-old woman explained. "They [the au-thorities] give it to those who are not from here, and they should give it to those from here . . . because the poor [those of the district seat] really need the land, but they [the outsiders] come from other places and offer something, then they [the authorities] give it to them and not to people from here." Others argued that outsiders should be able to get land, but "if you want to live here, you have to rent a house and wait until you have earned your position in the community. Then you can go and ask for any kind of land, even communal land if you want it. Then people will know what kind of person you are."

The history of communal land defines the community; it speaks to the community's defense of its pre-Hispanic land boundaries, to its patrimony, and to an ideology of caring for the poor that has persisted through time. When Tepoztecans say, as they frequently do, "We are a poor community, but we know how to defend what is ours," they often mean communal land. Many elders proudly accompanied me on the arduous journey to the top of peaks from which one can glean the vast patchwork of farmland, pasture, and forest that surround Tepoztlán. "All of this is Tepoztlán's land. Our ancestors fought to defend it," they proclaimed. And when they solicited the help of the Mexican president in their battles over communal land, they attempted to bring the weight of history to bear on his decisions:

> we know . . . that there have been sales of great extension of forest land that we are sure has always been the type of resource considered to be for the benefit of the whole community as part of the patrimony of the population. In accordance with the presidential resolution [of 1929] that gave to us and restored our land, we have been advised that the government of the revolution has declared all the forest land and trees a public utility and has agreed that it should be considered a community benefit that we are obliged to protect and conserve. (Letter from Tepoztlán to President Adolfo López Mateos, September 12, 1961)

The presidential resolutions of 1929 granted Tepoztlán 23,800 hectares of land classified as land belonging to Tepoztlán and restored to Tepoztlán 2,100 hectares of land that had been taken from the community by a neighboring hacienda. The act specified, "This resolution should be considered as establishing communal title to the land for the purposes of legal appeal and for the purposes of defending the total extension of land referred to in this document." And it declared the community's responsibility to defend the land: "That having declared as a public benefit the conservation and propagation of forest and trees in the entire nation, the beneficiaries of this act should be advised of their obligation to conserve, restore, and defend the forest and trees contained in the territory granted to them by this act" (Departamento Agrario, Acto de Deslinde de Tepoztlán).

Tepoztlán's presidential resolution of 1929 was only one of many land grants made in the state of Morelos during that year (Womack 1968:377). These land grants were the culmination of a decade of struggle during which former Zapatistas occupied offices at the state and local levels of government, although in the latter case many officeholders became "Zapatistas" overnight, ideologically transformed for reasons of political expediency (Womack 1968:359–70).

If the 1929 resolution represents the culmination of agrarian struggle, it also marks the beginning of a period in which Mexican president Plutarco Elías Calles (1924–28) would oversee a less reform-minded and increasingly dictatorial government (Miller 1985:314). The first state to experience agrarian reform, Morelos would also become the first state in which agrarian reform was halted. By the 1930s, peasants in the state of Morelos who requested plots of land received *derechos a salvo*, promises of land when it became available. For the most part, these promises were empty (Sanderson 1984:72).

The legal resolutions pertaining to Tepoztlán's land acknowledged a bond between land and people solidified by the recent memories of the blood spilled in the years of fighting. But memory alone cannot account for the contemporary link between land and identity. Memory has conspired with land law, local lore, and historians and anthropologists' written work to expand the temporal significance of communal land. Scholarly and popular writings about land law link Zapata's agrarian reform movement to pre-Hispanic categories of land use and to an indigenous identity. Emiliano Zapata's struggle emerges less as a peasant struggle than as an indigenous movement grounded in pre-Hispanic patterns of land tenure. Morelos, thus, was the birthplace of an agrarian struggle that links tradition and modernity, Aztec and Spanish, in a mestizaje that echoes the imagination of Mexican nationalism. For the many Morelenses whose family history links them to this historic struggle, they themselves are the center of the nation, for its history and their own are one. Or, this was true at least up until Mexico began to embrace neoliberalism.

Nationalism is often understood in terms of the imagination of a "fixed sociological landscape," one dotted with comparable institutions that define this place, this nation (Anderson 1983:35). Indeed, nationalism has become synonymous with this capacity to imagine oneself as similar to others who share a bounded territory, an ability that Anderson argues coincides with the mass production of newspapers and novels. The expansion of the print media, according to Anderson, fosters an homogenizing vision of space and time so that attachments to regions and localized communities vie with the ability to imagine oneself as similar to those one has never met. But perhaps this vision of nationalism is flawed empirically and insofar as it leans on a notion of an apolitical homogeneity. Contemporary nations are internally divided by race, class, gender, ethnicity, and any other number of differences one cares to name. In contrast to Anderson, Goodman notes that "Early Chinese nationalism built upon native place sentiments" (1995:395), an observation that accords with my own experience in Mexico. Moreover, as useful as Anderson's attempts to recapture the almost "religious" dimensions of nationalism are, we cannot afford to ignore the fact that claims to national homogeneity often obscure underlying diversity. As Duara notes, "Nationalism is rarely the nationalism of *the nation,* but rather marks the site where different representations of the nation contest and negotiate with each other" (1995:8, emphasis in original). Even when members of a nation claim nationalist identities, they may be envisioning the nation from different locations (Duara 1995:10–11). Perhaps, then, we would do better if we thought of the nation as a problematic space within which universalism and particularism are always in contention. Lomnitz-Adler seems to be calling for such an approach when he maintains that "Thus, at one level one has a collective conscience based on likeness and identification, and at another level differentiation, individuation, and a collective conscious based on interdependence" (1992:6).[1]

In Mexico certainly, geographic and ethnic diversity challenge the construction of the nation as a homogenous space and time, but Mexican nationalism incorporates diversity into a vision of the nation. The discourse of diversity taunts the notion of universal, homogenous time and space with the seductive powers of a dangerous particular. As ethnic conflicts around the world suggest, the nation's universality can be disrupted at any moment by unruly particulars that may make their own counterclaims to universality, and Nelson (1999) reminds us that the particular may be viewed as a festering wound in the nation's body. But as a lingering source of concern within the body of the nation, the particular invites unusual scrutiny. In the case of Mexico, postrevolutionary nationalists turned to the debates initiated in the colonial period by Franciscan missionaries and colonial scholars of jurisprudence to shape national institutions in accord with the geographies of culture and race bequeathed to the nation as a result of colonialism. The narrative of nation building that emerged mapped the particulars of ethnic and cultural diversity along a historical continuum so that regions became noted for their place in the nation's history.

In New Spain, the colonial production of difference crafted what might be termed a *geography of alterity* that later emerged to taunt nationalism's universalizing pretensions. This geography of alterity intersected with the emergence of the nation as a place where the "oneness" of nation remained in tension with a nationalist narrative that attempted to embrace regional, racial, and cultural differences as representatives of different temporalities in the movement toward nation building. Thus, in the nation's imagination, its oneness issued from a contemporaneous coming together of different time periods, analogous to a museum exhibit that displays different time periods all in one space. If Mexican nationalism formed from a strategy of geographic containment of differences, however, it is also true that these differences escaped their containers, shaping subjectivities that emerged to confront the nationalist narrative. Thus, those in the state of Morelos who attempted to defend communal land during the neoliberal onslaught of the 1980s crafted a dialogue drawing on writings from the early colonial period, the postrevolutionary period, and the present to fashion a defense of communal land. In other words, colonial categories persisted to do what Stoler terms different "work" in different periods (2002:206).

Chronicles of the Conquest read as a movement from periphery to center, with the goal being military, political, and economic control of the Triple Alliance, whose seat of power was the Aztec capital Tenochtitlán, near what is today Mexico City. Florescano writes of the impact of this conquest of the center on Nahuatl culture and civilization: "The conquest and destruction of Tenochtitlan represented not only the loss of the Mexica capital, it was the demolishing of the center of the cosmos, a disruption of the sacred order that, beginning in Tenochtitlan, the naval of the world, united the celestial power with those of the underworld and established the relationship with the four directions of the universe" (1994:100).

The center of the country became the new seat of colonial power. Colonial rulers often established their own palaces directly on top of the site of Aztec palaces. Moreover, the center later assumed importance as the core of the colonial economy's sugar production for domestic consumption and mining for export. But the colonialists sent to the North to pacify the native population encountered very different conditions than did those in central Mexico. At the time of the Conquest, there were few settled populations in what is now northern Mexico, but rather groups of nomadic warriors who raided colonial settlements (Wolf 1959:191–95). Unlike central Mexico, where Aztec domination prepared the way for Spanish control of Indian land and labor, the nomadic people of the North sickened and died when they were put to work on ranches (Wolf 1959:191–95). In the North, in the area adjoining the Chichimeca frontier, and in the South, east of the Yucatán, nativist millenarian movements emerged, promising that with the expulsion of the Spanish and the restoration of indigenous gods there would be no poverty, no work, and no rules of monogamy (Florescano 1994:106–9). Hostility between the indigenous population and the settlers, encouraged by awards given for bravery in battle against nomadic populations, soon developed with the settlers asserting that the indigenous people were uncivilized, bloodthirsty barbarians. In fact, in the North, racial mixture led to a progressive "whitening" distinctive of that region:

> According to this invented tradition, the conquest and settlement of the frontier had been carried out by Spaniards, that is, whites, and miscegenation with Indians had been negligible, and with blacks, impossible. . . . As ethnic affiliation became redefined in Chihuahua and in the North as a whole, whiteness became central to the creation of a regional sense of community and personhood. This invented tradition of origins is very much alive today, and is regularly evoked in the construction of a distinct norteño identity, opposed to that of the Mexican[s] of the Center, who are subjectively apprehended as "less white" and disparagingly referred to as chilangos. (Alonso 1995:68)

In the end, the North was settled by Indians and poor Spaniards fleeing the settled conditions of the South. Eric Wolf describes the impact of the migration of these different groups:

> All, however, were individuals who found little to recommend in the settled and stable existence of the southern frontier. The North would organize its communities by drawing together such individuals in associations of common self-interest. In contrast, the South would always rely upon the Indians, old upon land long before the conquest. . . . In the South, the Indian would persist, increasingly unwill-

ing to forego the security of living in communities of men of his own cultural kind. In the North, as later on the frontier of the United States, the only good Indian would be a dead Indian. (Wolf 1959:194)

Overall colonial policy conspired with geography to organize the already existing diversity of New Spain into a form that would prove useful in the reconstruction of nationalism. The establishment of Indian Courts, the use of existing power structures to serve the needs of colonial exploitation of land and labor, and the mixture of Spanish and Indian that resurfaced as mestizaje in Mexican nationalism drew inordinately on the experiences of the country's center. These experiences governed the reading of the national landscape, rendering the diversity of Mexico's regions as a historical document that stretched from colonialism to contemporary nationalism.

Colonialism in New Spain, although clearly aimed at exploitation of resources and labor, was dogged by religious and legal notions that were often at odds with its economic agenda. The early observers of the Americas believed in "universality of most social norms and in a high degree of cultural unity between the various races of man" (Pagden 1986:6). This commitment to universality raised the problem of how to justify the Conquest. Moreover, unlike the colonial experience in Tswana in Africa, where missionaries paved the way for capitalist labor practices with notions of discipline, as described by Comaroff, some missionaries in colonial Latin America fought to keep the native population separate from the Spanish. Thus, rather than a fixed set of discriminations, colonialism in New Spain produced multiple and contradictory lines of difference that generated conflicts and alliances between different actors.[2] For example, Franciscan writings on the indigenous population founded distinctions that differed fundamentally from those made by settlers who needed the native population for labor. Romantically portraying the primitive as the embodiment of their own vows of poverty and simplicity, Franciscans argued for the protection of the native population from the corrupting influences of Spanish culture. Although this view produced a powerful argument for the preservation of the racial divide that shaped colonialism, it also shaped confrontations between Franciscan missionaries and those who sought to exploit native labor. At the same time, however, the Franciscans ruthlessly asserted the distinction between their own true religion and the false worship of pagan idols among the indigenous population.

In a manner similar to the Franciscan attempts to defend their own religious vows by pointing to the indigenous population's "natural" simplicity, some colonial scholars of jurisprudence pointed to the indigenous population as the embodiment of natural law. I discuss this work more fully later in relationship to communal land, but for now it helps explain patterns of court use by the indigenous population throughout the colonial period.

Even before the Crown established special Indian Courts in the Americas in 1592, Indians took cases to Spanish courts and made full use of the appeals process. The profiles of court use make it clear that the indigenous population actively resisted the most abusive forms of colonial power while deploying colonial courts in their battles with one another. Borah notes, "The conquerors were amazed that subjects so meek showed such ferocity and tenacity in litigation" (1983:40). The Crown had its own reasons for encouraging, or at least for allowing, the indigenous population the use of this forum for their complaints. The Spanish had learned from the destruction of the indigenous population in the Antilles that colonists who were given free rein to exploit the indigenous population might well destroy colonialism's cheapest source of labor (Borah 1983:25). Moreover, the Crown mistrusted any sector of the colonial population that appeared to be gaining too much power. So, with the Conquest complete, the Spanish monarch turned to the task of controlling the colonists.

Reports from Spanish legal scholars, records of court cases, and ethnographic data produced by missionaries provided the Crown with information on the colonists' behavior. In a well-known example, don Martín Cortés—the son of the conqueror Hernán Cortés and doña Marina, his indigenous concubine—was reported to earn a yearly income of 150,000 pesos from tribute payments by his vassals. When the Crown heard of this fabulous sum, it commissioned Alonso de Zorita to make a count of don Cortés's Indians. The Crown's actions almost sparked a revolt among the colonists, who resented the Crown's interference in colonial exploitation (Vigil 1987:202–3). And when the Crown became anxious about the Franciscans' increasing power, it sought to enhance the secular clergy's power so as to weaken the missionaries (Baudot 1995:299–301).[3]

The fracturing of difference that characterized colonialism in New Spain made the deployment of racial and cultural difference a strategic matter for all concerned. Thus, the Franciscans used racial and cultural difference to argue for the need to "preserve" the indigenous population, and colonists anxious to exploit the indigenous population's labor argued for the indigenous culture's inferiority. Into this fray, indigenous rulers, encouraged by the meager legitimacy given them by the Spanish Crown, sought the privileges accorded only to colonialists as a way of differentiating themselves from the rest of the indigenous population. In Tepoztlán, one indigenous ruler used the courts to petition for the privilege of riding a horse and donning Spanish dress. In other cases, however, the indigenous population challenged elections of mestizos (of Spanish and indigenous ancestry) to positions reserved for Indian rulers (Borah 1983:201). In short, the value and legitimacy of difference were a constant source of political struggles, with the fate of the indigenous population dependent in part on their geographic location.

Postindependence Mexico turned against the indigenous population and notions of indigenous culture, with the majority of Mexicans viewing the Aztec past with disdain (Brading 1988:35). The liberal land reform of 1856 threatened Indian lands and by extension indigenous cultures and institutions, but to elite Mexicans who looked to Europe for models of art and architecture and for ideas of how to form a new nation, survival of the indigenous population was not a matter of concern. Indians, if they were to exist at all, were expected to integrate into mainstream institutions. Even the faces of the heroes of the wars of independence were whitened so as to minimize Indians' contributions to the nation. Indians did find an unlikely friend among conservatives, who argued for the preservation of Indian lands, but with the defeat of conservatives by liberals interested in the privatization of property, Indians turned to more radical ideologies, represented by revolutionary leaders such as Zapata. "To elites and ideologues, that shift might appear inconsistent; to villagers, it was a necessary adaptation" (Tutino 1987:243). The point then, as now, seemed to be to form strategic alliances that would foster the protection of indigenous institutions without regard to ideological purity.

With the end of the Mexican Revolution (1910–20), the indigenous past gradually came to occupy a more respectable place in national visions. By the 1930s, Mexican nationalism seemed to hold the Indian in higher regard than even the mestizo (Knight 1990). Anthropologists, historians, and artists played a major role in carving out a space for the

Indian in national ideology, if not in real life. The Mexican anthropologist Manuel Gamio, who received a Ph.D. under Franz Boas in 1922, introduced into Mexican archaeology and ethnographic techniques a theoretical orientation nurtured in cultural relativism, for which he was awarded a doctorate at Columbia in 1922.[4] But Gamio was not just an academic anthropologist. After receiving a master's degree in 1911, he returned to Mexico in 1912, just when the revolution was challenging the nation. In 1916, he published *Forjando patria*, a book that was widely read and that shaped the ideas of Alvaro Obregón, who became president in 1920 (Limón 1998:45). He served as undersecretary in the Ministry of Education during the presidency of Plutarco Calles but was dismissed from the government in 1925 (Limón 1998:47).

Gamio shaped what became known in the postrevolutionary years as Indigenismo, a movement to transform the place of the Indian in Mexican society, with an eye toward the eventual incorporation of indigenous culture into Mexican nationalism (Bonfil Batalla [1987] 1996:116). His *Forjando patria* lays out the problems that confronted Mexican nationalism on the eve of the Revolution of 1910—namely, the systematic dismissal of the indigenous population, a dismissal on which postindependence Mexico was built. Gamio argued that postindependence Mexico had been constructed around a minority population, with little regard for how the bulk of the population lived. The reigning laws, symbols, notions of art, and forms of industry could not possibly found the development of nationalism because they represented only a fraction of the population. Against this false universalization, Gamio attempted to develop a notion of nation building that relied on stages.

The creation of a homogenous nationalism represents the final stage of nation building, but Gamio called for a long intermediate stage that would embrace difference and call for Indianization of Mexico. Gamio attributed to the legacy of colonialism a pernicious cultural hybridity that undermined nationalism: the Mexican nation could not emerge sui generis out of the unity of its people. Rather, it needed a collective project of the state and people to be presided over by experts, in particular anthropologists, to turn a heterogeneous collection of people, small nations, into one. Toward this end, Gamio encouraged the racial mixtures that the Franciscans and the Crown unsuccessfully tried to resist. He wrote with lament of other nations whose people share the same flesh and blood, out of which emerges "the mysterious force . . . that opposes disintegration" ([1916] 1960:8–9, my translation in all quotations), but he remained confident that racial mixture would produce the homogeneity that serves as a strong foundation for nationalist sentiments.

Throughout his work, Gamio argued that unmixed blood inhibits the formation of nationalism so that physical marks of racial mixture emerge as markers of the progress toward nationalism. He applauded the mestizaje of Yucatán as reflected in its inhabitants' physical and linguistic features: "this racial homogeneity, this unification of physical type, this advanced and happy fusion" ([1916] 1960:13). Gamio defended the Spaniards, who—compared to other foreigners, who guarded their blood, mixing only with elite white women—allowed their blood to cross into the indigenous population ([1916] 1960:156). He wrote, "There is [in the colonial period] mixture of blood, of idea, of industry, of virtues and of vices. The mestizo type appears with pristine purity constituting the first harmonious product where original racial characteristics can be contrasted . . . nubile virgins with large black eyes, closely formed white teeth and tiny feet and hands which proclaim Indian lineage while a curly role of hair and pointy features that cover a golden down, are the clamor of Spanish blood" ([1916] 1960:66).

The reference to "mixing of blood" both invokes and undermines racial categories from the colonial era. Set against the Crown's and the clergy's efforts to resist racial mixing, blood mixtures became the foundation of the emerging Mexican nation. Gamio thus exonerated the Spaniards of New Spain for their role in the Conquest by showing them to be a different type of foreigner—one who embraced rather than rejected the colonized. In Gamio's excessively lofty portrayal, they were not people who thought of themselves as superior to those they conquered, but rather as one with the new land and people. They were therefore worthy of recognition as founding fathers. He acknowledged the exploitation of Spanish colonialism, but he found the Spaniards no worse and in many ways much better than other colonizers, such as the French and the English. Gamio deemed Spanish colonizers superior to those "nationalists" who presided over the postindependence whitening of Mexico and who elevated European art and architecture over that of Mexico. These whitened Mexicans, who considered themselves educated and informed, were Gamio's audience, for it was they who sought to construct the new nation in total ignorance of the indigenous population.

The mixing of blood that produced the mestizo physical type served as a promising metaphor for the future of the nation and as a correction to the hybridization that cultural mixing produced. Gamio seemed to see in the mixing of blood a democratic process that produced a new, harmoniously integrated whole, one in which neither Spanish nor Indian dominated. Here nature accomplished that which eluded a hierarchical social order that could produce only messy mixtures in which one culture's domination remained visible, as in the reigning ideas of governance, law, religion, art, and labor in Mexico. These hybrids suggested a process of rapid and thoughtless impositions of foreign forms; in contrast, mestizaje was the result of a gradual evolutionary process that would give rise to a new totality suited to its natural environment. Thus, hybrids were marked not only by their vulgar uniting of disparate entities, but by their violation of the natural fit between institutions and environment, as could be seen in the privatization of land (Gamio [1916] 1960:180).

Gamio's conception of mestizaje leans on a problematic notion of the "natural," problematic because it sets the natural apart from the social and cultural forces of conquest. He read the desires of the Spanish male for the indigenous women as natural rather than as socially produced and in the process ignored the pivotal role of his own work as a social production of desire. In this regard, it is significant that his work downplays power inequalities that underlay the "mixing of Spanish and Indian" blood, inequalities that Octavio Paz (1961) will later highlight when he stresses that mestizaje emerged from an act of rape in which Cortés violated an Indian woman. In raising Paz, my intent is not to criticize Gamio by more contemporary standards, but rather to highlight the symbolic load that mestizaje bears in Gamio's conception of Mexican nationalism. By naturalizing the process of blood mixture, Gamio attempted to create for Mexico what had been missing—a natural foundation for creating "one" from the "many." Naturalizing the founding act of mestizaje also clearly served to contest any possible resentment among the colonized for the descendants of the conquerors who continued to live in their midst. Positing this natural erotic attraction—always figured as the white male for the indigenous woman—invoked the kinds of "desires" Gamio needed to instill in his elite, whitened readers if the project of nation building were to succeed.

Gamio's arguments for inclusion of the indigenous majority in the construction of the nation rest not on the threat of violence, but on an appeal to what could be produced if the races were fused. He sought to convince his readers of the integrity and beauty of mestizaje, of its value in its own right, and, by extension, of the indigenous population's value. But the violence of racial mixtures as produced by the Conquest retains only a shadow existence in Gamio's notion of mestizaje, for he represented the indigenous population as passive participants in crafting the mestizo mixture. Even where indigenous people had been actively involved in armed struggles, Gamio suggested that they did not engage in those struggles with a clear sense of the project of incorporating themselves into society ([1916] 1960:94). Thus, the responsibility for producing mestizaje lay with the elites, not with the indigenous population, and the former needed to seduce the latter into accepting mestizaje: "In order to incorporate the Indian we do not intend to Europeanize him by force; on the contrary we need to Indianize ourselves somewhat, in order to present him with our civilization now diluted with his own, so that it [our civilization] will no longer appear exotic, cruel, bitter and incomprehensible" ([1916] 1960:96).

This remarkable proposal—advanced by a young nationalist—to Indianize a population so invested in considering itself white could take place only by invoking a founding, natural relationship of desire between Spaniard and Indian. Gamio evoked an imaginary harmonious desire behind the racial mixtures produced by colonialism to remind the hesitant reader not only of the glories of the Indian past, but of the desirability of indigenous culture. In part, Gamio's romantic reading of colonial sexual conquest leans on a double subjection in which indigenous women's desires remain invisible. These women appear mainly as objects of desire for the colonizers while giving birth to the nation by producing mixed race children. Their own desires must be subordinated first to the colonial men's project and later to the nation's project. Indeed, the project of nation building might be seen as justification for allowing the colonists' desires or, by extension, for allowing Gamio's contemporary, whitened mestizos unfettered access to Indian women's sexuality.

Gamio's work suggests that the postcolonial nationalist project—conceptualized as the creation of an integrated whole out of the various parts that make up society—places anthropology at its forefront. In short, if we read anthropology from the "margins," as it has been written by non-western European or U.S. anthropologists, the affinity between anthropology and colonialism that has been most often written about needs to be revised (personal communication with Longina Jakubowska, March

1991). In Mexico, where colonial policy sought to contain mixture, anthropology provided Gamio a seemingly scientific lens for promoting unity across the vast array of racial and cultural differences. Thus, the task of understanding the indigenous population became critical to the nationalist's project; anthropology became the science of nation building.

Similar to his teacher Franz Boas, Gamio pursued a commitment to a holistic vision of four-field anthropology (the unity of biological, archaeological, physical, and social-cultural anthropology), which led him to posit an adaptive fit between race, environment, and culture. This is especially clear in his discussions of the Maya of Quintana Roo, who, having avoided contact with whites by living in a difficult, isolated geographic area, preserved their racial purity and their cultural distinctiveness. In 1916, on the heels of the Mexican Revolution, they demanded of the new government that they be left alone, a request that the new government seemed disposed to grant (Gamio [1916] 1960:172). Manuel Gamio, anthropologist and nationalist, was forced to confront the dilemma this request posed for the nation. Would their isolation be permanent or merely temporary? he wondered. If it were to be only temporary, they should not be deceived into thinking that it would be permanent. Gamio's answer reveals an anthropology refracted through a nationalist lens: "It is unimpeachable that the Indians we are discussing have a sacred right to conserve the land in which they have developed and to continue the free existence that they have always enjoyed. But, it is also unquestionable that the various groups which make up the Republic have a no less legitimate right to avoid the collective prejudice that accompanies internal material estrangement and cultural divergence" ([1916] 1960:173).

To the inevitable contradictions posed by these competing ideals, Gamio proposed that, for the moment, the Maya of Quintana Roo be allowed to maintain their distinctiveness. After a thorough anthropological study, however, which would include an investigation of the conditions necessary for their incorporation into the nation, a process of change that would be fair to the Maya and to whites must begin. This proposal is consistent with the aim of Gamio's classification of cultural traits as well, where the anthropologist's expertise and objectivity serve to adjudicate which cultural traits are efficient and worth preserving and which should be changed. In the end, Gamio resorted to the promise of evolution to make his dream of a unified Mexican nation believable.

In Gamio's understanding, Mexican history can be read as part of a universal project of nation building in which the "nation" appears as a uniquely legitimate and modern form of governance. At the same time, however, the particulars of Mexican history and geography demanded that the "nation" produce forms adaptive to its specific predicament, such as Mexican land law, which, according to Gamio, needed to recognize communal land tenure. In this sense, Gamio anticipated contemporary criticisms of Western hegemonic control over the imagination of modernity. As Coronil (1997) and Mignolo (2000) note, Western narratives of modernity draw on a partial history of the West—one that erases forms of modernity that developed in the reluctant third-world partners of Western expansion. Tracing modernity in the third world provides specificity to the story of modernity, something that Gamio's work attempted for Mexico. For Gamio, modernity might be universal, embodied in the development of nation, but it was also specific as it responded to geographical and historical forces. In the final analysis, however, Gamio retained a modernist concept of the nation that privileges unity, even if that unity must be deferred to recover from the colonial past.

By emphasizing the specificity confronting the Mexican project of building nationalism, Gamio anticipated contemporary criticisms of the universalization of European notions of nations, but he remained a nationalist in the modernist sense. He understood nationhood as requiring a singular unity built around racial similarity, which, in the case of Mexico, meant mestizaje. Indeed, for Gamio, the nation was the foundation of progress and development, the ensurer of stability, and the font of good government. But his was a complex notion of unity. Unity functioned as a critique of postindependence Mexican nationalism, which failed to produce unity beyond that among those of European descent. Moreover, his unity was based not on exclusion, but on the hard work of inclusion. His work then was dedicated not to challenging the category of the nation itself, but to laying out in precise detail a project of *forjando patria*, of forging a nation.

Gamio's work was part of a larger movement to incorporate the indigenous population into the postrevolutionary Mexican state. Artists such as Diego Rivera, David Siqueiros, José Clemente Orozco, and Frida Kahlo painted murals celebrating indigenous culture and depicting the suffering of the indigenous and mestizo population under colonialism. Education minister José Vasconcelos encouraged composers to create music that drew on indigenous themes (Miller 1985:312), and schools began to teach indigenous dances as part of their curriculum (Vaughan 1997). The whitened faces of the prerevolutionary period lost their appeal as Mexico's racial mixtures were celebrated as leading to a more resilient and successful nation.

The focus on mixture emerged as a response to the problems that confronted the dominant elites after independence: How can those whose origins are linked to a colonial power carve a common space for themselves in the postcolonial society (Lomnitz-Adler 1992:9)? A tale of race facilitated forms of national development that emphasized the blending of native and Spanish not just in terms of blood, but also in terms of institutions. For example, the emphasis placed on religious syncretism in historical and ethnographic studies of Mexican Catholicism served to reinforce this nationalist project (see Lafaye 1976; Ingham 1986; Behar 1987). Indeed, Mexican intellectuals spent considerable time spelling out the complex dimensions of mixture that define mestizaje. Thus, Paz (1961) maintained that mestizaje emerged as a reminder of the violent birth pains of modern Mexico: the rape of the nation's economic resources by the colonial conquerors, the rape of Indian women by the Spanish conquistadors, and the forced imposition of Catholicism on the population. But mestizaje captures more than the psychosocial drama of postcolonialism, for the Mexican Revolution produced an economic mestizaje—an uneasy combination of a protectionist state and capitalist development (Basanez 1981; Hamilton 1982). Among the many contradictions produced by this strange brew was an Agrarian Reform Law that sanctioned both private property and communal forms of land tenure. This mixture gave birth to the kinds of struggles that I observed in Tepoztlán in 1984.

As nationhood became defined as the forging of a "cosmic mixed race," the indigenous population, even while celebrated for its history, was constituted as a problem. The postrevolutionary Mexican state, therefore, became preoccupied with the problems of transforming the indigenous population into a mixture not only in race, but in institutions and culture as well. In order to accomplish this mixture, the nation needed a count of the indigenous population, but a count required a clear definition of what constituted an indigenous population. Not surprisingly, most measures captured not indigenous identity, but the poverty and isolation in which the indigenous population had lived since the Conquest. Rural schools, with teachers inspired by the new rhetoric of nationalism, introduced Spanish to indigenous children along with notions of hygiene and discipline.

The important point is that although the 1920s and 1930s increased the visibility of the indigenous population, they did so within a framework in which indigenous culture and identity were fated to disappear. Even though many writers and authors of the period drew on the work of missionaries and others who tried to defend the indigenous population during colonialism, the turn to Mexico's indigenous population served a very different agenda in the postrevolutionary period. The point was not to make the indigenous population proud of its history and culture, for these elements were defined as in transition to mestizaje, but to enable mestizos to embrace the full scope of their history as part of racialized nation building. To the extent that the indigenous population lagged behind in the acquisition of Spanish language skills and the accouterments of modernity, they posed a problem for the nation.

By the 1940s, on the heels of Lázaro Cárdenas's expropriation and nationalization of the oil industry, the fervor for mestizaje had dimmed. In a sense, those who continued to speak indigenous languages and who had failed to embrace mestizo institutions seemed, in the eyes of Mexico's modernizers, to have failed the nation. The indigenous population became viewed as resistant to change and thus condemned to a life of poverty and ignorance. It is in this context that being *indio,* a derogatory term for Indian, emerged as synonymous with being backward and poor (see Friedlander 1975). The idea of transforming the indigenous population into a mestizo race gave way to the "timeless Indian," and Mexican nationalism began to draw on regional variation to construct a narrative of historical movement toward mestizaje. The passage of time came to be seen as reflected in the nation's diverse landscape. Anthropologists and historians contributed to this merger of time and geography as different regions became noted for the possibility of raising different research questions. Southern Mexico became known as the place where they "still" do things the way their ancestors did—at least in a commonsense map of Mexican geography. Aguirre Beltrán's (1991) term *region of refuge* evoked images of villages carrying on "traditional" ways of life, uninfluenced by the modern state. Here anthropologists described local strongmen, *caciques,* who, like their nineteenth-century ancestors, demanded loyalty from their clients and maintained personal armies to maintain control. Tourists journeyed to these "regions of refuge" to glimpse Indians in native dress and to find native crafts at bargain prices. Of course, in reality, southern Mexico was neither trapped in time nor isolated from state control (see Wasserstrom 1983; Parnell 1988; Nader 1990), although it was the region with the most monolingual Indian speakers and the poorest. If southern Mexico represented the past, the northern border spoke to Mexico's future. The North was the region with the fewest monolingual Indian speakers, where the U.S. economy and Mexican underdevelopment met in a confrontation that produced a very different Mexico, one noted for individualism and entrepreneurial spirit as well as for the worst forms of capitalist exploitation. It became known for its independent attitude toward the PRI and for being the home of the largest opposition party, the Partido de Acción Nacional (PAN, National Action Party). Thus, when the PRI finally did lose a presidential election, it was to a northerner, Vicente Fox (2000–), who could speak from personal experience of a new Mexico.

The centrality of regional identification to Mexican nationalism echoed in debates about NAFTA. In 1991, I attended what promised to be a fairly academic, although passionate discussion of Mexico's impending free-trade agreement. Two of the four speakers were guest academics from Mexico—one from Mexico City, in the center of the country, the other from Ciudad Juárez, on the northern border. The speaker from the North spoke optimistically of the impending free-trade agreement with the United States, whereas his counterpart from the center portended exploitation of Mexican labor, widespread environmental damage, and disasters for Mexico's small businesses. The discussion turned virulent when the guest from the North detected in his fellow citizen the claim that his own optimistic assessment of the agreement was owing to his rather mediocre sense of nationalism. He adamantly rejected the charge, arguing that what one purchased in the marketplace was no indication of one's nationalistic sentiments. Northerners, he explained, had for years been crossing the border to buy U.S. products without any concomitant loss of national identity. Years later, in 1994, the Zapatista movement in the southern state of Chiapas chose the signing of NAFTA to bring to world attention the blight of the forgotten Mexico.

The debates over NAFTA reflected a crisis in Mexican nationalism that pivots around consumption patterns. Although differences in consumption patterns affect all regions of the country, and the debate over the meaning of consumption can be carried on anywhere (Lomnitz-Adler 1996), different models of consumption can be mapped with different ideas of the nation in mind. The North provides a model of how Mexico should enter the postmodern, postindustrial world, opening its borders and competing on the global stage. But one must not forget that revolutionary fighters in Chiapas timed their own emergence as resurrected Zapatistas to correspond with the implementation of NAFTA. In drawing on the tradition of revolutionary struggles over land and against feudal labor relations, the Zapatistas sought to remind the world that Mexico was not even a fully modern, democratic nation worthy of playing on a global scale.

Although asserting the "oneness" of the Mexican nation, mestizaje challenged conventional notions of the nation that relied on primordial identities because it leaned on a processual notion of nationalism. The Mexican nation depended on history for its unity: the biology of a naturalized desire leaned on the passage of time for the forging of a new race. In the absence of a myth of primordialism to underwrite Mexican nationalism, Mexican nationalism remains an incomplete project continually worked upon and contested. To the extent that one can speak of Mexican nationalism at all, then, it is as an achievement with roots in the meeting of Spanish and native populations. An emphasis on an oversimplified regional diversity maps this achievement on the national landscape by deploying cultural and racial differences into the nationalist narrative. But the incorporation of differences into the national narrative raises the possibilities of unruly differences: the emergence of challenges to any "national" agenda that leaves out the indigenous population.

From Center to Margin:
Communal Land in the Discourse of Nationalism

Encased between the indigenous past of the South and a neoliberal economic future is the former symbolic and geographic center of the country, the area that figures so prominently in the Conquest and in the nation's subsequent development. But the global economy and Mexico's bid to strengthen its position within it challenge the geographic center's centrality to the nation's imagination. Current laws regarding liberalization of trade and investment and privatization of land suggest the magnitude of ideological change and its links to the nation's geographic imagination. For example, scholars have represented Emiliano Zapata's struggle for agrarian reform as founded on the institutions of communal land tenure believed to exist among Nahuatl villages in the center of the country. Thus, rights to a form of communal land tenure protected by Mexico's Constitution have figured in the alchemy of Mexican nationalism as representative of an indigenous Mexico. In this sense, communal land has occupied a privileged position in the nation's imagination even as it has continued to remain marginal to the contemporary state's plans and projects.

When Carlos Salinas de Gortari brought an end to agrarian reform in 1991 and offered communal landholders private title to their land, more than land tenure was at stake. The role of the geographic center, the institutions of that part of country, and the place of indigenous culture in the nation's imagination were challenged. As a result, those whose politics and lives centered around communal land found themselves displaced. Their institutions and ways of life were no longer at the center of the mestizaje that defined Mexico as a nation. Instead, communal land tenure was deemed an archaic, outmoded, and unnecessary burden on the nation's productivity. The shift of communal land from its place as part of a general meztizaje is underscored by the fact that the new changes in land law provided special provisions for indigenous populations to retain their communal land. The impact of this displacement needs to be traced along the juncture between geography and the subjective experience of place. Geography is not static, nor is it transparent (Soja 1989), and the movements of geography as socially imagined can be as dislocating as the movements of people.

Morelos provides an appropriate location for an examination of the confrontation between communal and private property, between the traditional and the modern, as these dichotomies played themselves out with the shift to neoliberalism. Although neoliberalism is an economic shift, it also disrupts the subjective experience of national identity as it is constituted in relation to regional identities and histories. Thus, Tepoztecans' struggle to defend communal land appears today as a confrontation with the state, but in another sense the continued existence of communal land can be read as one with the place of the "traditional" within the crafting of Mexican nationalism. To hold onto communal land is to hold onto one's place in the history of the development of the

Mexican nation. For many communities in Morelos, that place is defined in relation to the nationalist representation of Zapatista fighters as fierce defenders of their lands.

Jesús Sotelo Inclán implotted his 1943 exploration of the revolutionary movement in Morelos in his own confusion about Emiliano Zapata. Was the revolutionary leader a bandit who robbed and murdered? In Sotelo Inclán's own family, there was evidence for this version. Or was Zapata the apostle of agrarianism and the symbol of hope for the dispossessed whom he, Sotelo Inclán, learned about from his teacher, Díaz Soto y Gama, a faithful follower of Zapata? Sotelo Inclán discovered answers to this question in research in Anenecuilco, the Morelos community where Zapata was born. His "discovery" is worth quoting at length because I was introduced to his work by a Tepoztecan who wanted me to understand the struggle to defend communal land.

> I had to go to Tenextepango . . . in search of an old friend of his [of Zapata's], a fellow fighter who kindly agreed to accompany me to Anenecuilco and to introduce me to Francisco Franco. . . . In good faith and with the best of intentions I struggled to gain his support, something that I did not achieve in one day, but only through the repeated visits that I made throughout the year until one day he showed me, with a great deal of secrecy, a strong box out of which he removed some old papers. "Miliano put me in charge of these before he left: for these he struggled against Díaz and fought with Madero, Huerta y Carranza," explained Franco. "Zapata knew about these?" I asked hesitantly. "Of course, the old people gave them to him before the first war, the one against Díaz, so that he could defend the land of the community as they had done." . . . These papers completely changed the vision I had of Zapata, showing him to be the authentic representative of the hopes of his people. (Sotelo Inclán 1943:14–15, my translation in all quotations)

The major portion of Sotelo Inclán's text crafts Emiliano Zapata as one with his people and focuses on the documents that Sotelo Inclán discovered that day in Anenecuilco. He searched back in time to discover mention of the community in the Códices Mendocino in order to establish the community's pre-Hispanic roots. The oldest document in the Anenecuilco files, from 1560, is a request directed to don Luis de Velasco, viceroy of New Spain and president of the High Court, requesting his support in protecting indigenous land (1943:46).

Tepoztlán's communal land is distant both literally and figuratively from the commotion of the center of town.[5] The vast expanse of terrain that provides pasture land for animals, small farming plots for those too poor to purchase private property, and housing sites for squatters makes up the communal land. "Owners" of communal land inherit use rights over the land, but they may not buy, sell, or rent it.

Most Tepoztecans speak with pride of the continued existence of communal land and to the obligations that they have to their ancestors for protecting this land. Colonial authorities acknowledged Tepoztlán's pre-Conquest borders and used local rulers to reinforce the *repartimiento* system, a system that assured the conquerors a steady supply of labor.[6] The conquerors' use of local rulers modified existing systems while reinforcing the importance of communal land and indigenous tradition. This legacy upholds the notion that communal land belonged to Tepoztlán prior to the Conquest. Moreover, although in many places in Morelos *hacendados* took over communities' lands, Tepoztecans say that their ancestors fought to defend their town's land. Communal land, in the minds of Tepoztecans, thus stands for decades of resistance, first against the colonial government, then against the hacendados, later against government-controlled agrarian reform, and now against privatization.

Tepoztecans draw on the precolonial legacy of communal land to distinguish between communal and ejidal land, stressing the former land as an exclusive community resource, as the pueblo's patrimony. Casanova (1970) points out that the power of the postrevolutionary Mexican state over municipalities lay in the state's monopoly over scarce economic resources. By law, municipalities had to turn all local revenues from taxes over to the state government, leaving only fines and fees to pay the low salaries of municipal-level employees. They then had to request money for roads, schools, electricity, and so on from the state bureaucracy. State governors and their assistants disbursed these funds in elaborate celebrations, symbolizing civic participation, the governor's kindness, and the community's debts to the power structure.[7] These rituals surrounding government largess were the foundation of a political culture that left community members beholden to the state, a point I develop further in the next chapter.

To Tepoztecans, *ejido* land was part of these rituals of state power;

communal land was not. Because Tepoztecan communal land survived the Conquest owing to their ancestors' bravery, Tepoztecans acknowledge a debt to their ancestors, not to the government, for communal land. Thus, communal land is the only resource that can truly be termed the community's patrimony.

In Sotelo Inclán's text, Emiliano Zapata is transformed from a cacique, a political boss who rules through personalistic ties, into a *calpuleque*, a Nahuatl term that recontextualizes the revolutionary leader into a line of respected indigenous rulers who control rights to land. Zapata, no longer just a peasant leader, represents the indigenous past whose voice can be heard in the contemporary language of revolutionary struggle. Sotelo Inclán thus inserts into the understanding of revolutionary history and land struggles categories of difference borrowed from the colonial era.

For Sotelo Inclán, the colonial period marks a collision between the individualistic aims of the Spanish and the collective tradition of the Indians: "the *tequitatos*, the traditional leaders and representatives of the people remained silent without power to protest because the voice and rule was in the hands of new rulers, which were *caciques* with political positions. These rulers of Anenecuilco . . . considered communal land to be a personal inheritance. It was the spirit of individual ambition that already existed among the *caciques* in the prehispanic period, exalted by the example of the Spanish" (1943:55). According to Sotelo Inclán, the land documents of Anenecuilco tell of kind-hearted Indians granting land to the church, never suspecting that this friendly gesture will result in the formation of a hacienda that threatens the town's communal land (1943:56). The concern about individualism creeping into the indigenous community will endure for four centuries, culminating in Emiliano Zapata's struggle for land and liberty. This struggle, at least according to Sotelo Inclán, emerged as part of this long history of the battle for community against the seduction of individual ambition.

Images of ambitious and corrupt authorities figure frequently in Tepoztecan's attempts to account for contemporary problems associated with communal land. Many argue that the only reason "outsiders"—wealthy Mexican nationals, foreigners, and poor squatters from other states—get communal land is that corrupt authorities and creeping individualism lead people to sell land. As one man explained, "One must understand that it is not the people who have come to own the communal land that are at fault—they merely purchased the land. The fault lies with Tepoztecans who because of ambitions for money sold the land and with bad authorities who sell land to make money for themselves."

Tepoztecans who consider themselves the advocates of tradition distinguish between ambition for money and ambition for land. Owning land responsibly—that is, cultivating the land and maintaining it for one's children—preserves the community. Selling land for money and putting trust in monetary wealth betrays community. Tales of commitment to community often revolve around a confrontation with wealthy "outsiders" offering fabulous sums for a plot of land to respected citizens who repeatedly reject their offers. These commitment tales are juxtaposed to stories about people who sold land at what seemed a good price only to discover that with the depreciation of the peso in the 1980s they were left in poverty.

In contrast to self-proclaimed traditionalists, other Tepoztecans see the future as in the hands of those who have given up holding onto land to gamble instead on education. As one woman explained, "Those who sold land did so because they needed the money—it is crazy to try to defend land from being sold." Her perspective meets with agreement even among those who fight to defend communal land, for they, too, see the course of history as moving toward the continual expansion of the market. Paradoxically, the fight becomes all the more meaningful because it seems so hopeless. One day I found don Abram, a traditionalist leader within the Comité para la Defense de Tierra, quite depressed. After a long battle to take back a piece of land that had been illegally sold, members of the *colonia* (squatter settlement) where the land was located had voted to allow the wealthy foreigner who had illegally purchased the land to continue to hold it. Distressed by the turn of events, don Abram questioned the utility of continued engagement in the struggle to defend communal land. I described Camus's (1955:88–91) reading of the myth of Sisyphus to him, an interpretation that emphasizes Sisyphus's embrace of the task of pushing a rock up a hill that will always roll back down just as he reaches the top. In Camus's reading, Sisyphus smiles as he returns to push the rock once again, for the futility of the struggle fills his heart. Don Abram loved the story because to him it spoke to the compulsion to fight for justice regardless of the outcome.

The basic framework of communal land, as understood in Morelos in 1984, can be gleaned from Zapata's Agrarian Reform Law of October 26,

1915, and in less specific terms in the Plan de Ayala of November 25, 1911, in which the Zapatistas declared themselves "partisans of principles and not of men" (from Zapata's Agrarian Reform Law, quoted in Womack 1968:404). From its inception, the Agrarian Reform Law was a tool of state co-optation of opposition. When the Constitutional Convention met in 1916, Zapatista fighters in the state of Morelos were still engaged in armed struggle for access to land and for communities' rights. Emiliano Zapata had issued his Plan de Ayala in 1911. John Womack captures the significance of the Plan de Ayala for the Zapatista struggle and for the nation when he writes that "the Zapatista chiefs considered the plan a veritable catholicon, much more than a program of action, almost a scripture. They would brook no compromise of its provisions, no irreverence towards its projects—which were to issue in a classic Mexican millennium. . . . Afterward the Ayala plan became famous as the premier banner of modern Mexico's most remarkable and controversial experiment, agrarian reform" (1968:393).

The Plan de Ayala called for the return of properties usurped from communities; expropriation, with indemnification, of a third of the land of powerful *proprietarios* (private-property holders) to be redistributed in the form of "ejidos, colonies, and foundations for pueblos"; and the granting of pensions to the widows and orphans of victims of the struggle (quoted in Womack 1968:402). In Zapata's Agrarian Reform Law of 1915, the "fields, timbers, and waters" for which legal title existed dating prior to 1856 had to be restored to individuals and communities (Article 1), and the nation would recognize the right of pueblos, ranchos, and communities to administer communal resources (Article 3) (Womack 1968:405–11). Particular sections from the 1984 federal Agrarian Reform Law show that Zapata's Agrarian Law was echoed in what became Mexico's national law. For example,

Art. 52.—The rights over agrarian resources acquired by local population will be inalienable. . . . In no case, nor in any form whatsoever may [these resources] be alienated, given away, transferred, rented, mortgaged, taxed in full or in part . . . plots of land that have been belonged to *ejidatarios* [holders of ejido land] and become vacant because of a lack of heirs or legal successor, remain at the disposal of the corresponding population. (*Ley federal de la reforma agraria* 1984, Titulo Segundo, Capitulo I, my translation)

The law of 1915 defined as a natural right land for the subsistence needs of a man and his family and specified that the lands granted by the government should be considered to be inalienable and could not be mortgaged, although use rights could be inherited. In contrast to the contemporary Agrarian Reform Law, which defines the president of the country as the ultimate authority over land, Zapata's Agrarian Reform Law drew on the "traditional and historic" rights of communities to place the administration of communal land tenure in their own hands (Plan de Ayala, cited in Womack 1968:393–404). The difference is significant. Even today, control over communal land seems synonymous with control over community. Communal land, therefore, figures not only as an economic resource, but as a reminder of communities' potential independence from the Mexican state. As such, it is a thorn in the side of the state, which would prefer to treat communal and ejido land (land that was redistributed to the population after the revolution) as the same. Indeed, many Mexican scholars with whom I discussed my work patiently pointed out that all land in Morelos was ejidal, not communal. They would add that if there is communal land in Mexico, it is only in the South, where the population remains indigenous.

The Constitutional Convention that met in November 1917 included dedicated supporters of agrarian reform. Among the delegates was Francisco Mugica, a governor who had carried out a land reform in Tobasco, which then-president Venustiano Carranza (1915–20) refused to ratify, and Luis T. Navarro, from Puebla, who had served with the Zapatistas for eighteenth months (Womack 1968:272; Bazant 1979:148; Katz 1983:318). Drawing on the Spanish principle that property ultimately is invested in the king, Article 27 of the Mexican Constitution imposed restrictions on the size of private-property holdings, allowed for the expropriation and redistribution of land, and restricted foreign ownership of land (Bazant 1979:149). The inclusion of Article 27 in the Constitution is widely interpreted as an indication that radicals' wishes prevailed in the Constitutional Convention (see Cockcroft 1968:273; Womack 1968:273). But the radicals' "victory" in the Constitutional Convention eventually would serve to undermine the Zapatista struggle for land and liberty by raising questions about the wisdom of continued fighting (Womack 1968:283). Moreover, in giving ultimate right and responsibility to the president, Article 27 undermined community authority, something that continued to plague communities trying to defend land. By 1918, Zapata himself would sign a document that made no mention of the Plan de Ayala, and after his assassination at the hands of government troops in 1919, Zapatista fighters would be integrated into local Morelos politics (Womack 1968:303, 369). They and their descendants would form the new post-revolutionary power elite.

Property conceded to individuals and communities under the provisions of Zapata's Agrarian Reform Law is understood to be inalienable and cannot be mortgaged in any form, although it may be inherited. If the holder of a piece of property fails to cultivate that property for more than two years, he or she loses the right to the property. This notion that property needs to be continuously cultivated or worked in some way resurfaces again and again in contemporary struggles over communal land.

> Art. 85—An ejidatario or *comunero* [holder of communal land] will lose his or her rights over [land] and in general those [rights] he or she enjoys as a member of a collective of ejidatarios or comuneros . . . when:
> I. Failing to work the land personally or with members of his or her family, during a period of two consecutive years or more. (*Ley federal de reforma agraria* 1984, my translation)

The Colonial Roots of Mexico's Agrarian Reform Law

To what extent can one legitimately trace the Zapatista's Agrarian Reform Law to the pre-Hispanic *calpulli* form of land holding, as Sotelo Inclán did? Sotelo Inclán's notion of communal tenure draws on the work of Alonso de Zorita, who was part of the pro-Indian faction sent to New Spain to monitor judicial matters in the colonies. Zorita spent nineteen years, 1547–66, in New Spain, including Santo Domingo, Guatemala, and Mexico. In correspondence with the Crown, he attempted to convey the respect and admiration he had developed for the "*naturales*" and to counter the usual negative colonial representations of the inhabitants of New Spain. "These people are unjustly defamed for lack of reason and ingratitude, and when there is some demonstration of this among them, it is when . . . [they] are frightened by the cruelties that they have endured and continue to endure. . . . Although these and other things that I am about to say might be a bit outside official [views] I beg your Majesty's pardon, for all is with the intent to serve your Majesty" (Zorita 1963:26, my translation in all quotations).

Zorita then went on to explain that indigenous customs of succession and elections conformed in various ways, although the native people were unaware of it, "with Natural Law, Divine Law and Civil and Canonical Law. By this we can understand that they do not lack reason as others have suggested" (1963:28). Rather, the failure of reason lay with the colonists, who failed to appreciate the basic form of communal land tenure. He defined the calpulli or *chinancalli* as a "barrio of well-known people or ancient lineage, that has land dating back many generations . . . and those of this origin, barrio, or lineage and their land are called calpulli, that means land of that barrio or lineage. . . . The lands that they possess were divided when they arrived on the land and each lineage took its plots . . . and marked them for themselves and their descendants and from that point until today they have maintained possession of these lands" (1963:30).

The lands of the calpulli cannot be alienated, nor can they be given to those who are not part of the calpulli, but use rights may be inherited. If there is no one to inherit the land, the land remains in control of the calpulli: "When in some cases lands are vacant . . . they had and continue to have to keep careful account of them, so that members of another calpulli cannot enter into the lands. And, this has caused and continues to cause numerous quarrels as each tries to defend the land of the calpulli" (Zorita 1963:32). An individual who has use rights over the land loses the land if it is not worked for more than two years. Although the calpulli lands may be rented to other calpulli, rental is done only for the calpulli's benefit.

Zorita explained that the head of the calpulli maintains records in the form of pictographs detailing types of land, their boundaries, who is working them, and how much each person controls, which ones are empty and which have been given to Spaniards. He stressed that the head must be a member of the calpulli who is capable of defending it. That person is elected by the calpulli, and although there is a tendency to elect within families, the person must be the wisest and most capable and honorable (Zorita 1963:34). If a member of the lineage or barrio does not have land, the oldest member of the barrio or lineage in consultation with other elders may give him a plot according to his needs and the quality of land. The principle elder may never act alone in these matter but always in consultation with other elders.

According to Zorita, the alienation of calpulli land that had come about as a result of the blends of Spanish and Indian visions of land tenure had generated chaos: "upon seeing or hearing of lands that are not being worked they [Spaniards] ask the governor for these lands, and the people who the governor names to investigate are not very diligent in favor of the Indians, and if by chance the governor names a good Christian, those who have requested the land have ways of impeding him and of having another named in his place" (1963:32–33). Zorita advised the Crown, "Upon understanding the harmony of these *calpullec* or barrios, it is of value to sustain them . . . and not confuse them, as is now the case . . . there is no value in the *principales* contradicting what is said [by Spaniards, mestizos, and mulattos] and proclaiming that they are calpulli . . . because they are not understood and it is injurious to the rest . . . because those who are awarded [the land] sell and alienate it, damaging the calpulli" (1963:35).

It is important to place Zorita's visions of communal land within the play of colonial power relations. Zorita went to New Spain as an envoy of the Crown sent to monitor, among other things, the flow of resources from the colonies. In Spain, theologians and legal scholars were working out the moral justification for the Conquest, and many of the arguments hinged on whether or not the indigenous communities could be characterized as civil societies (Pagden 1998). In such a setting, reports on the rationality of indigenous land holdings became a primary focus of those who wanted to argue that the indigenous population enjoyed certain inalienable human rights. These concerns of the Crown are reflected in the steady parade of questions concerning modes of paying tribute among the Indian populations of New Spain, to which Zorita responded in *Breve y sumaria relación de los señores de la Nueva España*. In response to a question regarding whether or not the Spanish Christians had placed additional tax demands on the Indians, Zorita responded, "The things that the Spaniards did at first, and even now are [doing], in some parts [are] so exorbitant and excessive, and so beyond all reason, that if I were to answer everything . . . it would make this a very long process" (1963:130). Zorita went on to paint very humane images of work and tribute under pre-Hispanic rule, which he then contrasted with backbreaking and deadly work in the colonial period.

What does Zorita's work and its recovery in the postrevolutionary period tell us about the links between Spanish colonialism in the sixteenth century and Mexican nationalism in the twentieth century? For one thing, it seems clear that some Spanish colonialists looked to the indigenous population to confirm the legitimacy of their own institutions. Thus, to claim the legitimacy of "natural" law, vestiges of it must be observable even among conquered peoples, and in the Spanish conquerors' effort to legitimate their own law as natural, the thick line of colonial difference gave way to a dotted line of distinctions. Similarly, some missionaries underscored the natural affinity between their religious vows of poverty and the indigenous populations' lifestyles. Colonialists such as Zorita and the Franciscan missionaries scanned indigenous cultures to distinguish between that which was similar and that which was different. Theirs was not so much a plea to protect "difference" per se, but rather part of an overall project that defended their own moral position and their own visions of modernity within what Mignolo terms the expansion of commercial circuits that accompanied Spanish colonialism in the sixteenth century (2000:51). Years later, as postrevolutionary Mexicans once again tried to modernize their nation and mend the wounds left by colonialism, they recovered colonial debates to justify the incorporation of indigenous land tenure patterns into national agrarian law.

In 1951, Oscar Lewis supported Tepoztecan assertions that the town's communal land had remained in tack since before the Conquest. He maintained that in the early sixteenth century Tepoztecans presented maps showing the town's land boundaries under Moctezuma and that these titles were used by the Spanish to determine the town's land grants ([1951] 1972:114). Echoing Sotelo Inclán's description of the place of land titles in Morelos, Lewis reported that safekeeping of the land titles had always been a preoccupation for Tepoztecans, although the titles were lost several times, first to a hacienda and later when the land titles were sold by a local priest. Although Tepoztecans seem to have fought for their land, they did so mainly in boundary disputes often within the district itself and not so much with the Spanish, who found the land to be of little agricultural value ([1951] 1972:114).

The early significance of communal land as a symbol of community autonomy from the state is reflected in the battle following the 1929 presidential resolution over whether or not jurisdiction over communal land would remain in the hands of the municipal government or be given to ejidal authorities subordinated to the Mexican state. According to Lewis, the state prevailed, and control over communal land was ceded to ejidal authorities, but only after federal troops were sent to the community. But that does not seem to be the end of the matter, for in subsequent years control of communal land passed back and forth between ejidal and communal authorities. In 1984, communal authorities once again controlled communal land, although their power was subordinated to the Secretaría de la Reforma Agraria (Department of Agrarian Reform) rather than to the municipal offices.

In the first weeks of my research, I conducted a simple survey of seventy-two households, more to present myself to the community than to gather data. I asked questions about household composition, sources of household income, and parents' and grandparents' occupations. Because I did not select the households randomly, the survey results are not useful for generalizations about Tepoztecans, but they illustrate the power of working the land in many Tepoztecans' imaginations. Excluding those survey respondents who were older than sixty or younger than twenty (ten in all), all but two of the survey respondents reported that their parents were campesinos, and all reported that their grandparents were campesinos. The survey also reveals a wide range of contemporary income-generating possibilities, including teaching (four), domestic work (two), transportation (five), construction (six), and factory work (four). Four respondents described themselves as agriculturalists, meaning that they grew cash crops, either flowers or tomatoes, on their own land and used chemical fertilizers in the process, but more than half of the respondents described themselves as campesinos, which indicates that they engaged in subsistence crop production on land without irrigation or worked as day laborers in agro-industry. Further conversation revealed, however, that the category *campesino* disguised a variety of income-generating strategies, many of which seemed to dwarf the economic relevance of campesino identity. As one woman explained, "My husband works in the *campo* [in the fields]; he is a campesino, but now he is working in construction because we don't have any land to cultivate, so we have to buy all our food." Another described their household situation: "We don't have any land, so we borrow land here—we plant maize every year for the house—sometimes it is enough, and sometimes not. He looks for whatever work he can find, but right now he is not working." Another told me that her husband was a campesino, but because he farmed his own ejido land without irrigation, they could grow only maize for the house, so he also worked construction.

In many ways, my informants' explanations accord with scholarly definitions of the peasantry. Peasants are usually described as people who engage in subsistence crop production, but whose need for cash draws them into other forms of labor. As Kearney (1996) has pointed out for peasants more generally, however, the amount of food generated by today's peasants fails to provide for most families. Yet all these families answered my initial question about occupation with the term *campesino*, for the term seemed to capture something of significance for these people. Although *campesino* failed to describe the complexity of their material position within a broader productive process, the term spoke to their position in history, as I soon came to learn; their sense of the place they occupy in the larger national landscape; and, most important, their rights as defined by the Agrarian Reform Law. In short, even as the peasant mode of production contributed an increasingly paltry amount of food to the family, it remained salient in part because of the history I have described in this chapter. To work the land was to take one's position alongside those who had fought in the Mexican Revolution and those who continued to protect Tepoztlán's land long after the revolution was over. The category *campesino*, although economically marginal, remained politically salient because of its connection to regional identity.

Writing when the fate of the Zapatista revolution in Morelos was still being determined, Manuel Gamio argued for the development of a nation that incorporated diversity ([1916] 1960:177). Describing the population of Morelos as having a system of communal exploitation of resources, Gamio pleaded for region- and group-specific laws:

> The revolution has begun the return of lands expropriated from the indigenous population and has legitimated the holdings they currently have. However, more must be done. . . . The prohibitions imposed on the communities in terms of property and interests must be done away with. Clearly what [I] propose does not constitute a retrograde tendency, since experimentally it may prove advantageous for these groups [the population of Morelos] to offer them a system of communal interests. . . . In other words, man was not created to mold himself uniformly to laws, but rather that laws be made in accord with the needs of men, and because the groups that make up our country present diverse characteristics and needs, it is logical that our law—whether economic or another type—should be distinct. ([1916] 1960:180)

Gamio ultimately saw communal control as a kind of insurance policy for the indigenous population. Like Zorita before him, he worried that if communal property were to be individually divided, it would be easy for large landowners to take advantage of weak, isolated, confused, and ignorant people who might be lulled into selling their possessions ([1916] 1960:181). He stressed that the ignorance and confusion of which he spoke were not inherent traits of the indigenous population, but rather the result of being forced into a society built by a minority around its own institutions and culture.

It would be a mistake to overemphasize the power of nationalistic discourses to transform the Indian's position in Mexican society, but it would be equally erroneous to dismiss these discourses all together. They have shaped agrarian policy, and, for better or worse, they have provided the basis by which contemporary peasant communities in Morelos measure themselves against the past and in the process construct their own subjectivity. In short, they provide a lens into the temporal dimensions of nationalism. The image of the ancestors passing to future generations the communities' lands, defended since the Conquest, weighs heavily on contemporary communities in central Mexico. Contested concepts of self and community, in this case not easily separated, are interwoven around the issue of defending communal land. What kind of community "we" are is a matter of constant debate in places such as Tepoztlán. "The last brave men fought during the Mexican Revolution, now everyone is out for themselves. . . . When you return in five years, there will be no Tepoztecans in Tepoztlán," a man explained to me.

In 1984, Tepoztecans attributed contemporary problems in defending communal land to the emergence of egoism and ambition and to a fall from an earlier state in which community was the overriding principle of organization. Although the enduring conflict between community and state was central to this crafting of a sense of self-community, Tepoztecans' images of the past and their sense of debt to the ancestors are legacies of the cultural translations of Indian life in the colonial era, which were later refashioned by the process of developing postrevolutionary nationalism.

Manuel Gamio's *Forjando patria* established the foundation for state policy toward the indigenous population in Mexico for almost fifty years, during which time the government sought to incorporate the indigenous population into a mestizo nation. Beginning in the 1970s, however, that policy came under attack by those who envisioned a Mexican nation built around plurality and diversity rather than on the unity Gamio had privileged. In 1987, another Mexican anthropologist—who, like Manuel Gamio, was interested in the fate of the nation and its indigenous population—published *México profundo*. Echoing Gamio's earlier criticism, Guillermo Bonfil Batalla argued that the Mexican nation had been constructed around the institutions and ideals of the population's minority, who were enamored with Western civilization. Their Mexico was imaginary, ignoring the reality that Mexico possessed at least two civilizations: the Western dominant civilization and the equally valid, albeit unrecognized Mesoamerican civilization. Bonfil Batalla found traces of Mesoamerican civilization everywhere in Mexico: in food crops, in the use of space, in attitudes toward nature, and in the incorporation of indigenous terms in everyday speech ([1987] 1996:3–15). Despite this ample evidence for an extant Mesoamerican civilization, according to Bonfil Batalla, Mexico's institutions were shaped only around Western civilization, relegating Mesoamerican civilization to a primitive past.

Bonfil Batalla placed blame for the nationalist emphasis on mestizaje and the consequential erasure of Mesoamerican civilization on people such as Manuel Gamio and education secretary José Vasconcelos. He saw mestizaje not as the foundation for the creation of unity, as did Gamio, but rather as the justification for what he called "de-Indianization." Campesinos, like those I describe in this book, were not mestizos, but rather Indians who had been discouraged from recognizing and developing their Mesoamerican roots. They were doubly impoverished: economically poor and culturally denuded despite the fact that vestiges of Mesoamerican culture survived even in their communities. Nowhere did Mesoamerican civilization survive, however, in pure form. It always existed in tandem with Western civilization.

Bonfil Batalla asserted that Indian cultures have used resistance, innovation, and appropriation in order to ensure their survival from the time of colonial domination to contemporary, modern Mexico. Although he defined Mesoamerica as having a distinctive culture, he emphasized not an enumeration of the components of Indian culture, but the conflicts with colonialism and Western domination that underwrite the preservation of difference. In his work, Mexico's indigenous population is not a problem, but a resource for the nation, one that will help it address contemporary problems in a uniquely Mexican fashion. By embracing indigenous knowledge, Mexico can confront its problems in a way that does not merely mimic westernization and modernization.

Bonfil Batalla's prescription for Mexico is a full embrace of diversity through an elaboration and extension of the notion of democracy. Western notions of democracy do not work for his project, for they are based on modes of individualism that are at odds with an ethnically and culturally diverse population. Modes of election should be transformed to conform to local custom; administrative units should be changed to support the territorial integrity of various ethnic groups; and the state needs to recognize collective units and not just individuals. Creating a pluralistic nation, however, is not simply a matter of letting flourish what is already there.

Bonfil Batalla's project fits within what Mignolo terms *border gnosis*. Similar to Bonfil Batalla, Mignolo argues that colonial domination entailed the imposition of Western epistemology on other ways of knowing (2000:3–45). The vast stores of knowledge that had accumulated in Mesoamerican civilization as well as notions of what counts as knowledge were discredited in the colonial process and continue to be discredited today. Again, resistance becomes a salient analytical tool in the notion of border gnosis. Without the notion of a population that has resisted either consciously or unconsciously, however lamentable the loss of knowledge, such knowledge is not retrievable in a form that will challenge Western hegemony. But if existing populations retain that knowledge, then they and their contemporary allies might transform centuries-long acts of resistance into fertile ground for generating alternative notions of civilization and new ways of being in the world. For a scholar to engage border gnosis, therefore, is to become part of this larger project of legitimating and recovering knowledges deemed inferior under colonialism, and thus of challenging Western hegemony.

In Tepoztlán at the time of my research, the history of the indigenous roots of communal land and the notion of a long historical vista in which the ancestors fought to defend the patrimony weighed heavily in the politics of contemporary mobilizations. As demonstrated in the following chapters, the passions evoked by this history form a double-edged sword. In the face of threats to communal land from a well-defined source,

Tepoztecans came together in brave and often sustained political actions. At these times, Tepoztlán resembled the kind of communities written about in the history books. In everyday life, however, when the market continually inflated the value of land, Tepoztecans seemed powerless to stop the steady erosion of communal land, and many who knew the "history" were burdened with a deep sense of shame that they could not live up to their ancestors' legacy, at least as viewed through the place they had been allotted in the construction of Mexican nationalism.

As subsequent chapters show, however, a politics of loose connections emerged out of tense confrontations of persons, principles, aims, and objectives. On the one hand, many Tepoztecans engaged passionately in politics, viewing political participation as the repository of all that is laudatory about community. On the other hand, they greatly mistrusted the political arena. As this chapter has suggested, the weight of history, the sense of responsibility to ancestors, and the conviction that their community was a special community because of its history continually pulled Tepoztecans into the political arena. Chapter 4 describes, though, how Tepoztecans creatively elaborated on the primarily textual history I have outlined in this chapter. Indeed, the aura of truth and authenticity that surrounded Tepoztecan visions of history came from the way they drew on oft-repeated notions of communal land that carried the weight of reality.

In chapter 3, I turn to the other side of the politics of loose connections: the widespread mistrust of the political arena. Unlike this chapter, which highlights the ideological debates that shaped the formation of the Mexican nation, chapter 3 examines the practices of the Mexican state. More often than not, these practices ensured that the indigenous and peasant communities did not garner the benefits seemingly granted them in law. Indeed, the law constituted peasant communities as places where corruption and abuse of power were rife and the state as the protector against those abuses. In so doing, the law set up members of a community to turn against one another and to turn toward a state that, when viewed from poor communities' perspective, enjoyed unlimited power to co-opt opposition movements.

Chapter 3

Political Passion and the Troubled Mexican State

The juridical structures of language and politics constitute the contemporary field of power; hence, there is no position outside this field, but only a critical genealogy of its own legitimating practices. As such, the critical point of departure is *the historical present*, as Marx put it. And the task is to formulate a critique of the categories of identity that contemporary juridical structures engender, naturalize, and immobilize.

—Judith Butler, *Gender Trouble*

Chapter 2 indicated that in Tepoztlán those involved in the fight to defend communal land beginning in the 1980s and, to a lesser extent, Tepoztecans in general viewed themselves against the backdrop of a particular reading of history, one that drew on the place of communal land and mestizaje in Mexican nationalism. At the same time, however, Tepoztecans at this time were well aware that communal land and by extension their community were being displaced by the nation's turn toward a neoliberal agenda. They were viewed and, in a sense, viewed themselves as condemned to fight battles that they could not win to defend a form of land tenure that countered the "modernizing" trends of Mexican history. This position at the marginalized center of Mexican nationalism afforded them a particular view of the state, one that emphasized the relative omnipotence of the state against their own powerlessness.

In this chapter, I examine the dialogue between the representations of state-community relations in the Agrarian Reform Law and the institutionalized practices that Tepoztecans deployed over the years in their everyday lives when dealing with state bureaucracies. The politics of loose connections emerged, in part, as a by-product of a history of subordination to state bureaucracies whose functions were more than administrative. The agrarian reform bureaucracy and the laws that governed communal land shaped conceptions of community, produced and reproduced notions of proper gender relations, and fostered the development of the practices that gave birth to the politics of loose connections. Mandated by law, the political machinations required to secure services from the state produced a set of contradictions that shaped social relations at the level of community, which in turn created an atmosphere of mistrust. Just as the history of defense of communal land inspired Tepoztecans to enter the political arena in the first place (as discussed in chapter 5), the mistrust that is a by-product of the state's practices encouraged political participants to remain wary even as they joined political movements.

The state's power in Tepoztecans' everyday life is owed in part to geography. In some areas of Morelos, communities that lack resources are not given much state attention, and forms of community participation that differ greatly from those found in Tepoztlán flourish (Varela 1984). But a network of roads connects Tepoztlán to three large cities and a number of smaller communities for which the town serves as a market center. Buses travel to Mexico City every hour and to the state capital, Cuernavaca, every half hour, where Tepoztecans shop, visit doctors, work, and send children to high school. The rural police have an office in the municipal building, and on several occasions during my research in 1984 truckloads of soldiers, reportedly looking for drug dealers, traveled to town and took up positions along the streets in the center of town.

The state's presence in Tepoztecans' life has not generally been unwelcome. Tepoztlán's position as an administrative center creates opportunities for the town's bureaucratic elites to benefit personally from fees collected for carrying out administrative duties. In comparison with the surrounding communities that are part of the district, Tepoztlán appears wealthy with its cobbled streets, running water, electricity, and telephone lines. Although all Tepoztecans do not enjoy these resources in equal measure, on the whole they live better than those in the surrounding communities. Moreover, Tepoztecans have actively defended their rights in part because, living in an administrative center, they have more access to state officials.

This chapter explores the ways in which Tepoztecans' interactions with the state as they sought to defend communal land in the 1980s shaped their political imagination. Clifford Geertz has argued that people get the politics that they imagine (1973:313), but imagination is never disengaged from the play of power. Tepoztecans' imagination of the political arena drew on their history of interactions with the state but was also shaped by the power of law to produce particular kinds of subjects—women, peasants, children—and to endow these subject positions with relations to community and to need.

The legal system, particularly as associated with the Agrarian Reform Law, provided the primary arena for confrontations between the Comité para la Defensa de Tierra and the state. For most committee members and indeed for most Tepoztecans, their experience with the legal process demonstrated beyond a doubt the prevalence of corruption and abuse of power at every level of the state. Many distinguished between the laws, which at least in 1984 they saw as just (they traced these laws to Emiliano Zapata's Plan de Ayala), and the bureaucrats who enforced them, "the real problem." Despite Tepoztecans' favorable interpretation of the laws themselves, these laws have produced problematic visions of community, poverty, and gender. Thus, Tepoztecans' imaginations of the political process were inseparable from the role of law in constituting particular subjectivities.

By 1984, Mexico's Agrarian Reform Law had been modified many times to encourage the incorporation of ejido land into a market economy (see Sanderson 1984; Gates 1988), but assumptions about peasant communities had remained fairly constant. The law set up expectations, presumed to be grounded in history, about social relations in peasant and indigenous communities that became naturalized in legal categories. In the shadow of rights extended by law lurked a narrative about particular kinds of subjects that had to be deployed in order to demand one's rights. This is what Butler, drawing on Derrida, suggests when she claims, "Juridical power inevitably 'produces' what it claims merely to represent" (1999:5).

Laws are usually thought to be promulgated in the name of some preexisting persons—women, workers, minorities—who demand rights that are subsequently granted by a benevolent and informed legislature. But this perspective ignores the power of law to bring into existence certain kinds of subjects by recognizing "rights" as inherently linked to one's subject position (Butler 1999:1–6). The individual comes to exist not only as a way of thinking about the world, but also as a way of being in the world. The extension of rights is thus never innocent of power, but rather is one of the primary mechanisms through which power shapes the social body. Mexico's Agrarian Reform Law did more than extend recognition to Morelos' peasants. The authors of the law wrote into it an image of a peasant community complete with ideas about gender, corruption, and concepts of authority. Most important, the law created the peasant as a collective subject with rights dependent on participation in communal life.

Agrarian Reform Law centered the community as a locale invested with rights and privileges. Demands for technical assistance, credit, and public services required that petitions filed with the state include the names of the "collective" that would benefit from this extension of state resources. The collective might be residents of a barrio (neighborhood), parents of school children, or a colonia formed by those who demonstrated a history of residence in the community.[1]

The state's mode of dealing with local communities required that they organize collectively, but it also restricted the power of those collectives. The Agrarian Reform Law constituted local communities not only as dependent on the state but riveted with corruption that had to be monitored by the local population. For these purposes, the law mandated the creation of general assemblies, watchdog committees, and commissioners of ejidal and communal resources, thereby extending state power into the "community." In the overall scheme of state-community relations, the community was the base, the bottom rung in a ladder of power that placed the president of the country at the top rung. The president of the country restored or granted land, forests, and waters; enlarged already existing grants; created new population centers; recognized and entitled communal resources; expropriated ejidal and communal resources; established urban zones in ejidos and communities; and presided over all the provisions of the Agrarian Reform Law.[2] The Secretaría de la Reforma Agraria bore responsibility for carrying out the president's technical and administrative policies and for coordinating with Secretaría de Agricultura y Recursos Hidráulicos (Department of Agricultural and Hydraulic Resources) in developing plans for ejidos and communities (Agrarian Reform Law, Article 10, provision 5). At the state level, the representative of the Secretaría de la Reforma Agraria presided over the Comisiones

Agrarias Mixtas (Mixed Agrarian Commissions),which carried out and consulted with other bodies concerning agrarian matters such as the amplification, restitution, and granting of lands and communal resources and the creation of new population centers. The establishment of ejidos and communities created local social formations such as general assemblies, commissioners of ejido and communal resources, and Consejos de Vigilancia (Watchdog Committees) that were subordinated to higher levels of the bureaucracy.

My friends frequently warned me that I should be careful in my work with the Comité para la Defensa de Tierra because on the surface everything would look clean, but underneath there would be corruption. One man resorted to pen and paper to illustrate. Drawing a pyramid that reflected the appeal process of the Secretaría de la Reforma Agraria, he explained:

> This is the hierarchy of corruption. Here at the bottom level are the comuneros. If they want to resolve the boundaries, they have to go to the commissioner of communal resources to get his support. To do that, they have to pay him, they have to take him out to lunch. Now, if he accepts, he has to go to Cuernavaca. There, the commissioner has to do the same thing for the representative of agrarian reform—he has to take him out to lunch, buy him things, and pay him off. Then, if the representative agrees to help, he has to do the same thing with the deputies [*diputados*] up until the point that the case gets to the governor. But that never happens because by the time it gets to the deputies, there is a new commissioner of the Oficina de Bienes Comunales [Office of Communal Resources]; the comuneros have to start the whole process all over again because so much time has passed that there are all new authorities.

This view of the Mexican state, highlighting the history of unmet promises and co-optation of opposition, informed local gossip about políticos.[3] The state and federal bureaucracies clearly needed monitoring, but Mexico's Agrarian Reform Law concentrated monitoring functions at the local level, as though that were the only place corruption and abuse of power might be found. In fact, although legally empowered to investigate local authorities' behavior, members of local watchdog committees rarely issued formal charges of corruption. Fearing that official charges of corruption might cost them their lives, they contented themselves with adding to extant rumors of corruption at the local level. When Tepozte-cans also suspected state- and national-level bureaucrats of corruption, they had no legal recourse for demanding an investigation of their suspi-cions. In short, there were a number of provisions for monitoring the behavior of local authorities, but few avenues for monitoring authorities at the state and national level. Instead, the law described the relationship between various agencies at the state and national level as "coordination," not "monitoring and reviewing."

Of course, Tepoztecans' imagination was not entirely constrained by Agrarian Reform Law. Tepoztecans recognized corruption as endemic to the whole system—not just to their local community, as Agrarian Reform Law implied. Corruption at the local level, however, was distinguished from that which prevailed at higher levels by a specific set of meanings and practices. First, local-level corruption stood as a reminder of the failure of "community," thereby creating a sense of betrayal when neigh-bors and friends were found to be corrupt. Second, the watchdog com-mittees formed by the Agrarian Reform Law at the local level played a powerful role in spreading gossip about corruption. In short, the Agrar-ian Reform Law provided mechanisms for undermining the very "com-munity" that it chartered as the foundation for rights and privileges.

In addition to creating these social formations at the local level, the law designated the types of relations that exist between different bodies at the community level. The General Assembly had to meet the last Sunday of each month. Fifty percent of the ejidatarios or comuneros plus one had to attend the General Assembly for its decisions to be considered binding, but if this "simple" majority was not achieved, the General Assembly met the following month and its decisions were legally binding regardless of how many members attended (Agrarian Reform Law, Article 28). In addition to the monthly assemblies, the General Assembly met at the end of each production cycle to report on finances and to plan future projects. The Delegación Agraria (Agrarian Delegation) had to be notified of all assemblies. At the end of each General Assembly, a report detailing the meeting had to be written and signed by the representative of the Comi-sión Agraria Mixta or Delegación Agraria, local ejido or communal land authorities, and all the assembly members present, each of whom signed his or her name above his or her fingerprint. The final report had to be submitted within eight days to the Delegación Agraria.

The commissioners of communal or ejido resources represented the ejido or the communities and were responsible for carrying out the General Assembly's decisions. The commissioners, president, secretary, treasurer, and their assistants were elected in the General Assembly to serve a term of three years (Article 44). Members of the commission had to be *ejidatarios* or comuneros who had worked the ejido for at least six months prior to the election and had never been sentenced for an act that would deprive them of their full rights (Article 38). In addition to the commissioners, the General Assembly also elected a Consejo de Vigilancia made up of three members and three replacements for the president, secretary, and treasurer (Article 40). The consejo monitored the commissioners to ensure that they conformed to the law, reviewed the commissioners' financial records, and employed persons to audit financial records if necessary. With the General Assembly's prior approval, the consejo called a meeting of the General Assembly if the commissioners failed to do so and informed the Delegación Agraria of all matters that would modify ejidatarios' or comuneros' rights (Article 49). All contracts and agreements reached by commissioners and the consejo that were not approved by the General Assembly and the Secretaría de la Reforma Agraria would be considered null and void. As we shall see, relations between the commissioners and the consejos often became tense.

The Agrarian Reform Law revealed the dependency of representation on the legal construct of the community in land law. On the one hand, commissioners and Consejo de Vigilancia members had to be ejidatarios or comuneros or both, and they had to be considered members of the population nucleus, or community. In short, the Agrarian Reform Law viewed their relation to the community through the lens of identity: they were members of the group that they came to represent through their election as officials. But the group's identity depended on the legal construct of "ejidatario" and "comunero" as dependent workers and rendered authorities as managers. First, the law limited all local-level authorities and organizations to carrying out activities that ensured the productive functions of ejidos and communities. Local authorities could not grant land, nor could they amplify boundaries of ejidos or communities. Second, the law placed local-level authorities in the position of being informers. They had to notify the Secretaría de la Reforma Agraria of invasions of land and of changes in production systems. Thus, the law constructed ejidatarios and comuneros as laborers on their own land with control over the means and methods of production concentrated in the state's hands. In this way, the Agrarian Reform Law transformed commissioners and the consejos into state's representatives in the community, leaving the task of regulation and discipline to local community members. As a result, Tepoztecan community identity intersected with state and national identity, especially when the corruption Tepoztecans knew prevailed at higher levels appeared in local authorities' behavior.

In addition to constructing a dependent relationship between the community and the state, Agrarian Reform Law accented the family's reproductive role and women's dependent status. When the available land did not meet the population's overall needs, the law provided for determining a hierarchy of need constructed around the family as a reproductive unit (from most to least needs): peasants with children; married peasants without children; peasants, male or female, older than eighteen without dependents; peasants, male or female, older than sixteen and younger than eighteen without dependents (Article 72). The law specifically designated women's rights: rights to voice and vote within General Assemblies (Article 45), rights to retain their ejido or communal holdings after marriage, rights to a special zone for collective female agricultural or industrial labor (Articles 103, 104, 105). In "representing" women's interests, however, the Agrarian Reform Law also constructed a specifically gendered social role. The land dedicated to women's collective labor adjoined housing sites and was allocated at the same time as the land for schools. It integrated childcare, sewing and education centers, mills, and all other facilities dedicated to the service and protection of peasant women. In addition, the law specified that those who inherited land must sustain the dependent children of the deceased and his wife with the products from the inherited lands (Article 83). The Agrarian Reform Law further stipulated that ejidatarios could not make sharecropping or rental agreements or any other type of agreement that would constitute indirect exploitation, including the employment of salaried workers. But women with dependent children who could not work the land directly could enter into rental, salary, or sharecropping agreements to remain available to the minors who depended on them. In providing for women's "special situation," the law linked women's status to that of minors under the age of sixteen and those who were incapacitated. The only other exceptions to the sharecropping rules were those ejidatarios who would not be able to complete their work even if they dedicated all their time and labor (Article 76).

In 1984, the Mujeres Tepoztecanas added their voices to the struggle to defend communal land. Long before my arrival, the group had formed when these women decided to become involved in a contested election (see Martin 1990). By 1984, communal land had become a symbol of the future, a key element in the struggle between men and women, insiders and outsiders, and the Mujeres Tepoztecanas became involved.

Communal land was a women's issue, at least according to women in the group. Men, they claimed, had already proved they could not be trusted with such a valuable resource because men's politics was informed by self-interest, not by a love for children. Too weak to resist the lure of corruption, men had sold communal land without thought of their children and grandchildren. In contrast, according to the Mujeres Tepoztecanas, mothers held families together; they understood that if their children could not get land in town, they would be forced to leave. Moreover, mothers prove in their everyday life that they are capable of sacrificing their own interests, a trait that makes them the best guardians of the community's future.

The Mujeres' views of history captured yet another piece of the long, twisted tale of communal land. Population pressures and the community's attractiveness to wealthy outsiders had led to skyrocketing land prices. Most Tepoztecans willingly accepted the higher prices that outsiders and foreigners offered them for their land but found themselves begging for a piece of communal land when the peso was devalued. But even communal land could command lucrative prices from outsiders and foreigners. Corrupt officials could be persuaded to provide phony private-property documents to holders of communal land, and unsuspecting foreigners often purchased land without knowing if it was private property or communal land. Many purchased communal land without regard to its legal status.

From one day to the next, or so it seemed, squatter settlements would spring up along the mountainside. Many of the colonias' residents came to Tepoztlán from Guerrero or Oaxaca to escape the poverty of their own state. The Mujeres called these new squatters *paracaidistas* (parachuters) to capture the sense that colonias seemed to fall from the sky without anyone noticing until they were already formed. But some Tepoztecans had also appropriated plots of communal land for speculative purposes, and wealthy foreigners would purchase the land illegally to construct large multistory homes with spectacular views.

The threats to communal land posed by wealthy foreigners were insidious. They came about through a network of deals reached over a long period of time and involving many different players in the bureaucracy. When such a deal finally reached fruition and a luxurious home was under construction, there was little the women could do. Indeed, members of the Comité para la Defensa de Tierra argued that the women, because of their naïveté, often encouraged these kinds of deals with foreigners by supporting wealthy Tepoztecans' rights to hold several plots of communal land. In fact, the women did support wealthy insiders against poor squatters from surrounding states, claiming that communal land should be reserved for Tepoztecans. Moreover, many members of the Mujeres Tepoztecanas protested that Tepoztlán was full of its own poor who needed land—poor who were truly Tepoztecans and whom the community "knew": these poor had made a commitment to the town, and the town had a special obligation to help them when they were in need.

The legal jargon of Agrarian Reform Law disguised an overall picture of the type of "community" constructed in the law. Bestowing all powers to establish boundaries and to expropriate and redistribute land to the country's president, the law constructed ejido and communal land as a gift from a benevolent state to the community. The president bestowed land on needy communities just as a father provides for his needy dependents. Such an ethic established giving to the needy as a basis of community life. Continuing the theme of family relations, the definition of *need* centered around the presence or absence of children in families, making the community and ultimately the president responsible for families' welfare. In the final analysis, the Agrarian Reform Law constituted the community as subordinate to and dependent on the state. Tepoztecans' insistence that they had held communal land since before the Conquest was meant to contest this state-centered vision of land and is one reason that the struggle to defend communal land was at the center of so much Tepoztecan activity in the early 1980s.

Those who participated in and used the law in their struggles with the state used both the notion of a dependent community and the narrative that placed the origins of land in the pre-Conquest period. Drawing on historians' writings, Tepoztecan activists pointed proudly to their Zapatista heritage to argue for inherent rights to land and for the power of community unity. They viewed the law as representing the community's interests. Even if the experience of community always fell short of expectations produced in Sotelo Inclán's glorious images of the revolutionary struggle (see Martin 1992), the community was the locus of rights and obligations that should be demanded from the state. When corruption and abuse of power appeared *within* the community, however, the Agrarian Reform Law provided a paradigm through which Tepoztecans viewed themselves as dependent on the state for correcting their problems. Then Tepoztecans reminded themselves that the community was, after all, like a child in the family: it would grow and prosper if the president (the father) were good and just. If not, nothing could be done. People were only behaving in ways that the state implicitly sanctioned.

Out of the mélange of contested notions, community emerged as an object of contemplation, worry, and criticism. The disjuncture between images of the past and experiences of the present, coupled with the promise of "rights" guaranteed by law, unleashed an impossible desire for a unified community. Given the practices that prevailed within the state and the impossibility of disentangling the state from the "community" in everyday life, such unity was difficult to sustain. That did not, however, stop Tepoztecans from longing for unity. Many Tepoztecans proudly told stories of past unities, suggesting that underneath the apparent conflicts lurked a potential unity that might resurface at any time. Others were less optimistic about the future, but no less sure that in the past there had been unity. Few questioned the political, economic, and social benefits that might come if the community were united. Tepoztecans' interests in my own book as a "correction" of what they saw as Lewis's misunderstanding of Tepoztlán reflected the deep desire for unity that shaped their politics.

Technologies of Power

Historians, political scientists, and some anthropologists, fascinated by the unusual stability of the Mexican political system and PRI power, helped to construct a vision of the Mexican state as the perfect machinery of power. At least up until the 1980s, the state's reach seemed to extend far and wide, and its mechanisms of co-optation never seemed to fail (see Hellman 1978; Collier 1992; Middlebrook 1995).[4] Likewise, the popular press in the United States seemed mesmerized by the phenomenon of

"Mexican stability." My informants shared this view of the state, centering power in the structures of the state, at times creating too neat a division between state and civil society: the community seemed a victim of a state with nearly perfect powers of co-optation. This vision both overestimates and underestimates state power by ignoring the myriad of ways state power leaned on everyday practices located within the community. Although these practices can be analytically separated from the state, they have emerged as a strategy for gaining access to resources controlled by the state. They constitute a *habitus* in the sense described by Bourdieu, a system of nonconscious expectations structured by and structuring a history of practical experience (1990:53). They figure into everyday calculations of what must be done to get what one needs or wants. Although they do indeed have a history, it is a history disguised in the form of timeless dispositions and deeply held notions of the state.

The administration of Lázaro Cárdenas in the 1930s provides an appropriate starting point for a discussion of the practices to which I refer because his administration shaped Mexico's PRI, which ruled for more than seventy years. Lázaro Cárdenas organized his presidential campaign in part around appeals to the peasantry. Working through the press and peasant congresses, he publicized the agrarian reforms that he had carried out in Michoacán and won the support of peasant organizations in several states (see Craig 1983). The radical Liga Nacional Campesina Ursula Galván (Ursula Galván Peasant League), which formed from the agrarian revolts in Veracruz, was divided over Cárdenas's candidacy, but the more moderate faction endorsed Cárdenas's campaign. Cárdenas opened his campaign with the declaration of the CNC, an organization that played a pivotal role in securing the presidency for Cárdenas and that later served to channel peasant participation in the Mexican political system, including that of many older members of the Comité para la Defensa de Tierra.

Throughout his presidency, Cárdenas intervened in peasant and worker conflicts to see that reforms were carried out. One hour each day the telegraph office was kept open free of charge so that those who had complaints could wire them directly to the president (Hamilton 1982:134). The president frequently traveled around the country to oversee the implementation of reforms, at times spending more than a month in an area to monitor the expropriation and redistribution of land. He learned about rural areas from schoolteachers, who, after years of organizing against the government, now found the president supporting their socialist ideals of education (Hamilton 1982:136–37; Vaughan 1997).

Cárdenas succeeded in incorporating into the party the bulk of radical opposition to the government. The Confederación de Trabajadores Mexicanos (CTM, Confederation of Mexican Workers), established in 1936, came under control of Lombardo Toledano, who argued that the organization should support the Cárdenas administration's revolutionary acts by abstaining from strikes (Hamilton 1982:161; Cockcroft 1983:125). Hamilton explains, "The Cárdenas government in effect had given legitimacy to the state as representative of the revolution; this legitimacy in turn appeared to justify the linkage of the labor movement with the state" (1982:162). Likewise, peasants became integrated into the state through the Ejidal Banks that Cárdenas established to provide credit to ejidatarios and to oversee production and distribution of crops. Four sectors—labor; peasants; military; and a popular sector made up of state employees and teachers, organizations of small landowners, students and professionals, and women's groups—represented the party at its convention in 1938. The PRI thus formed into "sectors" that ostensibly represented extant social divisions, but that were created by the state. Participation in the various unions that formed to represent sectors became a vital link between the party and its various constituencies. As Collier notes, "in Mexico the heritage of incorporation and its aftermath became an important conflict-limiting mechanism that avoided or minimized polarization. The popular sectors were electorally, ideologically, and functionally incorporated into the dominant party, which helped to mediate relationships between them and the state. . . . With these resources, the Mexican regime attained a level of stability that had completely eluded it through the first three decades of this century" (1992:52). But if incorporation into the party helped the state control conflict, as a profile of contemporary radical Tepoztecan leaders illustrates, union participation also became a training ground for activism. At least in the peasant sector, bright, talented people gained opportunities to develop their skills as leaders and perfected a revolutionary discourse that would inform their sense of justice long after the party had officially abandoned it. Don Abram is an example of those activists whose political passions were nurtured in the state bureaucracy established during the Lázaro Cárdenas administration.

Don Abram was born in 1911 in the neighboring state of Mexico, and his experiences and skill at storytelling enable him to bring to life the history of Tepoztlán, particularly as relates to the land conflicts that have inspired his passion for justice.

Don Abram's parents died when he was only eleven years old. In telling the tale of his life, he emphasized the hardships that fall on those who are left without real relatives, but also the inherent goodness of strangers, something he claimed to remember when poor campesinos arrived from Guerrero and other surrounding states. He went to Mexico City when he was only eleven and found work in a store owned by a man whose relatives lived in Tepoztlán. The man became a surrogate father who made sure that the young Abram learned to read and write.

As don Abram explained with scarcely disguised pride, he developed a taste for "women and liquor" early on in his life, twin passions that landed him in jail. One night at a local dance he killed another man over a woman. Upon Abram's release from jail (it is not clear whether or not he served a full sentence), the shopkeeper who had raised him suggested that he go to Tepoztlán, where he could start a new life. Abram arrived in Tepoztlán in the late 1920s or early 1930s and began living with the shopkeeper's relatives in one of the poorest barrios in Tepoztlán, the district seat. He is proud of the relationship he established with his benefactors: he treated them as though they were his biological parents. Whenever he made any money as a day laborer, he turned it all over to his soon-to-be parents-in-law just like a good son would. They responded in kind, treating him as though he were their own son, and when Abram asked for permission to marry their daughter, they gladly agreed.

He and his wife had several children, but he remembers one baby for her stunning beauty. She had light skin and black hair that curled just a little at the nape of the neck. She was so beautiful that he worried that if his wife took her out of the house she would be afflicted by *mal de ojo* (evil eye). His wife disobeyed him, taking the child with her to the market, and the child became very sick. When he brought the child to the doctor, the doctor prescribed medicine that was "hot," and because mal de ojo is also hot, the two created a fatal combination. Abram then took the baby to a *curandera* (a healer) who reprimanded him for waiting so long to bring the baby. She told him that the baby would die and that it was his fault for not having brought the child sooner. Just to prove what she might have done for the child, she cleaned the baby with an egg. As she passed the egg over the child's body, the child calmed. Don Abram left with the baby, but as he was carrying the child into his house, her body stiffened in his arms, and she died. He realized that it was his fault and vowed to learn how to cure. Today he uses his curing skill to protect his own grandchildren.

Don Abram remembered that ever since coming to Tepoztlán, he had been involved in fights to protect the community's land. Although people sometimes challenged his right to be involved because he was, strictly speaking, an "outsider," he defended himself. To those who dared to debate him, he replied that he had never done anything to alienate community lands, whereas many "insiders" had not so respected the town's patrimony.

In the 1940s, don Abram became the local ejido commissioner and a member of the PRI, whose form had been shaped by the Lázaro Cárdenas administration. He remembers that during this time he fought fiercely to defend Tepoztlán's land (at this point there would not have been a division between the offices of ejidal and communal resources), but he also acknowledges that he took a plot of land for himself. He says many Tepoztecans did not love the land as much as he did, so he felt justified in taking the land. After decades of struggle in which he took cases to the Supreme Court and battled boundaries with neighboring communities, he came to realize what the party was "all about" (corrupt politics). He left the party and his post as ejido commissioner, but he continued to fight to defend land.

Don Abram recalled his involvement in a battle against a housing development for outsiders, a battle that took place on the same plot of land that Tepoztecans defended in the "golf wars" that I discuss in the epilogue:

In 1962, a group of people came to settle on Tepoztlán's land. They wanted to build a development. A group of us went to the land. We were met by two generals from Zone 25. They asked who the leader was. I knew why they were asking, so I told them that there was no leader. I said, "This is the whole pueblo." They answered, "OK, why are you here?" I told them, "This is the pueblo's land. You can go back to work now, but if you are not off by Saturday, we will kick you off." When Saturday came, people started arriving at my house, but by noon there still were not enough people. I wanted one hundred people. I asked, "Where are the rest—didn't you invite them?" They said that they had, but that the others were lazy or had work to do. I said, "OK, we will go with just ninety people." When we arrived, we were greeted by troops. One man grabbed me by the collar and shoved a pistol in my face. He tried to take me away, but I told him if he took me, he would have to take everyone. The people behind me started to say, "If you kill him, you must kill all of us." They asked us what we wanted, and we said, "We want to talk to the engineer responsible for the project." They tried to take me away, saying that we were going to talk to the engineer, but I said that we must all go together.

In the end, work on the project never went forward, although ownership of the plot of land remained in question. In 1991, don Abram asked me to find, in the files at the National Archives in Mexico City, the letter regarding the matter that had been sent to President López Mateos in 1961 (quoted in chapter 2). All these years he had doubted that the campesinos' letter had ever arrived and was surprised when I returned with a copy of it. As I describe in the epilogue, in 1995 a U.S.–owned firm tried to build a multi-million-dollar resort on the land, but Tepoztecans successfully stopped that project, although at enormous costs to themselves.

By the 1960s, there had been several changes in don Abram's life. His in-laws had died and left him the plot of land and the house in which he lived at the time of my research. Although their own children ignored his in-laws, according to don Abram, he cared for them when they became old and sick, just as a good son would. And when they died, their children did nothing to pay for the funeral expenses, so he assumed the whole burden. Nevertheless, after their death, their children tried to keep don Abram from inheriting the family land, but he defended his rights to the land, arguing that they had done nothing for their own parents. A few years later don Abram's first wife died as well.

Later don Abram became involved with a local woman, and they had a child. He says that she did not want the child, so he took the baby boy and raised it himself without a mother. He describes strapping the baby to the back of his horse so that he could bring the child with him when he went to work in the fields. In 1984, this child, at the time eighteen years old, lived with his wife and their three children in the house don Abram had inherited from his in-laws. I learned in 1994 that this son, who had meant so much to don Abram, had been murdered. Some Tepoztecans suspect that the son, like his father, became involved in politics and was murdered for taking a strong position against a landowner. Don Abram told me, however, that his son was killed by some people who worked for a wealthy land owner, but he thought it was in a drunken brawl.

Don Abram's life changed again when he converted from Catholicism to Seventh Day Adventism during the 1960s. He recalls that someone came to his barrio and went house to house talking to people. Because he always chats with people, he got to know the man, and they started to read the Bible. In the Bible, he learned that Saturday, not Sunday, should be the Sabbath and that people should not eat meat or drink alcohol. He studied very hard, and his teacher left him in charge of teaching the Bible to the rest of the class. To this day, every Saturday a small group of between ten and twelve people gather in don Abram's simple house with its dirt floor to study the Bible. On a Saturday in 1984 when I attended the service, they were studying Armageddon, and don Abram was teaching the group to interpret contemporary world events through the Bible's prophecies. They read Apocalypse 16:13–14. Don Abram questioned his dedicated pupils: "Who is the dragon?" The little gathering stared at him, waiting for an answer. "Ronald Reagan," he replied, answering his own question. "Who are the false prophets?" Again he succumbed to their anxious stares. "The pope, who says that he can save the world with his blessing—he could never do that because he is only a man—and people like Ríos Montt in Guatemala, who kill and torture people in the name of religion."

Although don Abram is no longer a PRI member, he continues to reap the benefits of his former position as ejido commissioner. In 1984, he worked as a gardener for a foreigner who lived in Tepoztlán. He recalled that one time when the minimum wage changed, his employer resisted increasing his hourly rate. He promptly took the case to the CTM. The employer was subpoenaed and arrived with several documents, seemingly well prepared to defend himself. He did not know, however, of don Abram's connections with the labor union. Don Abram boasts that his friends helped him. Later, he claims, the reluctant employer expressed surprise that he, a poor peasant, had so much power with officials.[5]

The weaving of radical politics and conservative religion has served don Abram well. His religious beliefs encouraged him to give up drinking, although he admits he is still attracted to women, and his commitment to sobriety has helped him to be a dependable and trustworthy leader. Moreover, as shown in the following chapters, his withdrawal from the rituals and ties of *compadrazgo* make him an appropriate mediator between "traditional" notions of justice and the modern demands of bureaucratic impartiality. In 1991, after don Abram became the commissioner of the Oficina de Bienes Comunales, a minister in the Seventh Day Adventist Church complained that don Abram's involvement in politics contradicted the teachings of the Bible. Don Abram referred the minister to Christ's admonishment to give to Caesar what is Caesar's. He told the minister that he took orders from no man—only from God's word—and in serving as commissioner of Bienes Comunales, he fulfilled his duty to the government. At the time, he was representing the comuneros in yet another bitter confrontation with the state.

When writing about the interrelationships between individual biography, community history, and state power in Mexico, many anthropologists and historians have viewed the Mexican Revolution as creating a new class of revolutionary elites who share an interest in maintaining a revolutionary discourse while subverting its intent in an effort to enhance their power and privilege. As my informants would agree, the state has maintained power by co-opting those individuals and groups who might challenge its legitimacy by offering them positions in the bureaucracy. These co-opted local leaders reap considerable financial rewards in their position. Discussing the ejido system, Friedrich explains: "The struggle for control of the ejido and the central role of ejidal office in the political life of the village is thus to be explained primarily on economic grounds. The story of this ejido [Naranja] resembles many other stories of Mexico past and present, where political success is the quickest and often the only means to a life beyond bare subsistence" (1986:124).

This process of co-optation so common in Mexican politics is usually assumed irreversible and undermines commitments between leaders and followers (see, for example, Hellman 1978:104–5; Lomnitz 1982). The stories of don Abram's political development and of don Pedro's, which I relay in chapter 4, suggest that for the generation of bureaucrats born in or around the time of the revolution, the term *co-optation* might be misleading. In the 1920s and the 1940s, to be a member of the agrarian bureaucracy—even at the local level—was to be revolutionary. Positions in the bureaucracy shaped identity by promoting a passionate and historically meaningful commitment to ideas concerning land reform, even for those who did not participate in the revolution. In such positions, peasants learned to equate a yearning for justice in land matters with legal rights based on traditional land tenure practices. The fact that so many peasants availed themselves of the opportunity to take a little for themselves does not negate the role of bureaucratic positions in creating a passionate attachment to agrarian matters filtered through constantly evolving state versions of Zapatista ideals. Although don Abram clearly acknowledged the transgression implied when he "took a little for himself," it is also true that having done so, he has regulated the land in compliance with agrarian ideals: he has used the land for his own purposes, and he has not sold or rented that piece of land. At the present time, when land is in short supply, the meaning of that transgression is very different from what it might have been earlier. Although the fact that he has held the land has afforded him many political advantages, as discussed in chapter 4, and some liabilities, the care he has exerted in managing the land in accord with agrarian and traditionalist principles has insulated him from the disdain usually accorded "corrupt" officials.

Don Abram's life and his passion for agrarian concerns suggest the productive power of law that I discussed at the beginning of this chapter. In describing his life, don Abram traced his own passions for agrarian matters in their intersection with agrarian law, dwelling on those conflicts that reveal the justness of community claims for land. To view don Abram's passions merely as co-opted by the state fails to acknowledge both the productive power of law and the limits to state control of that productive power. Don Abram's passions for land developed in conjunction with the emergence of a postrevolutionary nationalism that accorded a special place to agrarian matters. The scenario of co-optation would view those passions as having origins "outside" the structures of state power, a perspective that requires accepting a problematic divide between community and state. At the same time, however, to describe don Abram's passions as fully contained within the structures of the state is also misleading. Rather, revolutionary nationalism provided the terms on which don Abram's struggles for land were rendered meaningful as acts in pursuit of justice.

Under the PRI-controlled state, a political group grew in strength if it was able to get benefits for the community, and access to benefits depended on the establishment of ties with state- and federal-level officials. Although the Salinas de Gortari administration in 1991 expressed interest in changing this pattern, in 1991 the pattern was still very much intact in

Tepoztlán (see chapter 7). Party control over finances made the PRI the most effective political organization at the community level. Even the more recalcitrant organizations, those who claimed to be mobilizing against the party-state apparatus did not escape the PRI, for their leaders were cajoled and coddled by party officials in attempts to incorporate enemies into the party structure. But groups and individuals who did managed to resist incorporation into the state party apparatus were not therefore free from the state's influence. As I have already pointed out, to the extent that their demands were based on the legal categories, their goals were always already inscribed within the orbit of state power. And because the state/party apparatus depended on mobilization and organization, whatever tactics they deployed were also already indexed in local political culture as a request for incorporation into the party. In short, whenever someone emerged as a competent organizer, he or she was thought to be trying to enhance his or her political career in the party, as the following conversation between me and a Mujeres Tepoztecans member illustrates. The conversation concerned one of the most active leaders in the Comité para la Defensa de Tierra, the Maestro Jorge. It took place in 1984, when the committee, which had already defined itself as opposed to the party/state apparatus, had been in existence for only one year.

J.M.: Is the Maestro Jorge on the PRI list? [The list of local leaders that the PRI makes up before choosing its candidate for mayor.]
E: Yes, of course.
J.M.: How did that happen?
E: Not, with this mayor but with the one before, he [Jorge] made signs that he wanted to be mayor.
J.M.: What was he doing?
E: He was always arguing publicly with the mayor. He always disagreed with him and complained about the way things were being handled.

The Maestro Jorge maintained both publicly and privately that he had no intention of securing a political career for himself, and to date he has refused any offers to join the party and has not accepted any official positions in town politics. As I discuss in the epilogue, in 1995 during the battle against the tourist project, he was jailed on trumped-up charges of murder and served two years in prison. After being released, he did become a leader in the teachers' union, but he has never campaigned for any local office.

The fact that the Maestro's public opposition to the mayor could be understood as a request for incorporation into the party speaks to the power of the state's structures to condition the political imagination. At the time of my research in 1984, the emergence of a nonloyal opposition (one that had not already reached agreement with the PRI) was unimaginable. In the Maestro's case, however, his distrust of the PRI was not just political; it also was connected to his family history.

According to town gossip, the Maestro Jorge's older brother had been a member of one of the guerrilla movements that flourished in the neighboring state of Guerrero in the late 1960s and early 1970s. The brother was imprisoned in the early 1970s, but escaped from jail, and after his escape was assassinated. The judicial police ransacked the family home in Tepoztlán, looking for, as the complaint that I found in the local archives explains, "quien sabe que" (who knows what). Later in the same month, the Maestro Jorge and another brother were detained and beaten by members of the Judicial Police. In each of the instances, the Maestro Jorge filed legal complaints charging the governor of the state of Morelos, the state attorney general, the chief of the Judicial Police at the state level, and the local mayor with violations of rights to liberty. In each case, the authorities denied any knowledge of or responsibility for the events.[6]

The Maestro's family history was well known in Tepoztlán, yet after 1984 many continued to assume that his opposition to the state/party apparatus reflected a desire to incorporate into the PRI-controlled state. The assumption reveals aspects of state power: first, its ability to constrain the imagination, and, second, the use of gossip to reinforce constraints on imagination. The woman who shared the "tidbit" of the Maestro's name on the PRI list was a political opponent. One's political enemies frequently used such gossip to undermine the legitimacy of emerging opposition movements. If it could be believed that the Maestro's name was on the list, his political supporters would begin to question his integrity. But such gossip was believable because in so many other cases that was exactly what had taken place: opposition leaders became PRI candidates. This leads to the paradox that opposition to the state is unimaginable. Imagination is shaped by the past, and in Tepoztlán it is always fueled by examples of former opposition leaders who are now members of the PRI bureaucracy.

After the mid-1930s, the challenge facing all opposition candidates in the PRI-controlled state was how to be defined as "oppositional" in a setting where expressions of opposition were read as requests for incorporation, where the opposition and the official party seemed to have the same agenda, and where the state/power apparatus had already organized one's constituency. The shape that the PRI came to assume as a result of Lázaro Cárdenas's reform was not just the work of a clever political leader. In fact, the impetus for the definition of sectors came from the Constitution of 1917, which extended rights to peasants and labor. These "rights" incited political organizing throughout the country; Cárdenas deployed the legal constructs as a basis for campaign organization and created institutional channels to represent those conflicts. His presidency provided an early example of relations of power in the new, postrevolutionary Mexico, in which struggles to enforce rights guaranteed by the constitutions served to identify talented local political leaders who later became integrated into the PRI.

By 1984, the relationship between the state and community in Tepoztlán had soured not only the relationship between the town and the party, but also relations within the community as well. In a sense, Tepoztecans' experiences with the PRI were recast as indicative of the general state of human relationships. In short, the state was imagined as enjoying a kind of absolute power of corruption. One man told me, "The PRI won't allow someone else in power—they will destroy anyone who tries to get into power. I was in the PRI in the 1940s, but I got out because I figured out what it was all about." Another person remembered that a friend of hers had fought a labor dispute for ten years. After paying money for a lawyer, she lost the case because the lawyer was paid off by her opponent. An ejidatario engaged in a year-long battle over a plot of land complained that he wanted someone to come and "judge" the matter, but no one had come. "They make beautiful speeches from their offices, but the problem is in the countryside," he explained, highlighting the discrepancies between rhetoric and reality.

The community's intimate involvement with the Mexican state left many Tepoztecans feeling vulnerable to state control. And as they reflected on the corruption that they believed proliferated not only in the Mexican political system but throughout their community as well, they did so not with the curiosity of uninvolved outsiders, but with the uncomfortable awareness of painful introspection. They knew that they and their neighbors and friends had been a part of that system. Any discussion of the state/party bureaucracy produced an outpouring of tales of betrayal and politically motivated killings.

Tepoztecans viewed abuses of authority as the rule rather than the exception, an endemic aspect not only of politics, but also of community. For the most part, they were correct. Getting children into good schools, getting access to medical care, finding jobs, and getting enough water, all required Tepoztecans to "maintain connections" with their neighbors who had power in government bureaucracies. In hopes of getting her child into a better school, one woman reluctantly continued to sell Tupperware for a neighbor who had powerful connections in the high school. Another had joined one of the women's groups in order to find a job for her daughter. And with opportunities to be a "político" at every level of social life, the mistrust that characterized relationships with the state bureaucracy proliferated at the community level.

In Tepoztlán, most elements of "community"—collective action, ties of reciprocity, fictive kinship relationships—were linked to the regulatory role of the state/party apparatus. This means that Tepoztecans encountered one another in an overdetermined space. Relationships between friends and family members could be, and usually were, passionately close, marked by confidence, knitted together by ties of reciprocity, and at the same time instrumental and characterized by a constant mistrust. No underlying cultural code regulated this jumble of meanings, making trust the ruling emotion in one situation and mistrust in another, friendship in some domains and instrumentality in another. One cannot define a rule that explained where to use what code, as DaMatta (1991) suggests for Brazilian relationships between household and street.

Even the term *gente de confianza,* confidential friend, which Tepoztecans used again and again to describe to me the ties to other persons, captured the ironies of multiply invested interpersonal relations. Friedrich explains that a confidential friendship "entails a greater interdependence of feeling, and the inclination of habit of sharing in doings that are often private or intimate. . . . A confidential friend is also someone with whom one can discuss covert politics, even hatch a conspiracy. I participated in numerous whispered conversations between friends in which the 'egoism' and 'ambition' of others was [*sic*] laid bare to the bone" (1986:90–91).

Friedrich correctly points out that although such friendships may seem strong on any particular day or time, relations of trust often prove to be fragile with the passage of time and in relation to character differences. But in Tepoztlán friendship was even more fragile than what would be suggested by dimensions of time and character, for social distance and political necessity had to be factored in as well.

Certainly, a confidential friend was one with whom political intrigues could be discussed and conspiracies hatched, but there were levels of political intrigue. For example, members of the Comité para la Defensa de Tierra frequently described me as gente de confianza, but usually to those who were not committee members and certainly not to the inner circle of committee members (see chapter 4) who really ruled the committee. I was a confidential friend, but their confidence was predicated on an already existing mistrust that they believe filtered my access to information. In other words, in relationship to those who were not committee members, I could be trusted to reveal what I knew because it was assumed that my knowledge was limited.

Rather than a relationship that escaped the mistrust that characterized the political arena, trustworthy friendships were embedded in a more generalized mistrust. Trustworthy persons—persons trusted because what they knew was assumed to be already limited by mistrust—were entrusted with the task of making alliances between different groups. For this task, one could not trust a person who had already been trusted with deeper knowledge of intrigues because information might leak across the alliances that were formed. In short, the levels of trust and mistrust were already inscribed in the dynamics of political alliance formation. The intersection of trust and mistrust, of friendship and instrumentality, accounted for the frequent use of the term *gente de confianza* to describe workers in the state bureaucracy. To say that one had a trustworthy friend in the bureaucracy was to suggest that this was a person from whom one gathered information about "official matters."

A map of the gente de confianza claimed by a group or an individual provided a measure of political power, for to have trustworthy friends—in the sense described here—in high places was to have political power. Because the term was invested with this significance, claims to have trustworthy friends generated suspicion. Political leaders frequently promised followers that they had gente de confianza in high places who could be of use. The promise was always double-edged because, on the one hand, a person needed political patrons who were well connected, but, on the other hand, Tepoztecans suspected betrayal from those who were well integrated with the state bureaucracy.

The constant presence of these multiple and tense forces in social relations at the community level testifies to the power of the Mexican state to shape a politics of loose connections. Connections in the bureaucracy are necessary for any achievements, but at the same time these same connections might well lead political leaders to abandon their followers in pursuit of their own self-interests.

The role of the gente de confianza is pivotal to the politics of loose connections, for this person serves to connect organizations with the state or with other groups, but at the same time he or she also must be kept at arms length from an organization's internal intrigues. He or she is always a person "loosely" connected to the group, whose connection, as I mentioned earlier, is predicated on the instability of trust and mistrust. Ironically, the best gente de confianza are those in whom one has placed the least confidence.

In 1984, many longed for the emergence of a trustworthy opposition party and, with the same intensity, doubted that such an opposition would ever survive the PRI structure. Rallies held by opposition parties were a popular form of entertainment. People attended to hear the moving speeches, to enjoy the display of collective power, and to reaffirm their commitment to community. One young man described the rally that inaugurated the formation of the Comité para la Defensa de Tierra: "I really enjoy the public assemblies. I remember when don Abram stood up, tore his hat from his head. He was angry. He said, 'When the pueblo speaks, there is no governor, there is no president, there is only the pueblo.' It was so beautiful that you really felt like doing something. I wish they [the committee] would have more public assemblies." The desire this young man expressed for public assemblies speaks to the way desire linked community to ideals of rights and empowerment. This desire motivated Tepoztecans to become involved in numerous mass mobilizations around rights to land, water, and other resources. Activists proclaimed, "We are a poor community, but we know how to defend what is ours." In fact, periodic mass mobilizations did halt many unwanted development projects both before I came to Tepoztlán and during my stay in the community. But the organizations that formed around these issues rarely survived the onslaught of gossip that began shortly after the movement's emergence. Tepoztecans seemed passionately committed to activism, even as they readily exited groups torn apart by rumors of corruption and too close relations with state bureaucrats.

The gossip about políticos was believable because it was grounded in sociohistorical conceptions of the state that were not unlike those conceptions that dominated social science research on the Mexican state. Gossip illustrated long-existing patterns, so there was little need to validate tales of corruption with evidence. But it was not just distant políticos who were corrupt. The example of the development project included in my discussion of don Abram's life history illustrates that in terms of corruption and abuse of power, Tepoztecans did not establish boundaries between the community and the state. Deceptions by "insiders" weighed heavily in people's willingness to embrace negative assessments of the character of anyone who seemed willing to vie for political power. To most Tepoztecans, anyone, regardless of class or social position, was susceptible to engaging in corruption; to believe otherwise was to be stupid. "Here we have learned that everyone, when they first get a position, acts very well, but then after a while they start being político [corrupt]," a campesino in his sixties explained. Don Abram, however, contested the attribution of corruption to human nature when he underscored the connection between the party/state apparatus and beliefs about corruption: "The people mistrust everyone. First, they gossip, and when they gossip, everything gets exaggerated. But, more important, the government has so often promised things without delivering on their promises, and now the people trust no one."

The interplay between passionate commitment to community and rampant mistrust of politics played itself out in the trajectory from mass mobilization to depoliticization that characterized Tepoztecan political life. In Tepoztecan politics of the 1980s, words were thought of as unequally distributed. To *tiene la palabra* (strictly speaking, "to have the floor") was to have the power and ability to speak to the passionate commitment to community and to the demands for justice. Skilled political orators, those who had words, publicly represented the group and acted as leaders within the group. But their position was always precarious because they had to speak for those who claimed not to have "words." The latter sat silently through meetings and political rallies, rarely expressing their opinions in public, but readily engaging in gossip that carried their views of políticos throughout the community. In the analytic of power, such gossip often determined a group's fate. When those with words were deemed to be speaking out of self-interest or trying to manipulate a position in the PRI—as they frequently were—

group members were faced with choices. The motives of those who remained in the group would be questioned: perhaps they, too, were benefiting from their participation, or maybe they were just stupid. As corruption gossip took hold, those without words left the group, making the leaders appear more and more ridiculous: For whom were they speaking? Was not this proof that all políticos used beautiful words to disguise their self-interest?

The Mexican political system, as a legacy of its mestizaje, endorsed both the individualism of capitalist civil society and the communalism of tradition (see Lomnitz and Lomnitz-Adler 1988 for a discussion of this dynamic in the 1988 Mexican presidential election). Despite periods such as the Cárdenas presidency, the Mexican state remained committed to a capitalist path of development with a free-market system. But this commitment was tempered by the state's political role in defining sectors to be defended from the more dire effects of capitalism and in deploying those sectors as the base of the party / state apparatus. The elaboration of such an intermediate position created a set of paradoxes for both opposition groups and the state.

The revolutionary nationalism deployed by the Mexican state created ample reasons for opposition to the state. The Mexican Constitution, in extending rights to communities, such as rights to land, created the conditions for its own failure. For example, although the state of Morelos included the highest number of communities eligible for land according to the Agrarian Reform Law, by 1930 there was little land left to be distributed in the center of the country. Instead of being given land, peasants were given derechos a salvo, rights to land when and if it became available (see Sanderson 1984). In such a situation, the state inevitably became known as the purveyor of false promises (see Warman 1980; De la Peña 1981), but at the same time it had to be viewed as generating a desire that could never be fulfilled. Moreover, revolutionary nationalism celebrated opposition, encouraging citizens to value political unity and aggressive confrontations with the state. The volatile combination of the promises of revolutionary nationalism and the esteem given to acts of opposition meant that state power was frequently contested by communities who felt that they had been abandoned by the political system.

But if the Mexican state was weakened by promises, those promises also served to render the language of opposition extremely problematic. In a sense, the discourse of left opposition was always already inscribed in state structures, and opposition groups inevitably took up the same causes as those held by at least one faction of the official party, the PRI. With everyone—PRI candidates, the "loyal" opposition, and the "disloyal" opposition—clamoring for peasant rights to land, workers' and women's rights, it was difficult to distinguish among competing claims for political power. It was not that political rhetoric suffered from a loss of meaning, but that meaning became suspect. Rather than giving rise to playful resignation, the mistrust embodied in Tepoztecan views of politics produced the passionate vigilance implied in political gossip.

The tensions between the promise of unity in revolutionary ideology and the mistrust that surrounded political participation informed the ebb and flow of Tepoztecan politics, leading to periods of mass mobilizations that expressed a desire for a community unity, a unity that inevitably was undermined by gossip about corruption. It would be a mistake, however, to view these oscillations in Tepoztecans' organizing as an adequate account of politics. This is not a case of predictable shifts, for the content and form of politics changed drastically over the years. Tepoztecans were becoming increasingly powerful as a community and taking on different and more challenging issues, but the path they took was neither direct nor unproblematic, as I describe later in this book.

Viewed through the lens of the nation, the politics of loose connections in Mexico had its roots in the attempt to recover a space for civil society in the shadow of a PRI-controlled state bureaucracy that had lost legitimacy. Although a strong argument can be made that PRI control was never as total or absolute in some regions as is often implied (Knight 1990; Rubin 1997), in Tepoztlán the control that the Mexican state exerted over land, labor, education, social services, subsidies, and health care made it impossible for ordinary Tepoztecans to avoid the state. Moreover, their views of themselves as a community drew upon representations embedded in Mexico's Agrarian Reform Law and on the historic role that the community had played in defending its communal land. When I arrived in 1984, they no longer viewed the state as a just purveyor of these services, but rather as an all-powerful political machine with absolute power to corrupt. As I have suggested in this chapter, the impossibility of separating the community and the state practically or conceptually extended the state's legitimacy crises to the local arena as well, making it difficult to organize opposition movements. Yet Tepoztecans persisted in organizing, all the while keeping their gaze trained on exits from the political arena. The resulting politics mirrored the loose connections on which it was founded. Through loose connections with gente de confianza, who, I have argued, are better viewed through the lens of mistrust than trust, Tepoztecans made the connections they needed with state bureaucrats, all the while trying to keep the state at arm's length. Politics became ultimately a matter of trying to preserve a space for community separate from the state, an impossible task, but one that shaped the form of politics. Attention in the political arena became focused less on the support that could be given or exchanged and more on the formation of protective distances while one was participating in that arena. Those who attended meetings but refused to speak except in gossip were yet another manifestation of this protective distance, as was the mass exodus of members from groups when they judged leaders to be self-interested and possibly corrupt.

As this chapter suggests, the analysis of social movements from the perspective of rationally derived interests and strategically informed moves misses the important place of passion and desire in politics. One cannot make sense of Tepoztecans' repeated engagement in political struggles without attending to the unrealized and probably unrealizable desires for unity that pulled them to politics. As doña Rosa, the partura, exclaimed after reading a passage from her diary of political struggles, this one about the delivery of a garbage truck, "Me encanta la política" (I love politics). The verb *encantar* defines a specific form of love, one based on being charmed, captivated, and seduced by someone or something. To speak of politics in this way, then, is not to think of it as a kind of long-term commitment, lived out in everyday life so as to lead to deeper and deeper levels of consciousness and more clever strategies, but rather as a kind of passionate, irresistible pull that may well be destined to fail. Political passions are nurtured in that space between the desire for unity and the sense of its impossibility. It is precisely because those moments of unity are so precious and few that Tepoztecans leave their houses and risk their own lives and their families' lives to contest state projects. In other words, it is a kind of unruly play of desire that informs Tepoztecan politics. Indeed, one might see Tepoztecan politics as taking place in the space between Robert Redfield's depiction of the harmonious community and Lewis's representation of Tepoztlán as racked by gossip and mistrust.

My point is that if we theorize social movements without recognizing the play of desire within them, we risk transforming political participation into a kind of hollow form that, no matter how theoretically sophisticated it may be, moves farther and farther away from people's experience of politics. The fact is that Tepoztecans participated in political movements with playful excitement and passion, and not just with a cool calculation of their interests, although they did engage in the latter as well. We ignore the passion and desire that people bring to the political arena at the expense of accounting for why people are willing to stake their lives for political causes. As Benedict Anderson notes for nationalism, the question that needs to be answered is, Why are people willing to die for an imagined community? (1983:16).

Of course, having centered my analysis in the play of desire for unity, I have also emphasized that desire is produced rather than emerging sui generis out of some natural foundation. At base, Tepoztecans' desires for unity have been fostered and nurtured not only by the contemporary Mexican state, but also by the volumes of anthropological and historical writing that accord the fight for communal land such a privileged place in Mexican history. As I suggested in the previous chapter, the weight of this history hangs heavily on Tepoztecans when they feel their community challenged. It is at that moment that "memories" of the past come to bear on the present.

In this chapter, I have emphasized both Tepoztecan desire for community unity and the accompanying gossip and mistrust as products of the state's presence in the community. In the next two chapters, I take up the question of how these desires are produced and reproduced within social movements in Tepoztlán. Chapter 4 examines the desire for unity as it was produced as an aesthetic value by the Tepoztecan ancianos who shaped the struggle to defend communal land in 1984, and chapter 5 examines the gossip that traveled along the same surface as the desire for unity.

Chapter 4

The Crafting of an Aesthetic of Tradition

When I speak, I always say what I feel. The Maestro had heard me speak of land, and he liked the way that I spoke, so when he decided to do something about communal land, he came to me and invited me to participate.
—Don Abram, the seventy-four-year-old vice commissioner of the Oficina de Bienes Comunales in 1984

This chapter discusses the Comité para la Defensa de Tierra more fully. It focuses on what I term the *aesthetic of tradition* that legitimated the defense of communal land, examining how that aesthetic of tradition intersected with gender and class, and how it fared within the legal structure of the national Agrarian Reform Law.

I am drawn to talk of tradition as an aesthetic because the ancianos who worked in the committee often defended how things were "before" through a kind of argument of images that sustained only a tangential relationship to actual events. Indeed, a traditionalist aesthetic might be best understood as a kind of "collective fantasy" that took shape through the construction of binary oppositions that pitted tradition against the capitalist market in land (Weismantel 2001:268). Thus, the images of how things were *antes* (before) was rendered in its juxtaposition with the thematic of the present as a kind of fall. The final section of the chapter extends this critical argument by looking at the play of irony and parody through which members of the committee rendered a commentary on the contemporary Mexican state.

If the Mexican state is so omnipresent in Tepoztecans' lives, one might well wonder on what basis Tepoztecans can make a claim to an identity apart from the state. The term *inalienable possession* captures the importance of communal land. Annette Weiner points out that if social life depends on exchange between groups as Leví-Strauss argues, it is also true that those exchanges have little meaning without a prior group identity that is shaped around that which is not exchanged—that is, inalienable possessions. Possessions held back from exchange derive value in part from their "prestigious origins, succession, or an edifying authority connected to the past" (1992:37).

As with inalienable resources more generally, the story of Tepoztlán's communal land commands attention because it revolves around the struggle to keep this resource out of exchange, first with the conquerors, then with hacendados, and today with outsiders, some of whom are poor squatters from other communities or wealthy people who envision beautiful homes on communal land. Narratives about brave Tepoztecan ancestors defending their land emphasize the desirability of Tepoztlán, rendering the defense of communal land a form of impossible struggle. One might take don Abram's story of the loss of his beautiful daughter to covetous desires in the form of the evil eye as a metaphor for the struggle to defend communal land. In the minds of Tepoztecans and of many outsiders, the town's incomparable beauty provokes such desires. Indeed, just as don Abram lost his daughter by seeking the help of a doctor rather than that of a traditional healer, the fight to defend communal land in the absence of a return to tradition was doomed to failure. As Weiner notes, maintaining inalienable possessions is always a heroic venture (1992:48).

"Soon we will be eating *tacos de billetes*, money sandwiches—we must teach the young people to love the land," don Abram complained. His comment highlighted the absurdity of equating wage labor with subsistence work on one's own land. The notion of "love for the land" connects a mode of subsistence production with values associated with sustaining life. But even the notion of "subsistence" needs to be widened to capture the aesthetic involved in the idea of "loving land." "Loving the land" is not merely a matter of fulfilling human needs. Although the food produced on Tepoztlán's communal land contributes to nourishing the human population, in the ancianos' minds the work of humans in nourishing the land is equally important. Indeed, ancianos love the flowers that they often use to adorn their property as much as or more than they love the food they produce for subsistence. When water is in short supply, as it often is during Tepoztlán's dry season, many still manage to save a little for the flowers. To "teach" children to love the land means to teach them what the land needs: the special attributes of different types of manure in nourishing the land, how to work the land directly with one's hands rather than with machines, what plants need and when. Thus, love of the land is tied to an aesthetic shaped around a form of reciprocity that pulls land into the domain of social relations.

If under capitalism land can appear to have intrinsic value related to its place in the productive process, the notion of stewardship over the land as shaped by a traditionalist discourse brings human labor back into the equation. But human labor here is not the labor that creates surplus value—the past vestiges of laboring on the land in Tepoztlán produced little in the way of surplus value—but that which is engaged in as an act of love. When Tepoztecan ancianos speak of their love of land, they suggest that caring for land is akin to caring for children. They think of working the land as a male occupation, but it is also in many ways equivalent to women's roles in raising children. As in the case of rearing children who depend on their parents' proper guidance, land needs the ancianos' care so that it will *dar* (give). Indeed, Tepoztecans often complained that "la tierra, ya no da," the land no longer gives, a result of the way in which land had been abused.

When the situation is conceptualized through the lens of reciprocity, it is not that land saps human workers' energies, with land gaining a life that they lack (the form it would assume under commodity fetishism), but that land is pulled into the sphere of human exchange. Indeed, the land gives because of human labor; it ceases giving when humans cease to labor for the land. And yet, even in 1984, when the land ceased to reward human labor by providing for subsistence needs, ancianos continued to try to nourish the land, despite realizing that their work might no longer produce. Ancianos often referred to their work on the land as akin to black kernels of corn, a kind of useless product but one that they maintained out of their own love for the land.

This conception of land and of its links to human labor seems reminiscent of Marx's notion of nature as always socially determined (Berthold-Bond 1997:158), but the accent in the notion of love of the land is on reciprocity and not on the transformation of nature, as it is in Marx. Marx's understanding of human relations to nature must be viewed through his sense of human labor as the way in which humans objectify their existence in the world. Although under capitalism objectification appears as "a loss and as servitude to the object," objectification is the way human beings reproduce themselves actively in the world (Bottomore 1964:122, 128). To the extent that objectification, the form of human labor, appears as a loss, it is because of its connection to the creation of surplus value under capitalism. Marx recognizes a relationship of interdependence between humans and nature, but it is an interdependence based on humans' existence as "a part of nature": "To say that man *lives* from nature means that nature is his *body* with which he must remain in a continuous interchange in order not to die" (quoted in Bottomore 1964:127, emphasis in original). Although the absurdity of eating tacos de billetes certainly underscores human beings' place in nature, the notion of reciprocity underscores land's place in the social world. Land "gives" in exchange for that which is given to it, thereby taking its place in the social order. In short, land is not fixed, as is nature, but rather becomes social through its special place in the human social world.

Tepoztecan ancianos recognized subsistence land as located on the margins of nature and culture. Indeed, their references to reciprocity and to love of the land differed from the way they spoke about the flora and fauna that constituted the natural world. At the time of my research in 1984, ecological discourse had impacted Tepoztecan views of nature, and ancianos often reflected on the decline of species in the region. This decline they attributed to the impacts of human beings on the environment, but the lens of reciprocity, through which they viewed their relationship to land, was far less apparent in their discussions of the natural world. The natural world was a source of products that Tepoztecan ancianos recognized as having utility for them (such as the bat manure that they used on their fields), but they did not talk of nature as needing human stewardship. The by-products of nature were available for the taking, but they were not contingent on what human beings put into nature, although they could be diminished as a result of human action. In other words, the natural world could be transformed by human intervention, but it would never achieve the status of agricultural land, which was tied to the human world through reciprocity. To the extent that humans could care for nature, it was only by protecting it from the deleterious effects of human action; unlike agricultural land, nature did not give more as a result of what the ancianos could give it.

Talk of love for land intersected with the steady flow of market discourse concerning land in 1984. Although the image of eating money sandwiches seems to point to the fundamental absurdity of a system driven by the desire for money, ancianos did not equate capitalism with the unnatural. Although the ancianos believed that love for land could be attributed to their ancestors and therefore was temporally prior to land as a market value, they did not assume it to be natural. "It's natural—when people need money, you cannot expect them to turn down a good price for their land," explained an elderly woman. Unlike Taussig, who argues that his Colombian peasant informants found the commodity unnatural (1980:10), my own informants did little to dislodge a sense that capitalism emerged out of a natural order. Indeed, their commentaries on capitalist greed, divisions between rich and poor, the desire for commodities, and so on repeatedly emphasized not the historical origins of these "evils" in capitalism, but the timelessness and wide geographic spread of these things. Their discussions pointed to capitalism's affinity to the more base human instincts of greed and self-interest. Tepoztecans, according to the ancianos, needed to confront capitalism with the higher civilizing forces of tradition, a key component of which was love of the land.

Of course, images of the value of tradition cannot really be separated from a market logic, as evidenced when Tepoztecan ancianos explained why they wanted to protect communal land. The defense of communal land assumed importance against the backdrop of the expanding market in communal land: it is precisely because Tepoztecans recognized the market value of their community that land became an inalienable possession. In other words, the struggle to defend communal land took place in a space already dominated by the market value of land. More pragmatically, however, past experience, as ancianos explained, suggested the unstable grounding of exchange value. People who sell land for a good price soon find that they don't have enough with which to live. Communal land provides some protection from the devaluation of the peso not because it holds its exchange value, but because it provides one with a place to live and farm. In a world of unstable currencies, use value may take precedent over exchange value.

There was a great deal of slippage between how the ancianos talked of their land and how they behaved toward the land on a day-to-day basis. They would sell land, especially to finance their children's education, to pay medical bills, or simply to be rid of it because their heirs no longer desired to farm land. And they often lent communal land, illustrating its centrality to the social order, to enhance the ties of reciprocity that enabled them to garner political power. But it would be a mistake to view talk of love of the land as a ideological masking of the ancianos' "true" self-interests. Rather, the discourse of "love of the land" intersected with market practices. For example, one anciano refused to sell his corn because the price offered was lowered by the impact of corn imports on the market. He chose instead to stock the corn in his own home, but it went bad before the family could eat it. As he told the story to me, tears welled in his eyes while he complained that one loses the desire to labor when the value of one's work is so discredited. Another went through all the stages of selling land only to back out at the last minute, complaining that the price offered was too low. Although many Tepoztecans might have believed that these behaviors indicated the ancianos' irrationality, such behaviors make sense if we understand that ancianos were always negotiating the difficult terrain in which the market logic of land and the ethos of love of the land intersected.

At the level of Tepoztecan political discourse, indicators of poverty— homes with dirt floors, oxen- or hand-drawn plows, the conspicuous absence of stereos and televisions—become reworked as indications of "tradition." Tepoztecans themselves do not talk of a traditionalist viewpoint, but they do talk of the existence of segments of the community who continue to live, so they say, as they did years ago.[1] Although many Tepoztecans warned me that many traditionalists were wealthy, in the discourse of traditionalists the struggles between the *ricos* (rich) and the *pobres* (poor) can be recast into a conflict between the forces of "modernization" and those of "tradition," with modernizers being the rich and the traditionalists being the poor. In fact, by shunning conspicuous consumption, many traditionalists do manage to conserve their wealth usually in land that is both private and communal. Nonetheless, the poor, who in traditionalist discourse have keen insights into the problems of contemporary society, are not battling for more wealth. Rather, they seek to retain a distinct style of life—one that pits local rich and poor against one another in a rough and, as we shall see, problematic merger of class struggle, tradition, and Zapatismo.[2]

"Are there conflicts between rich and poor in Tepoztlán?" I asked, employing the language of Tepoztecan conflicts. I was walking along a dirt path with an anciano who had invited me to see his plot of communal land. "Of course," he replied, "the rich fight to defend what they have, their capital; we fight to defend what we have, which is our work, our land." The fight to defend capital and the fight to defend land are at odds with one another in part because those who have capital often get it by selling land and sometimes by selling land that is communal property. More important, in the absence of land, traditionalists cannot fulfill those relations that represent the aesthetics that define a traditionalist life, those that express love of the land. Love of the land is in many ways the foundation of a number of other social relationships embedded in reciprocity. As women pointed out, without land their children leave to find work, and without land family ties weaken as a result of the impossibility of fulfilling the reciprocal demands of marrying and raising children. In other words, the antagonism between rich and poor has as much to do with the impossibility of living out valued ways of life as it does with a fight over access to material resources.

Laclau and Mouffe use the notion of antagonism to underscore the impossibility of any identity to take shape as a full presence, noting that the relationship between landlord and peasant is not one of fully constituted identities confronting one another. Rather, they suggest, "it is because a peasant *cannot be* a peasant that an antagonism exists with the landowner expelling him from his land" (1985:125, emphasis in original). They locate the origins of social movements in "external" discourses that constitute such relations of subordination as oppressive. Although Laclau and Mouffe privilege democracy as one such "external" discourse, I think Tepoztecan discourses concerning love of land constitute relationships between rich and poor as oppressive by rendering love of the land as the foundation of proper social relationships. To be unable to live out the proper form of social relationships because of inequalities in the distribution of land constitutes a form of oppression.

For the ancianos, to defend one's work by defending land is not just to protect access to money; it is also to fulfill a particular relationship to the land that enables other social relations. This does not mean, however, that traditionalists have little need for money. Although their lifestyles lead them to reject many material possessions, they need money for food, clothing, transportation, and sometimes even fertilizers and pesticides, which they use on their land. It is in these settings, marked as fields of consumption rather than production, that they encounter the myriad ways the rich defend their capital and in so doing prohibit the poor from defending their labor.

Unlike when Lewis carried out this research in the 1940s, control of land and cattle no longer provide the primary path to wealth, and the poor are not necessarily laboring on the terrain of the local wealthy ([1951] 1972:177). Instead, the contemporary "poor" work as day laborers in construction or migrate to the United States in search of work. The "poor" are those who have difficulty meeting their consumption needs, understood not just through the lens of individual desires, but also through the lens of social demands. For example, young, newly married men often migrate to the United States in search of work to save money to purchase a home for the family, a kind of prerequisite for fulfilling the man's proper role in the family. The aesthetic of tradition—with its emphasis on the fulfillment of proper roles, beginning with the relationship between land and its caretakers and extending to family relations in general—shapes the political significance of the dilemmas of consumption around a division between merchants and those who must buy their products to live.[3] Merchants become, for the poor, the site of contestations over credit, rising prices, and appropriate relations between rich and poor.

The semiotic flexibility of discourse on rich and poor means that it cannot be read simply as an indicator of structural position; rather, such discourse stabilizes a body of tales of the past that can be continually called on to elaborate moral and ethical arguments about valued ways of living. What makes a person rich or poor is not structural position per se, which is always far more complex than the language of "rich" and "poor," but the use that a person makes of that position. To be rich is to boast of one's wealth, to refuse to donate to fiestas, to display one's wealth through open consumption of commodities, and to feel oneself better than others. Most important, the rich, similar to the land, no longer give. One older woman explained to me that in the past if you were poor, the merchants in the center of town would give you a bite to eat, but no longer. Then she paused and reflected, "Well, now the only time the rich give is when a poor person dies: then they will raise money for the funeral." Her observations speak to the way in which the rich seem to be moving outside the morality dictated by reciprocity. If they give only upon the death of a poor person, it seems to be as a compensation for their unwillingness to give to the living, but it seems directed less at the poor than at the threat of some kind of divine retribution.

In the tales that constitute rich and poor, traditionalist morality and ethical behavior fare better in the context of poverty than they do in the context of wealth, a kind of mirror of the arguments made by Franciscan missionaries in colonial New Spain (see chapter 2). Given the ambiguities of structural positioning in Tepoztlán, most Tepoztecans claim that they are poor and tell similar tales of the immorality of the wealthy even when they themselves might be relatively wealthy. The equation of poverty with morality, coupled with the reading of a lack of material possessions as an indication of a traditional lifestyle, lends tradition a peculiar moral and aesthetic force. Those who are driven to defend land because it is the pueblo's patrimony and who shun the material possessions of a capitalist society claim to speak for timeless and enduring community values.

For the investigator placed outside of history and community, the relative wealth of Tepoztlán's internal rich pales in comparison with that of outsiders—those foreigners and Mexican nationals who have purchased land in the town.[4] The latter live in architect-designed homes in the valley to which they retire on the weekends and in the summers. Some hire Tepoztecans to work in their gardens and to watch over their property, protecting it from thieves inspired as much by resentment and jealousy as by economic need. Although their wealth is often resented, it is far from most Tepoztecans' imagination, so these individuals are, in certain senses, outside the conception of hostilities between the ricos and pobres. Moreover, with few exceptions, outsiders have not acquired a place in this history of town conflicts between the ricos and pobres. In contrast, the social landscape of insiders in Tepoztlán is littered with the spirits of past political and economic struggles in which individual families established a reputation as either ricos or pobres. When I asked for clarity as to who were the ricos, I was told, "We know who they are—we know their families." Most peasants would name the same five families. A woman born in 1901 reflected on the Porfiriato: "I remember Porfirio Díaz [president 1877–80, 1884–1910] —he supported all the rich. No one had their own land, and everyone worked for the rich people, who did not pay them enough to live and often hit them. . . . When Zapata made his call for liberty and revolution [in 1910], the whole state of Morelos raised up in arms. The Carrancistas saw that the state [Morelos] supported Zapata, and they started persecuting the state." Indeed, newspaper accounts of the period tell of Carrancista threats to burn the community—something that they eventually did. One faction of Tepoztecans appealed to the governor for protection, stressing their willingness to reveal the whereabouts of Zapata to try to save the town.

Historians of Morelos argue that the revolution effectively destroyed the land base of the rich, creating a more egalitarian social structure, but categories of struggle from that period (for example, rich and poor, caciques and "indios") have survived to inform contemporary political discourse. The distinctions between ricos and pobres is thus an indication of class only if we understand that the terms refer to position in a process of consumption in which necessity is transformed into virtue. The limits imposed by economic necessity are not experienced as such, for expectations are adjusted in relation to objective possibilities so that people reproduce "in their verdict on themselves the verdict the economy pronounces on them" (Bourdieu 1984:471). In Tepoztlán, this process is facilitated by the fact that need, tradition, and poverty have acquired, through nationalist readings of the past, symbolic capital. Clearly, the act of representation always entails dimensions of domination, as I have stressed throughout this book, but the affinity between representation and domination tells us nothing about the dynamic processes through which representations are brought into play in the political arena, the topic explored in the next section.

Some of the ancianos who continue to live a "traditional" lifestyle can use their rights over land to control those who have no land. As I point out in chapter 3, many ancianos acquired their current land holdings in stints as officials in the agrarian bureaucracy. In the final analysis, traditionalist comuneros who hold their land supposedly on a basis of need can turn out to be and often are rumored to be land wealthy. This land enters into the vast array of lending practices that speak to structural positions ignored in the legal categories of comunero and ejidatario and in local distinctions between ricos and pobres.

Lending land is the one mechanism through which ancianos acquire the cultural capital to reinforce their prestige. Land is lent not only to help those who have no land, but also to gain access to better-quality land or to land that is closer to one's house. For example, someone who has a plot of poor-quality land might lend that land to someone who has no land and borrow from someone who has better-quality land. But not all lenders are equal; the ancianos who managed to accumulate land during their stints as officials are in a position to lend more land and also to lend land to those who can reciprocate only with labor exchanges and political loyalties. In fact, the Agrarian Reform Law inadvertently encourages such practices with its demands that land be farmed continuously.

As younger people leave Tepoztlán in search of jobs in Mexico City and the United States, those ancianos who have accumulated land often find that they cannot farm all the land that they have. The problem is exacerbated because the land is often spread out in small plots of less than one hectare of rugged terrain, which therefore cannot be farmed with mechanical plows. Under the Agrarian Reform Law, land that remains idle for more than two years can be confiscated and redistributed, with the result that the small number of ancianos who own a good deal of land and have no children to farm it must lend it in order to keep it in cultivation. These are the same ancianos who often emerge as prestigious political leaders at the local level.

Tepoztecans distinguish between *prestar* (to lend) land and *rentar* (to rent) land. The latter takes place within market mechanisms with precise agreements concerning the amount to be paid for the land and the dates in which payments take place. Moreover, those who rent land often do so to grow cash crops. In contrast, the terms on which land is lent are submerged in the pleasantries of traditional ethics of care and concern. Those who borrow land, according to the ancianos, reciprocate according to their free will and not in compliance with the demands of any contract. Although ancianos do become angry with those who accept their generosity without giving anything in return, they consider it abhorrent to have to ask for something or to have someone they have helped turn against them in political battles. In fact, within the traditionalists' group, such institutional arrangements effectively ensure the ancianos' prestige, and many are looked on as generous, kind leaders.[5]

Ancianos point to practices of land lending as examples of the higher cultural order of "tradition" and the denigrating influence of "modernity," emphasizing land lending as embedded in practices of reciprocity that overcome inequality. They argue that land does not need to be distributed equally but should be managed in accord with the community's needs. To the extent that ancianos control large expanses of land, they defend these inequalities by arguing that they have proved their love of the land and are defending it from those who might alienate the town's patrimony. The discourse of tradition does not disguise inequalities; rather, it justifies them. In this way, traditionalist ancianos seize on the cultural capital they glean from nationalist attention to the past, while reworking the terms of nationalism to fit their own circumstances. The place that ancianos occupy in the national imagination, as guardians of the community's patrimony, enable them to locate within a traditionalist aesthetic the practices of land lending that result in their accumulation of cultural capital. Perhaps it is not surprising that the contemporary work of ethnohistorians that draws on Nahuatl writings seems to support Tepoztecan ancianos' reading of inequality, suggesting unequal distribution of the land to begin with (see Cline 1984:293; H. R. Harvey 1984:91; Lockhart 1992:153) rather than the picture of idyllic equality that emerged in postrevolutionary nationalism.

I first met don Pedro Rojas in 1984 when I started attending Comité para la Defensa de Tierra meetings. He was one of the outspoken ancianos in the committee, and I quickly came to admire his direct manner of confronting foreigners who had taken over communal land.

Don Pedro lived in a house with a cement floor, but without the indoor plumbing that one finds in most Tepoztecan households. The main house where he lived with his wife and his teenage son contained an outdoor kitchen and two large rooms, and a television and a radio that Pedro liked to listen to in the mornings. In addition to the main house, the compound contained a tiny, two-room house for his daughter and granddaughter and another larger house for his son, daughter-in-law, and their two children.

Don Pedro did not hesitate to rule his family. When one of his daughters had problems with her husband, who was drinking and sleeping with other women, Pedro met with the husband's parents, and together they worked out a solution. His daughter would leave her husband and her three male children—Pedro thought those boys had been ruined by their father's bad blood—and return home with her daughter, who was still nursing. Pedro's daughter complied with her father's mandate because, as she explained to me, she was "a good and respectful daughter."

Like don Abram, don Pedro had once been an ejido commissioner. He had a great "love of land," and although he was orphaned at fourteen and left with nothing, he had managed to accumulate enough land of all types—ejido, communal, and private—so that each of his eleven children would be left with land. He boasted that unlike most Tepoztecans, he had also remembered his daughters in his calculation of how much land he needed to ensure his family's future.

An avid collector of Zapatista paraphernalia, he became the source of many of the stories I collected about Zapata. On the walls of his bedroom hung a banner with Zapata on horseback looking kindly down on a peasant dressed in white. Zapata's hand rests gently on the peasant's shoulder. The image is borrowed from a statue erected in Cautla in the 1930s and portrays what O'Malley (1986) has defined as the emergence of the paternalistic Zapata. Don Pedro remembered that he carried the banner in a parade in Cautla when he was ejido commissioner, and he liked the image because it is the "authentic" Zapata, who listened to the campesinos' problems. When don Pedro was plagued by dreams of columns of soldiers, he consulted an anciano, who told him that he was dreaming of the Zapatistas. The anciano explained that Pedro's father had been a Zapatista and that was probably why he was having these dreams. Don Pedro explained to me that maybe that is why he has such a "love for the land" and a strong sense of agrarian justice.

Although don Pedro continued to engage in subsistence farming, his children, with his support, quickly turned their inheritance to tomato production, thereby making the transition that Tepoztecans mark with the distinction between campesinos (peasants) and *agriculturalistas* (farmers). One son pooled resources with a friend to purchase a large truck to carry the tomatoes to Mexico City, where they could demand a higher price. In addition, one of don Pedro's children, his youngest, proved to have a mind well suited for schoolwork. Pedro had encouraged every child to get the education that he regretted never having; he was determined to help this son achieve his dreams of becoming an engineer. By 1989, the son was at the Universidad Autónoma de México (UNAM, National Autonomous University of Mexico) in Mexico City, and the family was trying to pay for him to live in an apartment that he shared with a classmate. The financial pressure encouraged them to sell one of their best plots of land to an outsider, who was going to build a beautiful home on the plot. Don Pedro now turned to investing the money so as to provide a continual source of cash for his son's education. By 1991, he had purchased a house for the equivalent of thirty thousand U.S. dollars in a town outside of Tepoztlán, which he hoped to rent to foreigners so that he could maintain a steady flow of cash. When I returned to Tepoztlán in 2002, one of don Pedro's daughters confided in me that her father had never rented the house because he did not trust any tenants. In the end, they just sold the property.

These transformations in don Pedro's status intersected with his withdrawal from the committee. In 1988, Don Pedro had been injured. He was hit in the head with a rock and knocked unconscious in a confrontation with the Mujeres Tepoztecans. Although the doctors could find nothing wrong with him, he continued to complain of dizziness and blurred vision, so his wife and his children encouraged him to leave the committee. One of his daughters, a single mother with two children, joined the committee because, as she explained to me, she had "inherited" her father's love of the land.

Tepoztlán's traditionalists refer to themselves as the poor and humble of the community. They represent themselves as limited by their lack of education or intelligence or by unique constellations of life circumstances, while proudly emphasizing that they treat others with respect and that they uphold simple patterns of life handed down over generations. In these ancianos' rhetoric, life's most basic truth is found in living out the proper form of relationships between people—including hierarchical notions of authority—and in sustaining an ethic of care, grounded in reciprocity, in relation to the land and to other human beings. Maintaining a level of control over one's demeanor (at least while sober), avoiding open displays of emotion, and controlling one's desire for consumer goods characterize a proper traditionalist lifestyle. As George Foster (1965) described for peasants more generally, this lifestyle means avoiding the extremes. But Foster's formation of "limited good" fails to acknowledge that in the Mexican case cultural capital accompanies the avoidance of excess wealth, at least for those segments of the population constructed in nationalism as representatives of the nation's agrarian roots. Ironically, as the example of don Pedro suggests, traditionalists not only can amass considerable wealth in land, but can use that wealth to convert their lifestyles. Of course, don Pedro did not widely advertise his new lifestyle, and perhaps no one knew of his rental property in the neighboring community.

In contrast to the Mayan ethnic identity as described by Nelson, in which women occupy a special, albeit problematic, place in the maintenance of cultural identity (1999:170–205), tradition dislodged from ethnic identity accorded little place for women among the Tepoztecans of 1984. As I have stressed, an aesthetic of tradition at this time was shaped around a particular understanding of how to produce on the land and was confined to the kind of work that men did. Ancianos often mentioned women's work, speaking of how in the past women used to wake up in the middle of the night to make tortillas before journeying to market, carrying the things that they would sell on their backs. This image of women's arduous labor provided the counterpart to the image of men working the land, but the ancianos represented contemporary women's lives as a total break with the past. Older women who continued to make tortillas by hand enjoyed a level of prestige for their labor, but because the aesthetic of tradition as shaped by male ancianos was crafted around ways of working the land, and women were not thought of as laboring on the land, they had no special place in the images of tradition crafted by the ancianos.

Of course, the absence of women in the traditionalists' aesthetic cannot be explained entirely by any actual disassociation from the land. For one thing, contemporary women did work land, and many requested plots of land from the Oficina de Bienes Comunales. Moreover, most requests for land that made their way to this office were not requests for land for farming, but for housing sites. Even those ancianos who continued to engage in agricultural production did so at a far less demanding scale than their ancestors would have. Dependent on cash, work on the land played a smaller and smaller role even for ancianos who supplemented their income by gardening for wealthy foreigners.

Among my informants were many elder women, but they rarely spoke of the past with the same sentimental attachment the elder men expressed. Older women boasted, with considerable subtlety, of their abilities to make tortillas and the special flavor of their tamales or mole as a lost art. Their daughters and granddaughters would encourage such boasting as though their mothers' abilities were rooted in a magical past when women knew such things. Nonetheless, women never shaped claims to political power around such traditional knowledge; instead, as I discussed in chapter 3, women's appeals to political authority were grounded in their "natural" affection for their children.

It is helpful to think about the traditionalist aesthetic crafted by anciano males against the kind of ethnic identity that Nelson (1999:170–205) discusses in her book to account for the nonexistence of women within the aesthetic. The ancianos' traditionalist aesthetic drew not so much on culture as on labor practices that, despite the fact that they were represented in opposition to contemporary capitalist consumption patterns, were very much tied to a peasant mode of production historically inseparable from capitalism. In its unacknowledged interaction with capitalism, a traditionalist aesthetic seemed somewhat lacking in its use of cultural references. It also seemed to draw on a public/private distinction that rendered women's work in the household invisible. In contrast to the situation described by Nelson, in which women are understood to be the guardians of cultural traditions, the only tradition rendered visible in the Tepoztecan traditionalist aesthetic was that of male labor in its association with land. Given that men did not acknowledge women's labor in relation to land, they did not conceptualize women as having anything of value to teach children. Indeed, the schools and not the household were held responsible for failing to teach children to love the land.

In the contemporary world in which labor is so often depicted as mechanized, speeded up, and impersonal, traditional labor practices have taken on the quality of a fetish not only for people in Tepoztlán, but also for global communities more broadly. Chatterjee describes the fetishism of women's labor on tea plantations in India as central both to the marketing of tea during the colonial period and to the marketing of tea today (2001:46–47). In the case of narratives about tea production, young women, represented as nubile virgins with hands adorned with jewelry, seem to pick tea at a leisurely pace. The female plantation worker's body is often represented as dismembered, with the focus on her hands. Among other goals, Chatterjee's work attempts to contest this fetishization of women's labor with its own description of hands broken and cut by the arduous work of harvesting the tea. Nonetheless, women develop their own narratives about their labor that hint at their own fetishization of the labor process and their special position as guardians of the tea bush (2001:224–29). These narratives are not unlike those developed by Tepoztecan ancianos as they elaborate a traditionalist aesthetic.

According to the Comité para la Defensa de Tierra, in 1983 the local commissioner of the Oficina de Bienes Comunales was a man who illegally sold communal land and did little to protect the town's patrimony. When the Maestro Jorge began to suspect the corruption, he organized a group to serve as a Consejo de Vigilancia. The consejo's first task was to replace the current commissioner with one that the comuneros elected in the General Assembly. They brought their complaints—that the man was an alcoholic, that he sold communal land, that he was not stopping *propietarios* (private-property holders) from taking over more land than they had purchased—to the state governor, who failed to respond. But one day when the group was meeting in the municipal offices, a governor's representative arrived. He asked about their complaints and, upon hearing them, suggested they go get the commissioner so that he could give his response to their charges. The comuneros returned with an intoxicated commissioner who could not even speak to defend his actions. Embarrassed in front of the governor, the commissioner gave up his post. The comuneros held a public assembly and elected a new commissioner, vice commissioner, and secretary of the Oficina de Bienes Comunales. Don Tomás, a campesino who had served as head of one of the parents' committees in the school system and had turned in fully balanced accounts, became commissioner. Don Abram, the Seventh Day Adventist described in chapter 2, became vice commissioner, and a female schoolteacher, Isabelle Ayala, became secretary. All were longtime residents of Tepoztlán, the district seat. Through the election of officers and the formation of a Consejo de Vigilancia—all Comité para la Defensa de Tierra members—the committee gained control over the local Oficina de Bienes Comunales at this time.

Although Tepoztlán seems to have had a strong faction of defenders of communal land for many years—local records suggest numerous disputes between the town and neighboring communities over communal resources—the 1980s witnessed a reinvigorated sense of the place of communal land in local politics. Tepoztecan communal land has historically been associated with those sectors of the community that live at the edges of modernization, and this association was reflected in the elections in which traditionalist ancianos won many of the positions of authority in the Oficina de Bienes Comunales. With traditionalists in charge, the defense of communal land became shaped by a traditionalist aesthetic even if the demands for land came from a variety of sectors.

By the 1980s, rising land prices, the desirability of Tepoztlán's land, the influx of migrants from other states, and Mexico's economic crisis repositioned communal land, making it a resource central to a variety of struggles. The communal land, which Tepoztecans had come to think of as marginally productive agricultural land methodically worked by traditionalists who had little interest in capital, became increasingly important. The influx of wealthy outsiders pushed prices of private property beyond affordable levels for most Tepoztecans. Moreover, the legal obstacles to selling communal land could be easily evaded, and communal land could command a good price on the market, especially when sold to outsiders who wanted the land to build homes rather than to farm. Even Tepoztlán's ricos began to think of communal land as important, for it could generate capital or be passed on to their children, who no longer could afford private property. Tepoztecans experienced all of these pressures at the same time as a burgeoning of immigrant populations from Mexico's poorer regions of Oaxaca and Guerrero made their own demands on communal land. Rumors abounded in Tepoztlán that the newly formed colonias where recent immigrants had settled provided safe havens for thieves and murderers. In 1984, Tepoztecans confided their fears to me that perhaps many of the new residents had been kicked out of their native communities for crimes they had committed.

The forces that converged around communal land—the women's groups, wealthy insiders, black-market traders in land, and immigrant populations—placed communal land at the center of the most important political debates in Tepoztlán during the 1980s. But it was not just a case of economic pressures on land. Communal land became metonymically linked to conflicts between ricos and pobres, men and women, insiders and outsiders, market and tradition. As Fernandez (1990) notes for boundary disputes in Asturian mountain villages in Spain, communal land in Tepoztlán came to stand for a variety of contested relations. Problems with land fueled discussions of the incompetent and corrupt Mexican bureaucracy, of the threat to a way of life posed by the influx of outsiders, and of the community's moral decline. Every sector of the population demanded protection of communal land. The issue was not whether or not communal land should be maintained—that was clear—but which sectors of the population would emerge as the legitimate guardians of the town's communal land base. This meant that the traditionalist aesthetic surrounding communal land would be brought face to face with the at times contrary images of legal rationality and bureaucratic malfeasance.

Of course, the place that communal land came to assume in Tepoztlán in the 1980s cannot be explained only with reference to local events. Mexico's economic crisis, its desires to lure foreign capital, and the massive movement of populations within the country linked local events to global movements of capital. In the country's efforts to lure foreign investment, Tepoztlán's land was constantly threatened. The expansion of Cuernavaca and its development of a modern industrial park encroached on Tepoztlán's communal land. Tepoztecans who visited government offices in Cuernavaca frequently discovered that their town had been targeted for a wide range of development plans, including roads, prisons, electrical lines, and tourist resorts. These projects provided the critical conflicts that fueled the struggle over communal land in the 1980s and 1990s. It was against the backdrop of increasing demands on communal land that the Maestro Jorge began to search for allies in the fight to defend communal land.

In 1984, a core group of seven people—teachers, students, and campesinos—directed the actions of the committee and shaped the interplay between class and tradition that characterized the committee. Of these seven, only two, don Abram and the maestra Isabella, held official positions in the Oficina de Bienes Comunales, but these seven defined the group and its activity through their association with the Maestro Jorge. The latter's politics and his family's history of left and even revolutionary political engagements defined the group as radical even for Tepoztlán (see chapter 3 for a discussion of the Maestro's family participation in left activities in Mexico). The Maestro surrounded himself with people whom he considered to have *consciencia* (consciousness) of the importance of the communal land issue. When crises emerged, this core group met to discuss options and strategies before bringing them to the full committee. When they brought cases to the committee, they passed the documents to one another, sometimes bypassing don Tomás, the elected representative of the Oficina de Bienes Comunales. They attended every meeting, participated in every inspection, and were members of every official delegation in which the committee brought problems to the governor, the Secretaría de la Reforma Agraria, the local mayor, and so on. And within this core group were the committee's three most vocal members, those who were considered to have the "words" to speak—the power to express the deep desires and passions of those who for lack of education or experience were reluctant to express themselves publicly.

The committee drew its more peripheral participants from the vast range of people interested in the issue of communal land. Many people who wanted a plot of communal land correctly perceived that participation in the committee would increase their likelihood of being given land if and when it became available. They began to attend meetings and to assist the committee on inspections of communal land, and in the process they gained information about how the committee functioned. Their participation was not a display of unambiguous political loyalty: if they did not receive land, they left the committee and spread gossip that discredited the group.

For the most part, people spoke openly about the interests that had motivated them to join the group. The Oficina de Bienes Comunales and, by extension, the committee had power over the resolution of disputes within colonias, and their support helped colonias receive services such as electricity and water. Some colonias sent representatives to the meetings at the Oficina de Bienes Comunales on a regular basis in hopes of gaining its support for long-term projects. Individual members of the colonias occasionally began to attend meetings; weeks later it might become clear, however, that the individual was involved in a conflict with another colonia member and was hoping to win the committee's support. Many of the more peripheral participants in meetings were those who had migrated to Tepoztlán and settled on communal land. Recognizing the insecurity of their position as outsiders, they attended meetings in hopes that their willingness to dedicate time to defending communal land would mediate their status as outsiders. Although many professed to believe in the committee's goals and its traditionalist ethos, all expressed skepticism about how realistic those goals were and expressed concerns about trusting the motives of the committee's core members.[6]

The committee's control over the Oficina de Bienes Comunales created a new domain for the playing out of different aesthetics as traditionalist leaders found themselves working with radical professors, government bureaucrats, and young students inspired by Marxist ideals. These different groups frequently complemented each other, and, as a result, lines were never clearly drawn. But points of contention emerged around particular issues as the committee sought to explain its decisions to itself and to outsiders only to find itself invoking principles that seemed to be at odds with one another: tradition and legal rationality; class struggle and patron-client ties between rich and poor; revolutionary fervor for change and the desire for timeless stability. Conflicts between different aesthetics ironically served to reinforce the discourse of tradition as the notion of tradition became elaborated to deal with a range of domains in social life. In the processing of cases, the traditional aesthetic confronted contemporary gender problems, relations between rich and poor, and the ever-present problem of the corrupt bureaucracy. But ancianos deployed a traditionalist aesthetic in a complex interpretive context, and they could not control the interpretations of their assertions.

"We are operating cleanly, we are operating within the law," the Maestro and others in the committee explained to those who brought cases to the Oficina de Bienes Comunales for resolution. The appeal to the rationality and universality of law justified the committee's position within the agrarian reform bureaucracy while distancing their actions from bureaucratic corruption. Under the Maestro's tutelage, peasants in the committee read the law books, learned their rights, and came to see that "in Mexico the law is good; it is the government that is bad," as committee members frequently explained to me. Law, with its limitations on the scope of authority, seemed to provide a counterpoint to the corrupt party/state apparatus. Moreover, as a local member of a newly emerging national left-wing party explained, "If the peasants learn the law, they will understand that the current state does not protect their rights."

In the committee, the reasonableness of law and the aesthetic of tradition came into dialogue with a system of bureaucratic corruption. Central to this dialogue was an attempt to disengage the law from its place in the agrarian bureaucracy while substituting the rationality of bureaucracy with the wisdom of traditionalism. As a traditionalist aesthetic was constructed in the ancianos' discourse, a wide chasm seemed to separate bureaucratic malfeasance and traditional authority. Against the clearly visible accumulation of wealth by government bureaucrats and officials, ancianos could point to the simplicity of their lifestyles, emphasizing the dirt floors in their homes, the absence of indoor plumbing, and their use of traditional farming techniques. A former *síndico* (trustee) known to have accumulated wealth from his position, seemed to give support to the ancianos' perspective when he reasoned, "A person who becomes mayor is usually more educated and therefore has more needs; he knows that it is wrong not to have soap when you bathe, but the position pays very little and so you take a *mordida* [payoff] to cover your costs." Compared to others who served in the state bureaucracy, the more traditionalist ancianos seemed to escape this desire for the symbols of progress and material wealth even though they had spent time in the bureaucracy. They continued living an austere existence that drew both respect and fascination from their neighbors. But the state/party apparatus had embraced traditional ancianos as well as those who desire commodities. Moreover, as noted earlier, ancianos admitted to having taken advantage of these positions to "take a little for themselves." If the authority of tradition depends not only on continuity with the past, but also on its unquestionability, the ancianos' stints in a bureaucracy characterized by corruption belied the notion of traditional authority. Yet committee members continually represented traditional authority as beyond corruption and ancianos as best suited to administer a law based not on written documents, but on local memory. This representation was part of the argument of images that made a traditional aesthetic seem beyond reproach.

"The reason people are passing through there is that it is communal land, and they have the right to do that," the Maestro explained to a wealthy outsider during a committee meeting regarding trespass through what the outsider considered his land. Señor Rivera, an outsider rumored to be wealthy, replied, "No, it is part of the property that I purchased, and I have the legal document to prove it. The land is registered in Cuernavaca, and they have the whole history of the land there." The Maestro questioned, "Up until what year? It has to go back to 1911, and if it doesn't, the documents are of no value."

In what must have seemed to an outsider an ironic twist, the universal and uncompromising application of law came to rely on the ancianos' traditional authority rather than on written documents, but the irony reveals the legitimacy problems of the Mexican state in the mid-1980s. Although Tepoztecans in the committee viewed Mexico's Agrarian Reform Law as "just and fair," those actually charged with administering the law had lost their legitimacy. By extension, legal documents could not be trusted, so written law came to depend on oral tradition. This paradox is perhaps more evident to outsiders than it is to insiders, who have always considered agrarian law not as a gift from the state, but as local practices and traditions codified. Therefore, when the Mexican state's legitimacy declined, it left not a vacuum of power, but rather a resurgence of anciano power as the true guardian of law.

Even if in practice the Mexican state seemed omnipotent, as suggested by the informant who described the pyramid of corruption (see chapter 3), communities such as Tepoztlán that retained communal land could at least imagine an alternative to the state through the imagery of a return to tradition. As I pointed out in chapter 2, the narrative of communal land leaned on nationalistic writings of history and anthropology even if the actual protection of communal land was imperfect. Nonetheless, the importance of communal land as a source of identity that challenged state hegemony is undeniable. The narrative of communal land legitimated structures of authority based in a traditionalist aesthetic that could resurface to challenge the state. Clearly, anciano authority was not immune to charges of corruption and abuse of power (a point discussed later), and Tepoztecans frequently challenged—if only in gossip—specific authorities' credibility. But when the notion of ancianos as a collective was invoked, as the Maestro did in this case, few would challenge that collective authority.

Tepoztecans take great delight in and are very skilled at verbal repartee, in particular those forms that employ irony. Drawing on ambiguity and subtlety, irony creates a form of attack on structures of power that is both safe and disarming, something that Tepoztecans relished as they found themselves drawn into relations with bureaucrats, tourists, and anthropologists in the 1980s. Once I had become a gente de confianza, I was privy to collective discussions of how Tepoztecans might deploy irony as a political weapon, one of the more humorous being to put an end to tourists with weeks and weeks of fiestas that never ended. When the tourists complained, they would be told, "But we are just a happy people," a play on the way traditional communities are so often represented in Mexican tourist literature.

The political uses of irony have been difficult to analyze precisely because it plays so clearly on ambiguity that its effectiveness as a political strategy remains questionable (Fernandez and Huber 2001:5). Irony seems, therefore, more akin to resistance than to revolution. Moreover, the ambiguities of irony have generated skepticism about the interpretive gymnastics in which the anthropologist must engage to render an unambiguous political statement out of a form of speech itself mired in ambiguity (Herzfeld 2001:75). But perhaps anthropologists have placed too much emphasis on irony's ambiguities, for even if irony plays with ambiguity to gain recognition, one's ironic statements must be seen as such by at least someone. Indeed, Kierkegaard's sense of irony highlights the distinction between those who "get" the irony, the discerning insiders, and those on whom its subtleties are lost (Cross 1998:129). To appreciate the moments when the ambiguity of irony gives rise to an unambiguous appreciation for its subtleties, we need to move beyond the ironic phrase to its place in a larger context where most people "get it" and use it to display their critical distance from structures of power with which they are otherwise quite intimate. Such performances were a frequent occurrence in the meetings held by the Comité para la Defensa de Tierra.

As I mentioned in chapter 2, defense of communal land, although seen as fundamental to community identity, was also viewed in the 1980s and 1990s as work in the most marginalized and impoverished sectors of the community. As the Maestro suggested, communal land was a resource for those whom modernization had left behind, those who had no education and little knowledge. Yet the aesthetic of tradition placed the defense of communal land in an altogether different light—as a reflection of Tepoztlán's proud heritage and as part of a broader network in which people sustained a proper relation to the land and to one another. This was fertile ground for irony, for the paradox of the superiority of tradition was forced to contend with its increasingly marginal position in the national imagination. Thus, the seriousness of processing cases and dealing with potentially life-threatening conflicts within the committee was frequently disrupted by jokes in which traditionalist leaders and sometimes even peripheral members used irony and parody to criticize what they saw as the paradoxical position of tradition. Behind the relative safety—"relative" in that it was not equally safe for all—of the committee walls, however, the ambiguities of irony were rarely left to stand, for they were quickly overshadowed, or sometimes foreshadowed, by a didactic voice.

As we waited for members of the Comité para la Defensa de Tierra to arrive for a meeting, don Pedro took the floor to tell a tale. "I went to see Duck Feet [a nickname he coined for a high-ranking official in the state-level agrarian offices] today," he began. He briefly explained that he had spent his whole day following Duck Feet from office to office, but his explanation was accompanied by a little charade. Rounding his shoulders and raising his eyes like a puppy pleading for food, he shuffled around the office, stopping abruptly as imaginary doors were slammed in his face. With each slam, he paused, a dejected look on his face, only to follow his imaginary official once again until yet another door was slammed in his face. Everyone in the office was now laughing at don Pedro's antics. The Maestro interjected with a tone of exasperation, "Why are you complaining—you got to see him, didn't you? What more do you want?" Again everyone laughed. Don Abram, however, felt compelled to draw a lesson from the little comedy: "For years, we go with our documents under our arms, and they slam the door in our faces, but after the revolution they treated us well and responded to our problems. They called us *señor*— now we need another revolution."

The Maestro's insistence that don Pedro had indeed "seen" the official was so clearly ironic that, practically speaking, his deployment of irony carried little of the dissimulation so commonly taken as definitive of irony. Moreover, his irony leaned on a form of parody in which the Maestro not only said the opposite of what he meant, but said what he imagined the official would have thought. In the unlikely event that the Maestro wished to take refuge in the evasiveness of irony, don Abram's response left little doubt about the lesson to be learned from the performance. In the absence of ambiguity, what did irony accomplish in this situation?

If irony is most often deployed by those at the margins, it may not be just because irony is a safe way to speak in opposition, but rather because the clever use of irony invokes the kind of social knowledge that comes from a marginal position. In order to deploy irony, one must know not only one's own context, but also the world in which one participates as a subordinate—in the case of Tepoztlán, the world of bureaucratic elites (see also Herzfeld 2001:70). Irony, especially when combined with parody, suggests the paradox of a disengagement with intimate power. It reflects critical distance on the social order from a marginal position whose value lies not only in its distance, but also in its awareness of alternatives, something that don Abram's intervention underscored (see Cross 1998, cited in Fernandez and Huber 2001:4). In the final analysis, the Maestro's irony worked because his statement "you got to see him" was so clearly the opposite of the alternative of proper relations that the committee and its ancianos championed.

For many theorists, the contemporary period is the age of irony, characterized as such for the instability of categories, the adoption of a distant and cynical attitude by most social actors, and the vision of language as devoid of meaning. But such generalizations about the contemporary age may overlook the fact that irony has a deep history in Mexico, illustrated for Tepoztecans by the fact that Emiliano Zapata, Venustiano Carranza's archenemy, was recovered as a national hero after his assassination by the government. The irony of Zapata's transformation was so deeply in-grained in Tepoztecan reality that ancianos were convinced that the statue of Zapata that stands at one of the entrances to Cuernavaca was itself ironic. "Zapata was never fat," some ancianos complained, "they made him that way to make fun of him." When I suggested that perhaps the government wanted to make him larger than he was in life to symbol-ize his power, ancianos patiently explained that the government had hated Zapata, and the statue was meant to fool the peasants into thinking the government honored him. Tepoztecans would surely agree with Frie-drich, who says that "Politics, the art of power, is predicated on not saying what you really think, on word and deed being continuously out of kilter. Irony is always a fact of politics, as when it becomes a component in a critical, antigovernmental, even anarchist ideology" (2001:230).

If word and deed are always out of kilter in the political arena, a persistent fantasy of those on the margins is the possibility of the slipup in which the platitudes of political discourse give way to honest expres-sions of attitudes. This fantasy emerged in the stories committee leaders told of the former commissioner of the Oficina de Bienes Comunales showing up drunk in front of the governor's representative, but in the absence of such real-life slipups committee members made up their own. Their miniperformances laid bare the absurdities of Mexico's postrevo-lutionary nationalism.

One day in July 1984, Tepoztlán was the site of a rally of left-loyal opposition parties. Under PRI rule—which, although crumpling in 1984, remained intact—parties competed in elections with the understanding that they would not win, but that they would be given a certain number of seats in Congress. As Bruhn suggests, the point of these elections was to stabilize the regime, not challenge it (1997:59). In such a setting, Te-poztecans held little hope for change through the electoral process, so when the parties began to hold their rally, only one anciano committee member attended. When he arrived at the committee meeting after at-tending the rally, the Maestro asked him if he had gone to hear the speeches. He responded, "*Pinche* [idiot] communists, socialists. Why do we need another group to rob the people?" After the anciano's lengthy diatribe against communists, which included many ironic twists and turns that left me very much in doubt about the anciano's position on communism, the Maestro queried a younger committee member, "What is the opposite of a communist?" The young member replied, "El papa" (the pope), to which don Pedro replied, "Porras papas, papas fritas" (dull-witted potatoes/pope; small potatoes/pope) skillfully using the similarity between *el papa* (the pope) and *la papa* (potato) to render the pope insignificant and dull-witted. With the room already convulsing in laughter, the anciano who had attended the rally once again took the floor. Standing up straight and raising his arm in a grand gesture, he proclaimed, "Everything for the revolution. Everything for the country. Everything for progress." A peripheral member who was often at odds with committee leaders stood and replied, "And for us, Señor?" The posturing anciano responded, "Shut up, you *pendejo* [jerk]." The Maestro joked, "You two should really make a team—you're great."

The miniperformance exposed the irony of political rhetoric, suggesting that indeed politics is the art of saying the opposite. At another level, however, the miniperformance also contained a theory of agency and ironic language. There was little doubt, at least in the audience, that this invented politician spoke truthfully when he told the campesino to shut up and called him a jerk. Although campesinos rarely hear such slipups from políticos, they are quite convinced that those moments reveal the true attitudes of those who seek their support in the political arena. Indeed, the ability to put truthful words—rarely heard given the ubiquitous use of irony in political discourse—in the speaker's mouth is what makes such performances so enticing. Thus, for Tepoztecans, irony was the creation of the ironist, who skillfully deployed the ambiguities of language for political ends. It was not that words were inadequate to say what one really meant, but that language users willfully deceived, which led to the paradoxical situation that those skilled at using language were both highly valued and associated with a skill often viewed as immoral. It is interesting to note that the two most skilled users of language in the committee, don Pedro and the Maestro, were never officially elected to any positions of power, and that don Abram, the elected vice commissioner, rarely used irony to generate laughs. Indeed, he sometimes used others' ironic phrases to erase the ambiguity that surrounded those ironic statements. The skilled ironist gets laughs, but he or she rarely is trusted. As shown in the next chapter, this mistrust can surface at any moment.

These ironies, although capturing a critical distance from societal structures, did not indicate an attitude of detachment, for they were ironies that needed to be viewed against the compelling belief that one's work should be rewarded with control over the products of that work. Indeed, the committee's organizing work, its deployment of tradition, and its use of law suggested not just ironic detachment, but a commitment to an alternative, making the ironies of the committee's situation truly bittersweet.

Conclusion

The collective fantasy that I have termed a traditionalist aesthetic represents not a desire to return to the past, but a kind of imaginative repetition of the past in the present that necessarily maintains a certain ambivalence. The motivation for this repetition comes from a desire to "name," from a position of authority, a difference that matters within the space of an encroaching market for land. The problem that Homi Bhabha raises for the enunciation of cultural difference more generally is relevant to Tepoztecan politics in the 1980s: "It is the problem of how, in signifying the present, something comes to be repeated, relocated and translated in the name of tradition, in the guise of a pastness that is not necessarily a faithful sign of historical memory but a strategy of representing authority in terms of the artifice of the archaic" (1994:35).

My point in this chapter has been to place a traditionalist aesthetic within the overall fabric of the desire for unity and political power that, I have argued, characterized Tepoztecan politics in the 1980s even as it contained the impossibility of fulfilling that traditionalist aesthetic. As becomes clear in the following chapters, the desire for unity made sense only as a desire that would never be fulfilled, but that fact did not render irrelevant those attempts to achieve unity through various arguments or images. Indeed, a traditional aesthetic did bring many people into the political arena, and it did inform the passion that ancianos brought to the struggle to defend communal land, however flawed it proved to be in practice. The important question to be asked about a traditionalist aesthetic has to do less with its practical applicability than with its appeal through a resort to images that drew on the peasant's place in the construction of Mexican nationalism, reinforced by the ancianos' interpretation of the contemporary significance of traditional labor practices.

Chapter 5

Communal Passions and the
Politics of Loose Connections

I'll tell you something else, Juanita, when I am on top of this roof constructing this house, I can see all the houses that have been built on that hill where it is all communal land. The commissioner [don Tomás] gives a citation to all these people, and they come in [to the office], but afterwards they [members of the Comité para la Defensa de Tierra] do not do anything. The rich stay with the land, and don Abram, don Tomás, and the Maestro divide the mordida among themselves. That's why I am not going to the meetings. I gave all my time, time without pay, while those three are getting rich.
—A peripheral member of the Comité para la Defensa de Tierra who stopped attending meetings in 1984

This chapter describes the politics of loose connections as a compromise between Tepoztecan desires for unity and passions for political engagement; it also discusses the impossibility of trust that emerged out of the community's history of engagement with the state. Peripheral members who feared the work the Comité para la Defensa de Tierra was doing believed that the leaders were corrupt, disagreed with central ideas about how communal land should be handled, and questioned how best to participate without jeopardizing their time or reputation—in short, how to negotiate the cost of participation while continuing to participate at some level. My analysis thus intersects with both Redfield's idyllic portrayal of Tepoztlán and Lewis's harsh depiction of gossip and betrayal in the town. I argue that gossip should not be viewed as betrayal; rather, it is a form of political practice that relies on a sense of the political game.

As I point out in chapter 3, the practices of most political groups in Tepoztlán, including the committee, were marked by a distinction between "those who have words," leaders, and those who remain silent, peripheral members. The former became the formal and informal authorities within a group, but those who remained silent shaped the group's identity through a variety of practices, including foot dragging, gossip, and nonattendance at meetings. Indeed, the interpretations these silent members crafted in gossip could determine the group's fate because a studied silence spoke with the clamor of moral authority. Refusing to speak marked one's humility and dramatized one's disinterest in positions of political leadership. Silence suggested a purity of intention that lent credence to the discourse of those "without words," at the same time as it spoke to their wisdom in not handing over their full loyalty to leaders who might well prove to be corrupt. At least in 1984, in the minds of peripheral members, "community" always failed when confronted with the lure of corruption and abuse of power that reigned within the state bureaucracies. Their silence at meetings, coupled with their whispered rumors of corruption outside of meetings, policed a fragile boundary between community and the state.

Any attempt to interpret silence is fraught with difficulties. As Visweswaran (1994) points out, the ethnographic interpretation of a refusal to speak results in the constitution of a subject endowed with intentions, motives, desires, and passions. The risk is not misinterpretation, wrongly ascribing motives and interests, but rather that the anthropologist engages in the colonizing demand that people emerge as subjects, a demand that resonates with the ways in which the West fashions itself as universal. In short, to interpret silence is to insist that ethnographic subjects behave sensibly and rationally and that their refusals to speak be translated in a way that makes sense. Making sense often means that silences be read as acts of political resistance. It seems impossible ultimately to treat silence as silence without resorting to some interpretive act that makes it a shadow of speech (see Chatterjee 2001) or that fills the silence with a historical and social analysis that forces it to speak. There seems to be no way out of these dilemmas, for anthropology is one of those human sciences that depends on confessional practices for its methods, and as Foucault (1990) notes, the act of confession is inseparable from the constitution of the subject.

In this chapter, I attempt to sidestep these dilemmas by focusing on the consequences of silence rather than on its utility for a subject who refuses to speak. Certainly, the chapter draws on the interpretations Tepoztecans made of their own silences, and it slips into historical and social analysis that renders such silences "sensible." But even if one can render such silences sensible, that sensibility can be distinguished from the consequences of the silences. Although I attend to the moments when those who refuse to speak suddenly erupt into discourse, these eruptions illustrate the difficulties of matching consequences to intentions. For me, the more pressing issue is the need to account for that which happens in a face-to-face confrontation with a refusal to speak. I am interested in the dis-ease silence provokes in those who speak and the impacts of that dis-ease on shaping the political landscape.

Peripheral members occupy an intermediate space in political groups. They are those members who do not give their identities over to the group, and yet they are unlike those who refuse to participate in any politics. Peripheral members participate while holding back. In the case of Tepoztlán, they represented themselves as the ones who try to protect community from the onslaught of corrupt politicians. In a world in which politics is so widely seen as corrupt, those who participate at the periphery of political groups negotiate the rewards of participating with the necessity of critical distance. Their gossip emphasizes the problematic intersection between leaders' self-interest and their own community interests, forming a kind of running commentary on the community's fate against the weight of self-interest. This is not to say that peripheral members do not bring their own self-interest into their calculation of the costs and benefits of political participation, but they often speak of their own self-interest as one with the community's needs.

I do not mean to suggest that leaders are self-interested and peripheral members are not, but rather that those who participate on the periphery of political groups engage in a performance that distances them from political leaders. As Lomnitz-Adler notes in his study of Tepoztlán, engaging in politics is dangerous to one's reputation (1982:304–5). One is taken to be either a político who reaps personal benefits from political participation and has facility with words and social skills or a *tonto* (idiot) who participates in politics without understanding that políticos are taking advantage of him or her. Lomnitz-Adler concludes that when faced with this opposition, most Tepoztecans adopted an apolitical demeanor, refusing to become engaged in political battles and maintaining a studied silence when confronted by politics. Although Tepoztecans tended to use Lomnitz-Adler's dichotomies when they spoke of those engaged in politics, I believe that the reality of political participation is far more complex than suggested by Lomnitz-Adler's dualistic scheme. At moments of mass mobilization, many Tepoztecans abandoned an "apolitical stance" to participate in the name of community. Moreover, as this chapter illustrates, those who participated from the periphery of political groups were mindful of the dangers of being referred to either as a político or as a tonto. Indeed, their style of participation traversed a fine line between these two categories. Those who managed to walk this line successfully emerged with reputations as defenders of the community against the políticos' nefarious ambitions.

When I speak of the "peripheral members" of the group, I am referring to that segment that participated in the meetings at the Oficina de Bienes Comunales often without speaking. As one peripheral member explained, "We just go and watch, and then we learn what is going on. . . . We don't say anything because that might be divisive." In the Oficina de Bienes Comunales, however, those without words who attended meetings came from different sectors. As I mentioned in chapter 2, under Agrarian Reform Law this office included a Consejo de Vigilancia, a watchdog group whose job was to monitor the authorities' behavior and to report violations of agrarian law to the commissioners. In the Oficina de Bienes Comunales, many of the peripheral members who attended meetings and participated as members of the Consejo de Vigilancia were also members of the Comité para la Defensa de Tierra. These people usually came from the district seat and were well acquainted with the authorities in charge. Because of the strong presence of members of the Comité para la Defensa de Tierra, the Consejo de Vigilancia and sometimes the Oficina de Bienes Comunales was called "the committee." The use of the term *committee* speaks to the continued importance of the popular mobilization that shaped the takeover of the Oficina de Bienes Comunales. In this chapter, I use the term *committee* to emphasize the grassroots mobilization that, although drawing on the legal framework of Agrarian Reform Law, went beyond the limits suggested by law. A second group of peripheral members was formed from the representatives of colonias and in some cases barrios. As I have already mentioned, colonias are housing settlements formed on the outskirts of either the district seat or of the subject communities. They are not viewed as desirable by those who have alternative possibilities, but for the people who live there—some of whom come from other places in Mexico—they are highly valued. Committee leaders often received the strongest support from these people, who were grateful for the plots of land they had received. Finally, Oficina de Bienes Comunales meetings were attended by a wide array of people who had problems with their land or who were seeking a plot of communal land or who were just curious about the committee's activities; representatives from the surrounding subject communities would also attend meetings occasionally. Although all peripheral members remained quiet for the most part during meetings, all did not share the same perspective. What one was willing to risk for communal land varied depending on how badly one needed land and whether or not one had received land from the committee.

Drawing on Weiner's (1992) analysis of exchange among Trobriand Islanders, Godelier (1999) posits that we must rethink the notion of exchange in society, recognizing that one preserves in order to give. He posits that capitalist notions of exchange, in which objects can be truly alienated from those who give them, blind us to the fact that in most gift economies that which is exchanged is never really alienated from the giver. Against Mauss's sense of the spirit in the object, Godelier argues that the giver always retains some ownership over that which is given, and it is this inalienable aspect of all exchange that forms the basis of reciprocity (1999:90–93).

Weiner's and Godelier's rethinking of exchange is useful for understanding the politics of loose connections. Loose connections emerge as a product of the tensions between giving and keeping in the political arena. Indeed, it is impossible to understand the strategies of loose connections without attending to what people fight to hold onto in the arena of exchange. Defined broadly, exchange includes not only tangible objects such as land, jewelry, food, and so on, but also intangible objects such as political support, knowledge, and senses of self.

In Tepoztlán, the process of protecting communal land as an inalienable possession gave rise to tensions over a different sort of exchange. Peripheral committee members viewed their participation as an exchange. As one member noted, "I joined because I saw that they [the committee] were doing good work for the community. Besides, you never know when you will need them, and if you don't help, they will say, 'Where were you when we needed your *ayuda* [help]?'" The political discourse of mutual help suggests that every exchange in the political arena also entails holding back. It captures a persistent alterity within politics: one can help only that which does not belong to oneself, and one helps by doing that which is truly the obligation of some other. When peripheral members described themselves as helping the committee, they asserted their goodwill and citizenship at the same time as they accentuated the distinction between their identities and the committee leaders' identity. Speaking of participation as "helping" highlighted one's distance from the unity that the leaders championed, a lack of unity that peripheral members expressed by refusing to show up for needed land inspections, evading the signing of petitions and letters to the president regarding communal land, refusing to offer their opinions in meetings, and frequently gossiping to undermine the support the committee might have enjoyed in the wider community. Holding back in this sense also protected an inalienable possession: their identities as members of the larger community. By holding back, the peripheral members enacted the critical distance that could preserve a communal perspective on land issues against the state's attempts to control all the resources that belonged to the community.

Weiner's (1992) point about reciprocity and exchange is that every exchange unites what is given with what is withheld, a point Godelier extends when he asserts, "the formula for maintaining the social sphere is therefore not *keeping while giving* but *keeping for giving*" (1999:36, emphasis in original). For Godelier, this means we need to maintain a double view when we analyze exchange, holding onto both the keeping and the giving as well as the tensions that emerge between the two. The politics of loose connections emerges out of this dynamic tension between keeping and giving in the political arena. The goal of politics is often expressed as unity, or, as in the case of Tepoztlán, as building community. But just as the model that takes exchange as the foundation of social life has ignored that which is not exchanged, so, too, the model that takes unity as the foundation of politics ignores the myriad ways in which politics is enabled by the position of holding back—which is often mistakenly taken only as a force of disunity.

On a day in late June 1984, the committee learned that a señor Rubino, rumored to be a wealthy outsider with connections to a drug cartel, had begun building on communal land in one of the colonias. Señor Rubino was known to travel with "bodyguards." The committee meetings in which his "case" was discussed took on a kind of hesitant bravado, for at stake in such cases was the game of machismo in which the threat of violent confrontation weighed heavily. As often happens in such cases, señor

Rubino had offered, or perhaps had been asked, to provide some adobe in exchange for being allow to build on the property. To accept the offer would be to enter into corruption and its benefits. To turn it down might demonstrate the kind of bravery Tepoztecans attributed to their ancestors. The following field notes reflect discussion at a meeting on July 3, 1984, when committee leaders tried to decide what to do about the offer.

The man who is one of the "bodyguards" for señor Rubino walked into the office. The Maestro explained that he [the man] was there to present an offer from his boss. The man stood and announced, "I talked with my boss, and he is willing to give one and one-half tons of *barro* [soil for making adobe]"; he added that his boss had said that at the cost of barro, three tons was too much [clearly, someone in the committee had begun to negotiate a payoff]. The Maestro was lying stretched out on the bench; don Pedro was sitting with his head lowered on a chair next to the desk. . . . Don José was sitting on the bench. Like everyone else, I put my head down and wondered, "Why are they discussing this while I sit here?" The Maestro broke the silence, "Well, Tomás, you're the authority; you have to make the decision." Don Tomás responded, "No, Maestro, we don't operate that way; the committee makes decisions here." The Maestro started to object, but don Abram interrupted, saying that the matter had to be discussed with the whole committee. Don Tomás said, "If it was up to me, I would say no." Don Abram interjected, "The whole committee has to hear the offer, and we all have to agree; we just can't make this decision among ourselves, but I am telling you, if there is not agreement, there could be big problems—you heard Pablo's [a peripheral committee member from the district seat] reaction the other night, and if Pablo is not happy, it will go out through the whole pueblo." The Maestra [Isabelle Ayala], who rarely speaks in meetings, interrupted don Abram: "Don Abram, there is nothing to be said now, we have to wait until we treat *asuntos* [business] on Saturday." . . . Don Pedro said to the worker, "Now you have your answer; we cannot tell you anything until Sunday." The man sat there for a few more minutes and then left.

The following Saturday the Maestro Jorge told señor Rubino's workers that the offer of barro was rejected. In an interview, don Abram told me that if they had accepted the barro, they would have been unable to enforce the law regarding illegal land sales because everyone would say that the rich were allowed to do things that the poor could not do. But the decision did not end the matter because the committee was required by law to hold a General Assembly in the colonia to determine what to do with the land and the water well. That meeting would effectively undermine the committee's resolve to take back the land.

The first meeting in the colonia took place on July 29. Don Abram announced that the committee was going to take back the land and turn the land and the pump over for community service. Someone stood and argued that because señor Rubino had already started building, they should let him keep the land and should instead demand some kind of community service from him. After four hours of angry discussion, the colonia finally agreed to let señor Rubino keep the land and to demand a bell for the church as compensation.

This case with señor Rubino, similar to others, gestured to what had been said outside the meeting as well as to what might be said after the meeting. During the discussion, at least nine members of the Consejo de Vigilancia, in addition to those involved in the conversation, were in the room, but the only people to speak were the Maestro Jorge, don Abram, and don Tomás—those with words. Clearly, either someone had asked señor Rubino for barro, or he had offered, and the negotiation had begun, although Pablo, someone who rarely attended meetings, had already begun to "talk" about the matter. The meeting itself was a pause in a process well under way. Those in the room who refrained from speaking were, in accordance with Mexico's Agrarian Reform Law, fulfilling their obligation to *vigilar* (to watch, to keep one's eye upon something), exercising, as it were, their disciplinary functions. As a member of the Consejo de Vigilancia once told me, "We do not speak because we are only there to watch." He pointed to his eye, emphasizing the physical feature that had to be disciplined to engage in watching. But this watchful silence hung heavy in the room. Its effects were not unlike those that Foucault describes for the panopticon, although its technology was somewhat different.

The disciplinary effects of the panopticon are predicated on the unnerving effects of being seen without being able to see: of "dissociating the see / being seen dyad" (Foucault 1979:202). In this case, those with words in the Comité para la Defensa de Tierra knew they were being observed, despite the fact that lowered heads indicated otherwise. What they did not know was what was being seen, and they would not know until it became processed in the anonymous gossip that drifted from peripheral members into the spaces of Tepoztecan everyday life. In a sense, the disciplinary structures created through the act of vigilance leaned on this delay, this waiting for a verdict from those who refused to speak.

The power of the committee's peripheral members lay in this position of silent, watchful waiting that epitomized the withholding that I have suggested shapes a politics of loose connections. To watch for diagnostic purposes without revealing a diagnosis or without ever having to account for what one might say in gossip captured the tensions between a refusal to participate and an apparent participation. In the face of this obvious refusal to offer an opinion on matters at hand, those who "had words" became caught up in speculating on the wisdom of their actions as viewed from the peripheral members' perspective. Caught by the silence of those without words, those with words had to speculate on what might be said, by whom, and under what circumstances. Thus, committee leaders came to discipline their own response to señor Rubino's offer of barro, a response that ultimately proved at odds with that of the colonia.

The peripheral members who maintained their silence in the meeting were playing the role allotted to them by the Agrarian Reform Law. As I noted in chapter 3, the law constitutes the community as a potential site of corruption and sets up the instruments of monitoring at the local level. In a sense, it constructs a human panopticon that creates among leaders the impression of constant vigilance without ever being sure what has been "seen." At the same time, however, by law, the "diagnosis" of the Consejo de Vigilancia was to be made to authorities higher up in the Secretaría de la Reforma Agraria. That members of the Consejo de Vigilancia preferred to render their diagnosis in the anonymous theater of local gossip captures a point of resistance within the disciplinary powers deployed by the state. The important point, however, is that these powers of discipline worked regardless of Consejo de Vigilancia members' motivations.

One should not overlook the extent to which fear played a dominant role in the lives of Consejo de Vigilancia members, which is the way most peripheral members who hailed from the district seat participated in the work of the Office of Communal Resources. As I discussed in chapter 3,

Mexico's federal Agrarian Reform Law established the basis for a tense relationship between members of the Consejo de Vigilancia and the commissioners of the Oficina de Bienes Comunales, giving the former the role of monitoring compliance with the law, reviewing accounts, and providing reports on questionable practices to the Secretaría de la Reforma Agraria. In addition, in Tepoztlán, consejo members monitored illegal takeovers of communal land and delivered citations to those who were in violation of the law. As I was told by many consejo members, their position was very delicate, for they could incur the wrath either of the commissioners if they were suspected of reporting the commissioners to the Secretaría de la Reforma Agraria or of those to whom they delivered citations. For those in the consejo, fear weighed heavily in calculating the cost of participating in the consejo, and for the most part their fears were not countered by expectations that their work in the consejo would be rewarded with land.

Rolando Medina, a single man in his late thirties lived in an adobe house with a cement floor and a brick ceiling. He was a member of the Comité para la Defensa de Tierra, and he served as a member of the consejo. His house had three rooms and a large back porch, where we sat and talked for hours about the committee and about differences between the United States and Mexico. He cultivated coffee, his main source of cash, which he sold on the international market through a cooperative. He was active in his barrio committee and in an agriculture collective that met to discuss crop diseases and the latest in agriculture technology. With no children, he would have had little chance of being eligible for receiving communal land of any sort, but he said that he had joined the committee because he loved land. He told me, "The best way to die is to die fighting for your land—that is how Zapata died, and it is an honor to die fighting for land." Despite his words, he was so fearful about the committee's work that whenever we talked on the front porch of his house, he would lower his voice as though we were surrounded by spies. He mistrusted the authorities but was afraid that if he spoke publicly about his suspicious that they were involved in corruption, it would be divisive and life threatening. At the same time, he was afraid to hand out citations.

One day in early July Rolando had the unfortunate fate of discovering that someone was beginning to build on a plot of communal land in his barrio. Before the meeting in which he was supposed to make his report, he confided in don Pedro and don Abram, hoping no doubt that they would deal with the matter without involving him. They told him to bring the matter to the meeting on July 3. When I arrived at that meeting, everyone asked if I knew Rolando's whereabouts. He was uncharacteristically late. When he finally did arrive, he walked over to the Maestro and sat down next to him, whispering his news. Later he came over to don Abram, and again in a barely audible voice, which I could hear only because I was sitting next to don Abram, he reported that someone was beginning to put barbed wire fence around a plot of communal land near his house. "I don't know who they are," he explained, "because they just drop some boys off to work in the morning, but I know the land belonged to someone who was murdered." Don Abram, speaking in a voice clearly audible to everyone in the office, replied, "Well, we have to do something with this situation that Rolando is bringing to us: maybe someone needs to talk to the *rurales* [the police] to have them knock down the fence." The Maestro disagreed, saying that by law they needed to give the man a citation so that he could come to the office. Rolando protested that he did not know who was doing the work because it was being done by hired labor, to which the Maestro responded, "Well, give it to one of the workers, and we'll have them tell us for whom they are working." Rolando contended that he could not give the citation because he was a neighbor, and he would then be the one whose life was in danger. "I just came here to report it to the committee, and from there you should handle it," he explained. Days later, don Abram's son went to the work-site and asked who was working the land. He learned that it was a local person. When don Abram told Rolando what his son had learned, Rolando argued that there was no way that person could afford to put so many workers on the land. In private, Rolando confided in me that he feared that the commissioners at the Oficina de Bienes Comunales had accepted a payoff from the man, and he was being asked to risk his life. He stopped coming to meetings and did not return until October. To my knowledge, he never offered an explanation for his absence, although don Abram did tell me that he was sure Rolando had become frightened.

At the time I was carrying out my research, I paid little attention to the warnings of committee members that my work might cost me my life. Because I never was convinced of the political leaders' inherent unscrupulousness, I never viewed don Abram, the Maestro, don Tomás, and don Pedro as a danger to me or to anyone else, although I did worry that they were putting their own lives in jeopardy with their work.

Nonetheless, although homicides are rare in Tepoztlán, there are several examples in my notes of people being killed over land conflicts, and I knew of cases in which committee members and the commissioners were physically assaulted while carrying out their work. Rolando would understandably have been concerned for his life in this case because, as he suggested, the previous owner of the plot had been murdered. But the fear committee members associated with their work was far more widespread than this particular case suggests. Some members told me that drug dealers were buying up Tepoztlán's communal land, and therefore everyone in the office was risking his or her life by pursuing cases against outsiders. Many times the committee took cases against outsiders whom they did not know very well, and tempers flared when people felt their land threatened. These situations were, as Rolando repeatedly reminded me, delicate matters.

Fear was clearly demonstrated as the classic case of holding things back from the exchanges that constituted the political arena: one's life was too much to give. Given Tepoztlán's supposed history of bravery in the face of threats to land, however, few of the committee's reluctant participants were willing to admit that fear alone had dampened their enthusiasm for participating in the committee. Instead, most peripheral committee members talked of the dangers of their work in the same breath as they talked of the corruption of leaders in the Oficina de Bienes Comunales, the arduous nature of the work, and their disagreements with other members of the committee over land distribution, which I discuss more fully later. As one committee member warned me before an investigation that he did not go on, but that I did, "You know, Juanita, these investigations are very difficult—you have to walk long hours in places where there are no trails—and on this one you will encounter people who are very *bravo* [hot tempered]. It's not worth it."

I would not want to suggest that the fears that surfaced in carrying out the committee's work were unwarranted. As I have already mentioned, homicides around land issues did take place, and Tepoztecans were particularly unnerved by their encounters with the wealthy and powerful residents now posing a threat to communal land. As Rolando's statement suggests, however, that fear was also part of a larger desire to die defending the town's patrimony, a desire that had been nurtured by stories of the ancestors. Such a death would be more meaningful than a mundane, ordinary death. Moreover, the desire for a meaningful death intersected with the desire for unity, for in death one proved one's distance from the self-interest that was believed to inform políticos' actions. Indeed, to die in the context of a political struggle is to emerge as a true hero. This was brought home to me when a journalist for the national newspaper *Excelsior* was assassinated. His articles on political networks in Mexico had not yet attracted Tepoztecans' attention, but after his assassination Tepoztecans began to read his reports and to talk about his death as an indication that he had stood up bravely to PRI's powers.

In his discussion of machismo in Nicaragua during the Contra war, Lancaster links honorable deaths in war with the values of risk associated with machismo. He states, "The risk of gambling is the risk of engagement in the world. . . . And in death, the game of risk is the men's last statement on life. It is as though to say: Life is a game, a gamble, full of chance and risks, and it always plays out to the same end" (1992:201). Men embrace this gamble, treating the prospect of death lightly, leaving it up to women to express fears that they feel but cannot speak of in a culture of machismo (1992:197). In Tepoztlán, men in the committee did talk of their fears, at least to me. Although this may have been because they did not feel the same social pressures talking to a woman as they would have felt in talking to a man, I believe more was at issue. By speaking of their fears, Tepoztecans involved in the fight to defend communal land associated their committee work with the struggles of the Zapatistas and of those who had continued that battle in subsequent years. Talk of fear was one with talk of the significance of the struggle and of their own bravery. At the same time, however, such talk also meant that the cost of one's life came to be calculated along with the other costs of political participation.

Concerns about corruption gossip so shaped interactions in the Oficina de Bienes Comunales that the authorities were often rendered impotent. They took land from people who they felt had genuine need or refused to give land to those who needed it in order to appease political enemies' appetites for gossip. Leaders in the Oficina de Bienes Comunales refrained from drinking alcohol for fear that people would say that they had made deals when they were drunk. The whole committee condemned any private conversations between authorities and individuals processing land cases. But these restriction were to no avail, for those who participated in the committee as peripheral members came to assume that although everything looked clean, it was really just politics as usual.

Under the tutelage of the Maestro Jorge, the solution to corruption gossip became collective management of land. Leaders in the Oficina de Bienes Comunales rejected notions of themselves as powerful patrons and instead encouraged members to engage in a form of participatory democracy (discussed in more detail later). They wanted peripheral committee members to see themselves as powerful guardians of the communal land, not because of their ties to political leaders, but because of their collective strength. Toward that end, committee leaders encouraged peripheral members to give more of their time to committee activities, demanding a level of unity and risk that most peripheral members resisted.

Tepoztecans who lived in the center of town considered Colonia Manantial an impoverished place for its lack of water and electricity, but its residents boasted about the clear spring water that they used for bathing and laundry and about the electricity they coveted from a nearby gas station. Many of the approximately thirty residents of Colonia Manantial were related to doña Melina, the female founder of the colonia, so that the colonia was united not only on the basis of residency but also through ties of kinship. Therefore, when a colonia member—also a relative of doña Melina—who had not built on his land for more than seven years refused to cooperate in collective work projects, the whole colonia met and decided to take back his land to build a church. Implementing the colonia's decision was not a simple matter, however.

On Thursday, October 25, 1984, the representative from Colonia Manantial arrived at the committee meeting with a group from the colonia. Don Tomás had not shown up at the meeting, and don Abram told the one woman who had brought a case to return when Tomás was there. After the woman left, Julio, the Colonia Manantial representative, spoke: "We are here for the same problem that we always come for: García is again starting to build on that plot of communal land, and his brother is beginning to work the land above his plot. The people in the colonia are beginning to believe that don Tomás and don Abram have given him permission to build, especially because García said that they have given him verbal permission to build." Don Abram replied, holding his palm flat up to mimic a document: "With what proof—with what is he saying that I have given him permission to build? If I had given him permission, it would have to be in a document signed by all of us." Julio replied that the people were starting to believe García because no one had stopped him from building. He added that he himself had stopped the work twice, but once García claimed that he had the authorities' verbal permission, there was nothing more Julio could say. Moreover, Julio complained that the case was causing him difficulties as colonia representative because García and he were in the same family, and the others in the colonia were convinced that he, Julio, was also involved in letting García build.

The Maestro Jorge interrupted: "We told Tomás if he did something like this on his own one more time, he was out, but Tomás is not here tonight. Why don't you unite all the people you can on Saturday night and confront him with this? We will give him eight days to resolve the situation—to designate the land for some service to the colonia—and then if he doesn't do anything, we will turn the land over to the colonia to do whatever they want with it."

Julio again repeated that the situation was causing him difficulty, and the Maestro again encouraged him to come to the meeting on Saturday.

On Saturday, October 27, the group from the colonia arrived at the meeting with Julio. This time don Tomás attended the meeting. He denied ever giving García or his brother permission to build. Don Abram seemed to accept don Tomás's explanation: "The people in Santa María said the same thing about me, and I never gave them permission to put anything up on that land. How could we give this man permission? It would be like a dog eating his vomit—twice he has sold communal land, and we are going to give him permission again. . . . When they say these things, they have to have proof—they have to have documents." Julio nodded his head in seeming agreement. The Maestro counseled Julio, "Why don't you get a commission of about five people together and go tomorrow, and if they are building, tell them you came to the meeting Saturday night, and Tomás said that he had never given anyone permission to build—you all heard it. Is there someone you know who genuinely needs the land?" Julio suggested the name of a single man, the grandchild of a committee member, but don Abram said that this person was not a good person for the land because he did not have *necesidad* for it. The Maestro reiterated, "Tell them to stop building, or you are going to take the land for service for the colonia—a school or something." Don Abram added, "You tell them that we respect the word of the colonia—whatever the colonia says, we would never go against it." The Maestro asked, "Can you get five people together and go tomorrow?" Julio looked at the group sitting with him. One man said OK.

On November 3, Julio was back in the committee again with complaints about García and his brother. Directing his comments to the Maestro Jorge, he explained, "García is still building on the land, and it is a very difficult situation because I am telling you he is very stubborn, and he will not stop." "Did you send the commission and go and stop him when he was working?" the Maestro asked. Julio answered, "Sometimes he works only for a half hour and then we go and we see that more work has been done, but he is not there. . . . No, this man is very *terco* [pigheaded]—if we go, he will say that don Abram and don Tomás gave him permission, and then there is nothing we can do." Don Abram angrily replied, "With what proof can he say that?" but the Maestro interrupted, saying "It doesn't matter. Julio, you have the document that was signed by the colonia taking the land away from him—you can just show him the documents." Julio responded, "We only have a copy." The Maestro told him it did not matter if it was a copy. Another committee member, also from the same colonia, supported Julio's position: "That man is very terco and no matter what we do he will not stop building." The Maestro responded, "That is why I am saying that you need to organize the colonia, and the colonia has to go and stop him. Only with people to people will you stop it—you are the representatives of the colonia, and you have the responsibility to do this. The colonia has spoken, and now you have to defend what you have decided." Again Julio answered that the situation was very difficult and that he really did not want to get involved in it, but if that was the way it would have to be, they would organize an assembly of the whole colonia. But he complained, "If I had known this a week ago, we could have organized it for this Sunday—now we will have to wait another week." The Maestro replied, "Organize the assembly, and don Abram and don Tomás will go."

As I pointed out in chapter 3, mass mobilization has long been an aspect of Mexico's populist form of governance, but it is often part of leaders' political strategy to gain incorporation into the Mexican state. For those seeking positions within the PRI, the ability to mobilize large masses of people symbolized the control a leader exerted over his or her followers. The point was to create a mass mobilization that could potentially threaten PRI authority, and in response the PRI often found a place for those who could mobilize their constituents. Vélez-Ibañez (1983) has termed the practice "rituals of marginality." Although scholars have viewed these "rituals of marginality" as culminating in the leader's deception of his or her followers, I believe the picture is more complex than mere deception would suggest.

In central Mexico, where the presence of the state is so dominant, leaders and followers alike understood and accepted the form of exchange that dominated this type of politics. Followers hoped that the leader would win a few benefits for them upon incorporation into the PRI, while at the same time protecting them from the more obvious dangers of mass mobilization. In short, a simulated participatory democracy combined with political patronage under the PRI. Although many people despised the co-optation of leaders that was common under the PRI, they also participated in the system, hoping to win a few benefits, or, as don Abram would say, hoping to be thrown a bone. Indeed, Tepoztecans generally approached politics with a kind of playful cynicism, enjoying lofty political rhetoric while anticipating the moment of deception. At the same time, however, they recounted with great passion stories of the town's mass mobilizations as though they were moments when community won out over the corrupting state forces. When the forces led by the Maestro took over the Oficina de Bienes Comunales in 1983, they intended to use these moments of "authentic" mass mobilization as a form of continuous minirevolution in defense of communal land. They failed to anticipate, however, the hidden appeal of the system of co-optation that had become an intimate aspect of the culture of politics in Tepoztlán.

The exchange practices that governed the link between leaders and followers under PRI authority entailed knowledge of the kinds of complex calculations needed to negotiate with the state. Authorities who followed the letter of the law, making no allowances for the time that followers put into mass mobilizations; who miscalculated the point at which a deal should be struck, thus losing all benefits for themselves or their followers; or who refused to assume responsibility for the more dangerous aspects of politics jeopardized understandings between leaders and followers. Violation of these practices as described in Julio's case stimulated the imagination of corruption. Julio's complaints that Garcia was pig-headed constituted a thinly veiled assertion that don Abram and don Tomás had indeed given him permission to build. The Maestro's contention that the colonia had the authority ignored the common practice of placing *la espina encima* (literally, putting a thorn in the side of the highest authority; figuratively, lighting a fire under those at the top), which the committee itself followed every time it took problems with land directly to the country's president.[1] Within a political culture in which hierarchical authority took precedent over legal rights, it made no sense to pursue a case in which a higher authority had already spoken. It must have seemed to Julio that either the Maestro himself did not understand the agreements that don Abram and don Tomás had made or that all three were involved. Moreover, as in the case with don Abram and his *compadre* that I described in chapter 4, kinship ties had to be negotiated if Julio were to resolve the matter, which made him particularly reluctant to take action.

Although Julio's reluctance to pursue a case of land evasion makes sense against the backdrop of practices of the Mexican state, his reactions also illuminate the politics of loose connections against the demand for unity. The Maestro Jorge, don Abram, and don Tomás looked to unity for insulation from charges of corruption and abuse of power. They reasoned that the more people participated in the committee and became involved in day-to-day decision making, the less likely the Oficina de Bienes Comunales was to fall victim to corruption gossip. Indeed, when Tepoztecans gossiped that the ejido commissioner was corrupt, they pointed to the fact that few people participated in ejidal assemblies. He doesn't want participation, they would claim, because then people will see that he is illegally selling land. Leaders in the committee believed that spreading responsibility among a wide array of participants would lead to better decisions and less corruption, but peripheral members viewed mass mobilizations as the appearance of diffused responsibilities to serve the interests of those exercising power in the committee.

By far the most serious threat to the security of Tepoztlán's communal land came from the fact that so many of the district's boundaries were in dispute. Boundary disputes between communities had long been a central feature in the history of Mexican land law. Borah (1983) reports that many of the disputes that indigenous people took to the special Indian Courts during the colonial period involved complaints between indigenous communities. Today, ambiguous borders make it easier for private developers, government officials, and expanding urban areas to claim the communal land of pueblos. Rectifying boundaries is an intractable problem, however. Different maps sometimes show different boundaries lines, as was the case for one of Tepoztlán's boundaries. If the committee followed the official map, they would lose land and be accused of giving away the town's communal land; if they followed the presidential decree from 1929 (usually taken by locals as definitive), they would inherit a colonia settled by outsiders.

Therefore, a primary goal of the committee from its inception was the rectification of Tepoztlán's boundaries. Doing so meant carrying out long, arduous inspections of boundaries, gaining the support of bureaucrats in the Secretaría de la Reforma Agraria, and, most important, getting the communities that made up the district to view themselves as part of the whole district. Having to show up at 5:00 a.m. and hike miles through uncharted terrain took its toll on busy peasants' participation in the committee, and rather than attend meetings where volunteers would be solicited for such excursions, many decided to stay at home. Those who did participate often found that the engineers who were supposed to verify the boundaries never showed up. But the most trying aspect of the effort to rectify the boundaries was the attempt to gain the support of surrounding communities, members of the district who for the most part had nurtured a long history of hostility to Tepoztlán, the district seat.

Tepoztlán is the seat of a district of more than twenty thousand people. As such, it is the administrative home of all government offices, and most occupants of these offices are residents of the district seat. Although sections of one barrio in Tepoztlán remained without electricity and running water in 1984, the other seven barrios had running water, electricity, and telephone lines. Buses run from Tepoztlán to nearby cities, making it possible for Tepoztecans to commute to jobs as far away as Mexico City, and many young people travel to Mexico City or elsewhere for postsecondary education. In short, despite district-seat Tepoztecans' tendency to describe themselves as a poor community and despite the presence of some poor families, the district seat enjoys economic benefits not shared with the other communities that make up the district.

Mistrust and tension characterize the relationships between the district seat and surrounding communities, but each subject community has a different manner of expressing this mistrust. Some communities, such as San Andrés de la Cal and Santa Catarina, have a well-developed internal political structure with local leaders who do not hesitate to bypass the district seat, taking their cases directly to state-level officials. Residents of Santa Catarina have a reputation for being bravo in politics and other matters; I was repeatedly warned not to go there by myself. Santa Catarina and San Andrés join with Tepoztlán for some political battles if only to exchange information, but they maintain a watchful eye for corruption and abuse of power by residents of the district seat. Other communities, such as Santo Domingo and San Juan, either do not become involved in larger political battles or contest Tepoztlán's opposition to development projects that they believe might help them. According to committee members, many of these communities were ruled by caciques who often supported the PRI.[2] In communities such as Amatlán and Ixcatepec, where electricity and running water are available, wealthy outsiders have settled and have changed the profile of each community's relations with the district seat. Viewing all legal dealings as state-level bureaucratic matters, these outsiders believed, wrongly, that district officials raised questions only because they wanted to be bribed. Accordingly, they ignored citations from the committee and refused to comply with their neighbors' request that they take disputes to the committee or to the district seat.

When I was there in 1984, Tepoztlán, the district seat, was not a source of identity for most members of the district. In a survey of eighty-two families that I conducted early in my research, I found few cases of marriage between residents of the district seat and residents of the surrounding communities. Where such intercommunity marriages took place, they linked families from the better-off communities, and my research in the National Archives revealed a long history of complaints directed to the president of the country from subject communities about relations with the district seat. Communities such as Santa Catarina complained repeatedly that residents of the district seat were encroaching on *their* land and water resources and that "development projects" were often carried out in ways that brought few if any benefits to subject communities. Lewis noted similar tensions in his study of Tepoztlán, arguing that a kind of moral boundary led members of a subject community to see communal land "as village rather than municipal lands" ([1951] 1972:117).

The ambiguities inherent in the discourse of community are traceable to the construction of administrative districts, first under colonialism, then by the contemporary state, and later reproduced in the postrevolutionary Mexican state's requirements for unity. As I mention in chapter 3, in the 1980s, when a "community" wanted to obtain needed services from the state—such as electricity, roads, telephone lines, and so on—its members had to show evidence of unity, often represented by the number of names collected on petitions. Because the Oficina de Bienes Comunales ostensibly represented the whole district, it needed to demonstrate support from the surrounding subject communities, but in practice its status as district representative was ambiguous, not only because of the manner in which it had been taken control of by Comité para la Defensa de Tierra members in 1983, but also because of the ambiguous place of communal land in the Agrarian Reform Law that existed in 1984.

The Agrarian Reform Law, to the extent that it dealt with communal land at all, treated communal and ejido land as the same, when in reality they originated out of distinct processes. Ejidatarios have to apply for distribution of ejido land as a group, so ejido land is not only a "gift" from the state but is also clearly marked as the responsibility of the group of ejidatarios who applied for the land, with the result that ejido land never raises the same questions regarding the boundaries of community that communal land necessarily raises. Who has responsibility for communal land, who can speak for the comuneros, and even who is a comunero are matters of some debate. These ambiguities sometimes served the state's interests, but they also created opportunities for subject communities to contest their subordinate status. When the state initiated a project, government officials would seek the support at the level most likely to obtain a favorable outcome for the project, exacerbating extant tensions between the district seat and subject communities. Authorities at the level of subject communities were often happy to entertain state-level projects even if they turned them down eventually, because being approached by state-level bureaucrats legitimated their distinction from Tepoztlán, the district seat. For example, in the fight against the golf course that I discuss in the epilogue, the governor's representatives are said to have offered San Juan status as the district seat in exchange for its support. Of course, when the community made demands on the state, the state could use the elasticity of the definition of *community* to demand the district's full participation.

Despite the rather obvious state-level manipulation of community discourse, it would not be accurate to presume that the state always profited from the ambiguities of community boundaries. Appeals to community incited genuine political passions that at times appeared to unify the whole district, threatening a widespread disorder that encouraged state officials to rethink development projects unwanted by the whole district. Tepoztecans of the district seat, however, drew the boundaries of community tightly around the district seat when it came time for elections, only to expand them after elections so that the district seat could speak for the whole district in appeals for government assistance. Thus, a paradox was created in which local officials who hailed primarily from the district seat needed the support of the whole district to govern.

Similar to peripheral committee members, residents of the surrounding communities engaged in political practices that enabled them to participate while at the same time retaining an aura of distance from the committee. In September 1984, the committee began a campaign to rectify the boundaries of Tepoztlán. To do so, they wrote a letter to then-president Miguel de la Madrid requesting a land inspection that would confirm the boundaries. An initial draft of the letter asserted that illegal land sales and communities encroaching on Tepoztlán's land had resulted in a loss of communal land, but residents of the surrounding communities objected to the letter. At a meeting, a representative of San Andrés explained:

> The issues are not the same because we have never sold our land—it is Tepoztecans [in the district seat] who have sold their land and the authorities in Tepoztlán who have given land away. This has not happened in San Andrés because the people are politically conscious and would not sell their land. Here in Tepoztlán you have mansions with swimming pools, and the authorities continue to give land away. The people of San Andrés have seen this, and when the authorities come to them with a letter, they say, "Why do they want to rectify the boundaries?"—they think that the authorities only want to make more business with the land.

Representatives of another community complained when the Maestro said that they could not send 150 people to deliver the letter. The Maestro argued that if they sent such a large contingency, the authorities would see only half the people and would then spread lies that a deal had been made.

For weeks, the committee worked to redraft a letter that would be acceptable not only to the district seat but also to the surrounding communities. Representatives from the communities argued that where the letter asserted that land had been illegally sold, it should make specific reference to the district seat, but don Abram contested that if the letter was going on behalf of the whole district, it should not mention specific communities. Exasperated, he complained, "This is what bothers me. . . . If it is just each pueblo fighting its own battles, we will never have any strength." During one meeting, where representatives again complained about lines in the letter, the Maestro took out his pen and crossed out several objectionable lines, asking if the representatives were now satisfied. They nodded their heads, but after they left the meeting, the Maestro rewrote the altered sentences and said, "We'll just leave the letter as it is."

Although representatives from the surrounding communities were more forthright in voicing their objections to the letter, in the end they engaged in the same kind of foot dragging that peripheral members within the committee used to express dissatisfaction. The representatives would leave each meeting promising to return with signatures, never to return. In the meantime, the Maestro boasted that the committee had collected eight hundred signatures, but he admitted that most were from the district seat. In late October, a group of about seven members, all from the district seat, finally went to Mexico City to deliver the letter. Rather than deliver it to the president, they went to the Secretaría de la Reforma Agraria, where they were warmly received by a woman who proclaimed that she was on their side and that she herself was from Morelos. Two years later the boundaries remained unrectified.

Intracommunity tensions within the district might well be seen as the product of a mandated unity between groups that have little practical interaction. The state has certainly shaped relations between the district seat and its surrounding communities, usually not for the better. For example, the relative privileges that the district seat enjoys came to it by virtue of its role as a district seat, and these privileges in turn have created class and educational divisions between the district and the surrounding communities. Moreover, the political games that the state plays in pedaling its controversial projects where they are most likely to be embraced, sometimes in violations of the law, have provoked further tensions between communities. To mandate district unity on top of these tensions, however, does not render politics impossible. Instead, it produces the terrain of loose connections at the district level.

The surrounding communities, in behaving as they did in 1984, were not merely resisting the committee's authority; rather, they were engaging in a form of political participation. For one thing, at issue in the rectification of boundaries was a direct attack on the integrity of the communities as separate entities; San Andrés and Santa Catarina community members' responses seemed calculated both to retain relations with the committee and to hold back their support. The fact that they sent representatives to meetings and kept checking on the status of the attempt to rectify the boundaries, all the while evading the problem of collecting signatures, is reminiscent of the strategy of peripheral members who continued to come to meetings on Tuesdays and Thursdays even after the committee leaders agreed to close the office on those days. In short, the surrounding communities tried to keep their feet in the door while refusing to support the district seat's desires to rectify boundaries, but their strategy of evasion was tied to the particular issue of the problem of land boundaries. In other cases, as shown in chapter 6, the communities did participate with the committee.

Viewed through the politics of loose connections, the example of the struggle over the boundaries reveals that state-imposed territorial units speak not so much to the unimpeded power of the state, but to its power to shape the terrain on which forms of political participation take hold. Viewed through a framework that values unity, the district's problems seem to condemn political projects to failure, but attention to a politics of loose connections suggests that in the absence of unity we find not failure, but ways in which state power has been kept in check. As becomes clear in the chapters that follow, the failure to rectify the boundaries did not weaken the committee's ability to defend itself against unwanted projects. Boundaries are limits in multiple senses. Although they would have enabled Tepoztecans to validate some claims to land, they would have undermined others. More important, the mapping of Tepoztecan territory would have left the committee in the position of administrator of territorial divisions dictated by the state and might well have facilitated the privatization of communal and ejidal land that President Salinas de Gortari began in 1992.

A fundamental issue for the guardianship of inalienable possessions is to whom this important role should be allocated. Weiner (1992) suggests that women play a central role in the protection of those treasures that speak to the continuity of a group through time, but in Tepoztlán the control over communal land, at least in the postcolonial period, was monopolized by men, as noted earlier. However, during the time I carried out my research, women began to use the associations of women with motherhood and family to argue that communal land was "their" issue. Male relatives often preyed upon widows, confiscating land left to them by parents and husbands, and in some cases sons tried to take land away from their mother upon their father's death, something don Abram judged a distasteful outcome of the abandonment of tradition. More than half of the cases processed in the Oficina de Bienes Comunales, therefore, involved women seeking the committee's support in conflicts with relatives or asking for a plot of land because their own had been confiscated by a relative or because they had not been left any. Except for the Maestra Isabella, who was Bienes Comunales secretary, women requesting land had to appeal to male authorities. Although these men displayed considerable concern for the plight of the single woman with children, the image of men deciding the fate of many women was not lost on the more politically active women of Tepoztlán in the Mujeres Tepoztecanas.

As in most Tepoztecan groups, the Mujeres Tepoztecanas was divided between a core group of leaders and more peripheral members. In fact, it was women in the group who explained to me the unequal distribution of "words." In the case of the Mujeres Tepoztecanas, two of the three women leaders were mothers who had raised children without the help of spouses. The other woman, Rachel, was a teacher in town who quickly moved up the educational bureaucracy during the time of my research. In addition to teaching, she ran a restaurant in the center of town. The Maestra, as she was called by the group, publicly thanked her spouse for allowing her to do this work, but appeared to be economically and politically independent of him because she had cultivated powerful networks among state-level bureaucrats and was an astute politician.

In 1984, between ten and twenty women attended each meeting of the Mujeres Tepoztecanas. Every evening during the week the women gathered in the plaza or in the courtyard in front of the church. Standing in small clusters of four or five, they exchanged information on the latest illegal land sales, water shortages, and injustices wrought by the corrupt bureaucracy. Later, when the Maestra Rachel appeared, the clusters gave way to a circle, the Maestra in the middle. Some women toted young children, but most of the women had children old enough to watch their younger siblings at home. One impoverished woman, her clothes in shreds, her feet flapping in oversize men's sneakers, arrived every day with her dog. Doña Rosa, who boasted that she was still politically active at eighty years old, shuffled slowly into the meetings, greeting everyone with a wide smile.

The group included mestizo women of different economic backgrounds. Four of the women owned small businesses in the center of town, and the rest sold handicrafts or worked as maids for foreigners. The group occasionally pooled money to help a woman start a business or a sick member see a doctor, benefits that were certainly appreciated in the economic crises of the 1980s. The Maestra Rachel often used her ties to help members of the group collectively and individually, particularly in matters of health care. Like the peripheral members of the Comité para la Defensa de Tierra (later the Coordinadora Democrática), most members of the Mujeres Tepoztecanas expected this kind of help from their political participation in the group. Unlike the committee, however, the Mujeres tried to fulfill these expectations while at the same time maintaining the image of a mother caring for the entire "community" in need.

The following excerpt from my field notes, dated May 11, 1984, speaks to the fit between individual need, collective need, and community in the Mujeres Tepoztecanas' discourse.

> Doña Juana started to cry and said that she was not going to feel shame in front of the group. "I will tell you I am going through a difficult time because I am having these problems with my kidneys, and the doctor tells me that I have to buy this very expensive medicine." The Maestra Rachel replied, "We should never be afraid when we have need; if it is not need of money, it is need of companionship or friendship, and we should help one another in this because we all go to church on Sunday, and we all know that God said we should help one another." . . . Then the Maestra Rachel told the group, "When I had need—I remember my husband was participating in the election, and we had no money— I would ask people for money, and they would say, 'No,' that I had everything with my restaurant, with my store, and with my job. But they didn't know I was paying five hundred pesos a month for lights, for the telephone." The woman sitting next to me replied, "Of course you had need."

The discourse of need figures into many political struggles in Mexico and was used by the Comité para la Defensa de Tierra to justify land takeovers (see also Díaz-Barriga 1996). Indeed, in the case of communal land, one demonstrated need by squatting on a piece of land. The discourse of need is most often analyzed as an attempt to shape radical class consciousness, as it was used by the committee, or as a general practice of subordination whereby the poor come to view themselves as dependent on the wealthy, part of the process of state co-optation (Díaz-Barriga 1996). In the hands of a skilled rhetorician such as the Maestra Rachel, need was revealed to have far more complexity. Disengaged from its economic sense, need became universal and a source for a community ethic of care.

To view this discourse of universal need only as a disguise of subtle class differences underestimates the extent to which this discourse shaped women's experiences of the group. The concept of universal need, used in the context of class differences that pervaded the Mujeres Tepoztecanas, was not about establishing patron-client relationships—even though these relationships existed within the group—but about overcoming the shame of being subordinated to needs by recognizing the universality of need. To be sure, the discourse of need constituted a group identity that was antithetical to a focus on class differences. The Mujeres Tepoztecanas crafted a view of community in which economic differences fit into an overall pattern of harmony. Internal differences in wealth, occupation, and social status contributed in their eyes to the group's overall strength and importance. Differences in power and resources complemented disparities in need. In contrast to the view that emerges in Western social thought, *community* signified for the Mujeres Tepoztecanas not an underlying similarity, but a force field made up of different resources on which they could draw.[3] For the Mujeres Tepoztecanas, community relied on differences as a source of strength.

The boundaries of community for the Mujeres Tepoztecanas were not nearly as inclusive or as ambiguous as those drawn by the Comité para la Defensa de Tierra. Although the Mujeres Tepoztecanas often tried to help those in the poorer communities of the district by distributing social services in these areas, the group itself did not include residents of these communities, nor did it try to include them. More important, the help to surrounding communities always inspired contentious debates as to which Tepoztecans from the district seat might have more need than the surrounding communities.

The Mujeres Tepoztecanas operated very much within the framework of political practices that have retained hegemonic control in Mexico at least since the 1940s. Leaders in the Comité para la Defensa de Tierra often pointed to the Maestra Rachel as the last of the great caciques, a turn of phrase calculated to evoke both the corruption of her power and the ironies of her attempts to carve a space for women in the male-dominated political arena. Clearly, she wielded a type of "cacique" power, using her connections to help loyal supporters and exacting political favors in return. She expended considerable time and energy, often successfully, trying to form connections with those at the top of the bureaucracy, and she was always careful not to challenge the boundaries that many Tepoztecans of the district seat drew around their community. In the eyes of committee leaders, her inclusive notions of need, combined with her exclusionary notions of community, made hers a politics that served the interests of the wealthy and powerful.

That I ended up working with both groups during my initial research period in 1984 speaks to the fact that both were neophyte organizations not yet clearly marked in the landscape of Tepoztecan politics. Indeed, the person who first introduced the committee to me also told me about the Mujeres Tepoztecanas, whom he described as very aggressive in defending the town's land. Months later I realized that the stories he told me about the women's bravery in confronting authorities were actually tales of confrontation between the committee and the Mujeres Tepoztecanas—this, despite the fact that he recommended both groups to me as good examples of local-level grassroots organizations that were defending the community. In fact, the two groups were beginning a battle for control of community politics, a battle that was most often waged through competing corruption charges and that would resurface around the 1988 elections (see chapter 6).

Early in April 1984, I first heard a story from doña Juana about the committee that alerted me to the tensions between the two groups. She told me that about eight months before I arrived in Tepoztlán, the then-commissioner of Bienes Comunales, don Miguel, together with don Pedro, don Tomás, and the Maestro Jorge were going to sell communal land to people from "outside" of Tepoztlán for five thousand pesos per plot. "It doesn't sound like a lot of money, but you can imagine how much money they would have made when they put it all together. . . . All the women from the Mujeres Tepoztecanas went there the day they were going to sell the land and stopped them from measuring." She concluded, "Now these people are all in the Comité para la Defensa de Tierra, and you would talk to them and think they are wonderful people . . . don Abram included. Now, he is so *digno* [righteous], saying that we must all unite to protect our communal lands . . . but when he was in the position of commissioner of ejido resources thirty years ago, he was selling land like crazy."

Most everyone agrees to the outlines of this story. The Maestro Jorge led a move to distribute land (some say it was communal, others say ejidal) and those who would receive the land would pay five thousand pesos for a plot. But there agreement ends. Leaders in the committee argue that a local Tepoztecan, a wealthy store owner, was going to sell the land so that a factory could be built, and the Maestro, responding quickly, organized a repossession and redistribution of the land, claiming that it had not been cultivated in more than two years. The fee of five thousand pesos covered the legal cost of processing land documents. Unfortunately, the would-be holders of the land were teachers, and the Mujeres Tepoztecanas could and did argue that as teachers they did not really have "need" because they all had a salary. In the end, the land was not redistributed, and the Mujeres Tepoztecanas boasted that the incident showed the strength of their stand against corrupt male officials.

Gender figured prominently not only in the Mujeres Tepoztecanas' attempts to argue women's natural ability to resist corruption, but also in the charge that women did not fare well when they had to process cases with male authorities. In fact, most people who were trying to get a plot of land or to win a land battle pursued the case through as many political channels as possible, using competing political leaders simultaneously, another aspect of the politics of loose connections. The same women who took their complaints and requests to the Oficina de Bienes Comunales also took them to the Mujeres Tepoztecanas. The clusters of women who talked together before meetings were most often talking about land issues: who was illegally selling land, what women had cases before authorities, and how those cases were being handled. Because many peripheral members of the Mujeres Tepoztecanas had spouses working in the committee, a steady supply of information and disinformation flowed between the two groups, and when the outcome of cases was critical to the community, this information fueled gossip about corruption.

As I stressed in chapter 3, Tepoztecan politics took shape around the establishment of connections, but relations established through those connections were rarely ties of unmitigated trust. One always needed connections but could never depend on any one line of connection. Therefore, it was not uncommon for individuals to participate in multiple groups at the same time, many of which were at odds with one another. From the perspective of a peripheral member, all political leaders tended to be at least potentially corrupt, and therefore no specific leader deserved one's loyalty. Moreover, one could never know who might be in the best position to emerge victorious in a political struggle, and therefore it never made sense to give full loyalty to any specific group. But participating in multiple groups' positions enabled one to hear gossip for every side and reinforced the notion that one should always hold back when engaging politically.

In this chapter, I have highlighted the tensions that shaped a politics of loose connections within the Comité para la Defensa de Tierra. I use the term *tensions* to underscore that they are not points of contradiction that move toward resolution, but rather stresses and strains that, although related to the particular moment in history in which I did my research, have endured. Political movements must always grapple with these kinds of tensions, however, for they exist in tandem with the forces that pull people into the political arena in the first place. The most striking thing about Tepoztecan politics is not that these tensions existed, but that Tepoztecans and in this case the Oficina de Bienes Comunales endured and were often successful despite the tensions that pitted committee and organization members against each other.

Clearly, one of the enduring tensions is the thriving market in what is held to be an inalienable resource. This tension is reflected not only in illegal sales of communal land, but in the necessarily intimate relationship between the value of private property and Tepoztecans' demands for communal land. As foreign and domestic outsiders purchase Tepoztlán's private property and often communal land as well, Tepoztecans themselves look to communal land for housing. When they do, they find not only that there is a dwindling supply of this land, but that friends and neighbors are holding plots of land for their children without working those plots, and that migrants from other places in Mexico have settled on the land. Moreover, because the boundaries between communal land and private property are vague, as the market value of private property increases, so, too, does the market value of illegally sold communal land. In fact, over the years, Tepoztecans have sold communal land among

pivots around the power certain words come to have not because they convey information or knowledge, but because of their power in battle. Favret-Saada argues that in order to understand—read "catch"—the sense of witchcraft, one must allow oneself to become "caught" in the words, much as French peasants do as they turn to witchcraft to explain an unfortunate series of events. Her sense of the need to be "caught" in order to "catch," as she points out, stands in opposition to the poststructuralist attempts to avoid being caught in language.

Clearly, talk of democracy differs from talk of witchcraft, for the latter is often spoken about in hushed tones to evade the critical gaze of those who define witchcraft as backward or primitive, whereas the former is loudly proclaimed and celebrated as evidence of modernity. But democracy shares with witchcraft that ability to catch speakers who find themselves caught up in a social problem, even when those speakers are academics who pride themselves as social theorists. In such a situation, talk of democracy speaks to being caught up in the desire for a solution to a series of seemingly unresolvable contradictions. Moreover, the invocation of democracy silences those who would pollute the water, for to be antidemocratic, although theoretically possible, is unthinkable practically speaking—by which I mean speaking from within a set of social situations. As such, a theory of democracy is probably best arrived at by careful attention to the situations in which the word *democracy* is used and not as an abstract theoretical formulation. In short, democracy cannot be spoken of as having an absolute meaning derived from its place of origin, but rather in a situational sense derived from its enunciation at a particular point and time and in relation to specific "problems." For example, to capture ethnographically what democracy meant to Tepoztecans, one has to become, at least for a time, caught up in how to rescue a collective political life in a community internally divided by mistrust and disagreements. In this predicament, Tepoztecans rallied around the word *democracy* not cynically, but passionately, deploying its power to deal with the intractable problems of sociability.

Chapter 7
Transnational Politics and the
Imaginary of Sustainable Development

> Rather than thinking of the struggles as relating to one another like links in a chain,
> it might be better to conceive of them as communicating like a virus that modulates
> its form to find in each context an adequate host.
> —Michael Hardt and Antonio Negri, *Empire*

When I returned to Tepoztlán in 1991, the Coordinadora Democrática, formerly the Comité para la Defensa de Tierra, was engaged in what the Maestro and others described as *la lucha* (the struggle) for the very existence of el pueblo. They had uncovered government plans to connect a previously unconnected section of Mexico's rail system by running tracks across the mountains that surrounded Tepoztlán. Multinational capital was financing the project, which portended widespread ecological disasters according to Coordinadora members and the ecologists who worked with them. The multinational financing, the potential magnitude of the ecological disruption, and the international connections made by Mayor Robles encouraged Tepoztecans to appeal to the global environmental movement. Echoing the multinationals' strategies, Coordinadora members sought to use computers and fax technology to influence global power structures and to gain control over Mexico's economic future. In the process, many of them began to rethink their notion of the world and of globalization.

In 1984, I asked a middle-aged woman to describe the relationship between the president and the pueblo. She explained, "The president is like a father to us, and just like in the family, if the father is good and just, the children grow and prosper, but without a good father the children cannot prosper. It is like that with the pueblo: if the president is good, we grow, but if he is not, we will be nothing." Tepoztecans often deployed the patriarchal family as a metaphor for relationships between those in positions of power and the community in 1984. Such talk expressed the intimate link between state power and gender ideologies. When I asked the Maestro Jorge how so many foreigners were able to buy land in Tepoztlán, he explained, "Because this *pinche* [lousy] government has drunk the water." "Drunk the water?" I asked. Everyone laughed. "Don Abram will explain to you." Later, don Abram told me that many years ago Emiliano Zapata's son had been madly in love with an actress. The woman would leave Zapata's son to take care of her ranch and go into Mexico City for days at a time; the son would await her return. One day when the lover was away, don Abram and his friends went to visit Zapata's son at the ranch. They found the son crying because his lover had been gone for so long. Immediately the men knew that she had "given him the water." She had, according to don Abram, put menstrual blood in his tea. When I expressed skepticism, don Abram responded, "But, of course, why else would Emiliano Zapata's son be so controlled by a woman?" Indeed, as the story is structured, "drinking the water" transformed Emiliano Zapata's son from a macho to an effeminate male prone to respond to a woman's orders.

To say that the government has "drunk the water" is to invoke not only a macho ideal, but also that ideal's profound vulnerabilities in the face of a seductive power. Viewed from the perspective of gender ideologies, Mexican history can be written as a series of challenges to the state in which its leaders' machismo is constantly tested. Ever since Lázaro Cárdenas expropriated foreign oil companies in 1938, thus "standing up" to foreign interests, the international arena has tested the Mexican president's machismo. Foreign capitalists are not represented within this gender iconography as macho males, however. Rather, they command a feminine power, the seductive promises of riches that tantalize leaders into abandoning their loyalties to the nation in favor of a subordinate role to those international capitalists. Just as the incredible strength of Emiliano Zapata's blood was not enough to counteract the "water" given to his son, the strength of national identity, also a blood tie, can be undermined by the seductive lure of foreign capital.

Why is it that the traits of machismo are not extended to the foreign capitalist? Lancaster points out that machismo is a gestural system in which the male must prove himself "active": "Every gesture, every posture, every stance, every way of acting in the world is immediately seen as 'masculine' or 'feminine' depending on whether it connotes activity or passivity. As a gestural system, machismo has a steep temporal dimension, and yesterday's victories count for little tomorrow" (1992:237).

Value as male is always at stake in this interplay of gestures, and men must continually prove their abilities to take risks, to assert their opinions, to fight, and to conquer women (Lancaster 1992:236). Lancaster directs his discussion of machismo to the politics of sexuality, but his analysis is pertinent to the political arena as well. The elements of risk taking, fighting, and making and meeting challenges center politics. I would argue, however, that the world of global capital does not follow the form of risk Lancaster describes.

For many Tepoztecans, the kinds of deals that allowed global capitalism to take ever more control over national territory take place on life's backstage. Tepoztecans often joked when Mexican government officials, in the seemingly never-ending processes of debt renegotiation, made eloquent speeches about the nation's good never being compromised. "They are so macho in public, but then they go behind closed doors and sell the country down the drain," don Tomás joked. This kind of "backstage" negotiation could not fit within the scheme of a male-to-male contest for power in which public gestures weigh heavily. The world of global capitalism was not perceived as "a steep slope" in which yesterday's gains count little in tomorrow's contest. Such a game has a certain logic of fairness to it that global capitalism does not have. Tepoztecans clearly recognized that in contests between the Mexican government and foreign capital, the latter held the upper hand. They criticized the Mexican government nonetheless because it was unwilling to take the kind of risks that standing up to foreign interests entailed. Foreign capitalists also lacked machismo because the whole game of capitalist money making was perceived as outside the logic of machismo. From many Tepoztecans' point of view, capitalist industry made money by a gradual and rationalized exploitation of labor, which, in contrast to the face-to-face confrontations between macho men, remained anonymous and almost invisible. If, as Lancaster claims, machismo is a game between men in which women figure as intermediaries, and if we are to factor foreign capitalists into this gender warfare, foreign capital represented the silent intermediaries of the feminine domain.

The global imagination, no less than the national imagination, stirs up a myriad of passions. In the contemporary world, domination of space has become a critical factor in the exercise of power. Control over the means of communication, the ability to move rapidly for strategic economic advantage, and, most important, the ability to break through spatial barriers (to cross the boundaries of nations, regions, and communities) give capitalism unique advantages in contests over power (D. Harvey 1990:226–39). The control over space implies the ability to create new spaces and new ways of imagining space, while displacing, or at least disrupting, already existing spaces, a process that David Harvey, following Deluze and Guattari (1983), refers to as *deterritorialization* and *reterritorialization*. Thus, for example, multinationals, together with receptive host governments, created the Free Trade Zone, a space carved out of the national territory in which capitalism was given a free reign. And as scholars flocked to these regions to study the whole issue of contested, negotiated, and debated boundaries, borders and identities took center stage in literature and social science.

Domination of space as described by Harvey (1990) involves processes of distancing and separating, of the sort involved in mapping the world. Profound implications are associated with this global perspective. Ingold argues that such a perspective implies that human beings have dominion over the world as over a piece of property: the world belongs to us, but we do not belong to the world (1993:39–42). Humans do not think of themselves as living within the world, but as journeying across its outer surfaces (Ingold 1993:36). The globe becomes a free space over which human beings can wander without any center from which to explore it. This global vision, assumed to be the superior vision of the world, is then contrasted with the "bounded," "limited" local vision of the world, which Ingold argues is closer to everyday experience. But local visions of the world are not necessarily bounded and limited; their mode of knowledge about the world is enriched by the passions associated with place.

Local visions deploy metaphors that understand the world by linking the global with more familiar social fields. The nation and its location in the global economy become the site of intersection of various discourses of power, including those of family, sexuality, and gender. Thus, global conflicts suture together multiple fields of experience and transform the abstract processes of debt negotiation, foreign-trade agreements, and the like into a complex narrative of domination and control that resonates across various social fields. To say that the government has "drunk the water" is to invoke not only the state's impotence in the face of foreign capital, but also male anxieties about losing power and authority to women both in the home and in the formal political arena.[1]

Drawing on the sex-gender domain for a description of the machinations of state power in a global economy creates a kind of passionate engagement in the process of imagining the world. Harvey's emphasis on spatial abstraction overlooks such passionate engagement. We might best understand the differences between abstract global visions and passionate local visions by contrasting Ingold's notions of the local with Harvey's notion of time-space compression. Harvey argues that advances in computer technologies, infrastructure development, and the speed with which the media bring together images from around the world have resulted in an experience of the world as a place that is physically smaller and moves at an ever-increasing pace (1990:284–307). He attributes to this time-space compression a disorienting and disruptive impact not only on politics and economics, but also on the experience of self in the world. But his depiction of time-space compression fails to take into account different experiences of the impact of a restructured global world order. For example, at any given period of time, most Tepoztecan families have members working in different parts of the United States, giving many a feeling of camaraderie with me. They cheerfully inquired if I knew their loved ones and encouraged me to look them up on my return to the United States. Perhaps because I had traveled so easily to Mexico, they presumed it would be easy for me to cross the United States and look up their relatives wherever they might be. They were acutely aware, however, that "travel" was not so easy for them or for their relatives. Tales of their own "travels" to the United States highlighted the difficulties of movement because of poor transportation, legal obstacles to crossing the border, and the barriers to communication with loved ones who lived miles from home. Their discussions of travel emphasized a journey from the familiar and comfortable place of home across difficult and *distant* terrain. Time and space were not compressed, but lengthened and exaggerated. The arduous nature of the travel, coupled with the notion of the endurance of physical and cultural separation, rendered the journey to the United States deeply meaningful as a transforming and knowledge-seeking experience.

The difficulties of travel and the passions for el pueblo that Tepoztecans experienced did not translate into a global-local divide that would envision a clear boundary or a perspective bounded by the local. Whenever discussions of immigration policy emerged, and they frequently did,

Tepoztecans reminded me that they only wanted to go to the United States to see how things were different. Hadn't I come to Mexico for the same reason? they asked. And in 1984, when don Abram heard excerpts of one of Ronald Reagan's Central American speeches on the radio, he sat and composed a letter to the U.S. president. He wanted to take issue with Reagan's representation of the fighting in Guatemala. The global world was alive in Tepoztecans' imagination, but without the sense of conquest that is stressed in so much writing about the global world, which takes globalization as a kind omnipotence. In other words, in Tepoztlán, the global entailed the local, with all the specificity that implies. The United States represented a special place, for it was recognized as wielding power over Mexican presidents and other officials. It was where the movies were produced, the celebrities lived, and the multinationals did business. A journey to the United States represented the traveler's ability to operate in circles of global power. Thus, in 1991, when the Coordinadora declared it was willing to take the battle over the proposed train project "all the way to the United Nations if necessary," they were threatening the Mexican government with a new form of taking problems to the top.

The linking of the train line entailed blasting tunnels through the mountains, and engineers and ecologists feared that the tunnel blast would divert the water supply. "We need to organize everyone who is sympathetic to us to stop the project," explained the Maestro. I did not realize that he meant me and some of the wealthy foreign residents of the valley, nor did I envision at the time that the Coordinadora would indeed take the struggle to the United Nations. Since my previous visit in 1988, several new groups had formed in Tepoztlán, and others who had a longer history now viewed themselves as members of the Coordinadora. In addition, the PRI was engaged in a full-scale campaign to regain power in the town, which included mass organizing of young people into the party, replacement of the local priest with a conservative, charismatic Catholic priest, and use of Programa Nacional de Solidaridad money (discussed in detail later) to shore up support for the party. If the PRI was engaged in a full-scale restructuring of power relations, however, so too were the numerous opposition groups in Mexico. The latter drew heavily on notions of sustainable development and the emerging politics of ethnic identity.

Since 1984, the valley where wealthy outsiders lived in luxurious homes had been forbidden territory for me. Although I knew that some of Mexico's prominent left intellectuals spent their summers and vacations there, my own struggle for legitimacy within the Comité para la Defensa de Tierra encouraged me to ignore these residents. Contacts with the dreaded outsiders could only further complicate my already delicate position. Indeed, I had come to view residents of the valley in much the same terms as my informants: as a homogeneous block of wealthy outsiders who destroyed the town's economy, who contributed little or nothing to local fiestas, and whose weekend visits disturbed the tranquility of community life. Of course, I knew that some of the wealthy outsiders expressed a desire to help Tepoztlán and that among them were Mexican intellectuals for whom I had great respect. As one outsider told me in 1984, "We know that we are part of the problem, but we also want to be part of the solution." By 1991, progressive outsiders had formed a group called the Vecinos de Tepoztlán (Neighbors of Tepoztlán), a name that tactfully underscored the limitations of their claim to call Tepoztlán home. They initially formed to do something about the problem of the garbage that always seemed to pile up in the ditches alongside the roads— which Tepoztecans blamed on the outsiders and outsiders blamed on Tepoztecans. Later, they were drawn into land tenure issues and, as events unfolded in the summer of 1991, into the struggle to defeat the train project. They played a pivotal role in linking the Coordinadora and progressive ecological groups in Mexico.

In 1991, the Coordinadora appeared much more similar in form, if not in composition, to the Comité para la Defensa de Tierra, which I had first studied in 1984. Once again, it appeared to be a grassroots organization that shunned involvement in electoral politics, in contrast to its involvement in the 1988 elections. No longer in control of any municipal offices, it focused on stopping unwanted development projects. In a world that seemed very distant from the high-powered organizing that the Vecinos de Tepoztlán envisioned, don Abram served as the commissioner of the Oficina de Bienes Comunales. The former commissioner, don Tomás, had been removed from office amidst charges of corruption and abuse of power. Now don Abram assumed sole responsibility for any complaints dealing with communal land. He worked from his home, where a hastily constructed meeting room had been added onto his house. He was now almost ninety years old, and he found the constant barrage of complaints tiring. "People are calling him before he gets out of bed in the morning, and they are here past midnight," complained the daughter-in-law who lived with him. Worse still, when he gave people documents for their land, they gave him nothing in return. Don Abram complained that people assumed his salary covered the cost of everything. They did not realize that he had to go to Cuernavaca to file the documents and had to purchase out of his salary the paper on which these documents were written. "A man in the Secretaría de la Reforma Agraria told me to set a fee for giving out documents, but I want people to give according to their consciousness and their will," he explained. "They tell me they are going to get rid of this position—I hope they do because it is nothing but service for the pueblo," don Abram sighed.

In the kind of ironic twist that happens when history and passion are out of step, don Abram, the man who had dedicated his life to the defense of the pueblo's patrimony, now had no heirs for his own land. Only two of his children had remained campesinos. One, his last-born son, had been murdered in what was rumored to be a political struggle. The rest had their professions (teaching, accounting, storekeeping, and so on). He reminded me again, "I told the Maestro to teach the children to love the land, but the schools have not done that, and now everyone wants their profession and their cars and houses. . . . Soon we will be eating tacos de billetas." But there were young people in the Coordinadora who worked hard to defend the town's land.

The Coordinadora's youth committee was made up of about fifteen secondary school–age young men and women. The constant flirtation that went on during meetings lent a lively cast to the proceedings as every discussion became loaded with double entendres that combined the intricacies of politics with those of sex. At one meeting I attended, a young woman taunted the handsome male leader of the group: "I came looking for you at your house yesterday." The leader, glancing at the other guys in the room, responded, "You came looking for me?" "Of course, you were supposed to have the leaflets ready," she said, coolly unraveling the politics from the sexual politics.

Despite the playful sexual politics, the youth committee was serious about its work. Its members composed many of the leaflets distributed by the Coordinadora, inspected damage to communal land, and worked hard to overcome tensions between the district seat and the surrounding communities. An offshoot of the group the Maestro had formed in 1984 to fight the rising cost of bus transportation, the youth committee had since developed its own independent leaders and had assumed responsibility for a much broader political agenda.

As with many sectors of the population, Tepoztecan women also had their own committee within the Coordinadora. Many of the women in the group were originally members of the Mujeres Tepoztecanas, but, according to one of the group's leaders, they had left the group because they had discovered that the Mujeres' leaders worked only for themselves. Their committee, as they told the story, had existed long before the Coordinadora and had started as a sewing cooperative to help women make money. They had joined with the Coordinadora during the mayoral election of Humberto Robles, but only some women in the group had attended the Coordinadora meetings. Separate from their connections with the Coordinadora, the group had maintained connections with a group in Cuernavaca that opposed NAFTA and supported Cuba and the struggles in Central America. These political positions, although acceptable to the leaders of the women's committee, had held little interest for rank-and-file members. Indeed, the women who participated in both the women's committee and the Coordinadora had seemed more interested in local issues than in broader Latin American political issues.

Against the backdrop of local organizing, President Salinas de Gortari tried to revive and modify the PRI by creating local community support as a foundation for party strength. On the heels of Miguel de la Madrid's austerity measures (see chapter 6), Salinas de Gortari's Programa Nacional de Solidaridad, which became known as Solidaridad, represented a sharp boost in social spending (an 85 percent increase from 1988 to 1993). Solidaridad, built on the findings of Salinas de Gortari's doctoral research in rural communities in Puebla and Tlaxcala, claimed to be a modernist approach to social welfare, one that removed the political conditionality historically associated with the distribution of government monies. In place of the peasant, labor, and popular sectors, Solidaridad emphasized the community as the locus of development initiatives and responsibilities (Cornelius, Craig, and Fox 1994:18–19). Of course, although perhaps subordinate to more inclusive categories such as "peasants" and "workers," "community" had long been politically salient in Mexico, for it had structured rights to land and to government services.

The distribution of Solidaridad monies in theory would bypass the normal political channels, removing any possibility of political strings attached. As I described in chapter 3, Mexico had a long-standing pattern of resource distributions centered on those in positions of power. Monies were distributed in rituals in which the governor or the president journeyed to a community and with much fanfare announced some benefit to be given to the pueblo. Like a sensitive, all-knowing father, the official knew beforehand what the community needed. In contrast, under Solidaridad, each community formed a development committee that made up a list of projects and participated in supervision, implementation, and evaluation of those projects. In the words of Enrique González Tiburcio, secretary of Solidaridad's Consultative Council, "Solidarity turns the old method of social policy on its head, promoting organization from the micro level upward in both social and geographic terms. Because Solidarity does not work with political parties, but with citizens and social organizations, it opens a democratic political space for a more productive and beneficial relationship between the state and society" (1994:73).

The evidence of Solidaridad's ability to remain independent of PRI power structures is mixed. On the one hand, leftist groups and independent community-based organizations have used Solidaridad funds to their advantage (see Moguel 1994). On the other hand, there seems to be some quantitative evidence that municipalities that voted for the Cárdenas opposition in 1988 were punished by the distribution of Solidaridad funds for education (see Gershberg 1994). More precisely, the qualitative data suggest that Solidaridad may have encouraged communities and groups to align themselves with the PRI to gain benefits for their communities (Haber 1994). In Tepoztlán, a community where Cárdenas was victorious in 1988, the PRI was determined to regain lost ground; Solidaridad was a key element in its strategy.

During the summer of 1991, I worked in the municipal offices trying to recover some of the local history from badly preserved and disorganized archives. As I pored through dusty file folders with dates scribbled on the outside, I came to understand a side of Tepoztecan politics that I had never before observed from the inside—PRI organizing. The municipal offices were busy preparing for a visit from the governor of Morelos, Antonio Riva Palacio, who would announce the formation of a Solidaridad program. PRI officials visited the municipal offices in the weeks that preceded his arrival to ensure that a "Solidaridad" development committee would be formed. Meetings of various town organizations, excluding those connected to the Coordinadora, were held, with special attention being given to the young people.

By the day of the governor's arrival, a development committee had been made up. The local band entertained the crowd that waited for more than three hours for the governor to arrive. Newspaper reporters from a variety of Morelos newspapers wandered through the crowds with cameras ready for the first sight of the governor. Coordinadora members hung on the outskirts of the crowd, awaiting an opportunity to present the governor with their complaints about the train. Finally he appeared, surrounded by a coterie of local- and state-level officials who would make their own speeches. When the speeches began, these officials laid out the goals of solidarity (to form development plans that reflected the local conditions of each pueblo, to bring together people who would work with the government to improve the conditions of the pueblo, and to use a form of democratic participation by local groups to achieve development objectives) as well as the amounts of money to be dispensed and the groups already formed to work with Solidaridad in the surrounding communities.

The governor swore in the new development committee, which included representatives from each of the surrounding communities, local town organizations, and the colonias. No one from the Coordinadora had been named to the committee. Then he called on someone from the Coordinadora to read a letter addressed to him. A man who is a teacher stood and read the letter, which explained that the people of Tepoztlán had learned of this project (the train line) through the news media and that they were concerned that the project would lead to deforestation, to incalculable damage of a pristine ecological corridor and communal land, and to a diversion of the water supply on which the peoples of Tepoztlán depended. The letter concluded that the project, furthermore, would not bring any benefits to the people of Tepoztlán. The letter asked the governor not to allow this important issue to become a matter of politics and to order work on the project suspended immediately, thus taking into account Tepoztecans' opinions.

The governor responded that his office had been monitoring the project not only because of its impact on Tepoztlán, but because of potential impacts on the whole state of Morelos. He assured everyone that if the project were carried out, it would be done without damage to the land, and under no circumstances would it be carried out without full consultation with the comuneros. "Nothing can be done behind the back of the pueblo, and everything should be done for the benefit of the pueblo," he concluded. He then began addressing the newly formed development committee: "We are beginning a new stage . . . we want to work together: the pueblo and the governor in a form of planning based on coordination destined to achieve regional development." He told them that the amounts of money they had heard of today were for information only because each pueblo needed to develop a plan according to its own needs, giving priority to the poorest sectors of the population. He invited opposition parties to enter the planning phase and to debate, in a realistic manner, the pueblo's aspirations. He added:

> At this time, the governor, your friend . . . is going to tell you something more: that your plan . . . should be ready in at least thirty days. . . . Why in thirty days? Because I am going to return in thirty days because I don't want to announce today how much money I am going to allocate to Tepoztlán because I want to [disperse funds] in response to what you tell me we should do in the municipality. But I want you to tell me in an order [of priorities] . . . so that I can say we are going to do one through nine, but we do not have the funds for ten—but it will be you yourselves who will have told me how you will carry out the programs of the government.

Before the governor ended his speech, he made an exception to the thirty-day rule. He announced that funds from the state and federal governments and from Solidaridad would be used to open several new schools in Tepoztlán. His announcement won him a resounding applause.

Contrary to Salinas de Gortari's expressed vision for Solidaridad, the money was being effectively used at the state level to bring new people into the political process, solidify relations between the party and its new and old allies, and to punish groups such as the Coordinadora by exclusion. The Morelos governor effectively used Solidaridad funds to create a new base of support for the PRI with his insistence that funds be tied to the newly formed development committee's ability to work together. The governor's speech attempted to unite the pueblo by casting anyone who refused to work with Solidaridad as an enemy of the pueblo and of the poor. As Solidaridad was implemented, however, its politics became more complex.

Months after the governor's visit, a young man who had been active in both the Comité para la Defense de Tierra and the Coordinadora and who described himself as a Marxist interested in peasant revolutionary struggles told me that he had been given a job with Solidaridad. When I expressed surprise, he assured me that Solidaridad was a different kind of program. He said that it was really to help the poor and that there was no expectation that people who received Solidaridad monies would become PRI supporters. He elaborated his point by explaining that he was currently working on a project to help San Juan, one of the poorest surrounding communities, form a crate-making industry. "You know, Juanita," he explained, "when we are fighting things like this train, the poor communities are often not with us because they are so poor that they believe it when the government promises to help them, and they go along with the project. We must help these communities so that they are not so vulnerable to false promises." I suspect that the project he spoke of was never realized. I certainly never heard anything about it. But the fact that he saw Solidaridad as a significant departure from past practices of PRI funding for social welfare was important. Moreover, his analysis of the problems poverty posed for the left in Mexico spoke to a paradoxical overlap between Mexico's emerging neoliberal agenda and left politics. Neoliberalism promised to dismantle the paternalistic relations between the state and society that had so long hampered the development of independent left movements in Mexico, but a less-involved state with more bureaucratic and impersonal distributions of welfare monies might also create opportunities for new forms of opposition to emerge.

In the new political terrain that took shape after the 1988 presidential election, opposition movements such as the Coordinadora became imaginable. Their links with outside groups gave them a measure of independent power. The proliferation of NGOs throughout Mexico and the world provided new venues through which local, community-based organizations could pursue complaints against the state. Playing NGO politics did not require that local communities transform fundamentally their notion of politics. Local organizations were accustomed to taking issues to a variety of offices in the state-level bureaucracy in the hopes that anyone might respond. In each of those offices, people found friends who supported their struggle and wanted to help them. In the minds of those who pursued such support at the international level, NGOs were not by definition more trustworthy or more deeply concerned about the issues that plagued the local communities. They were merely another avenue to garner power in ongoing struggles.

At seven in the morning on a July day in 1991, the Maestro, a representative from San Andrés, don Pedro's son, a female member of the Vecinos de Tepoztlán, don Modesto, and I met in front of the home of Marcos, another member of the Vecinos de Tepoztlán. Marcos had connections with leaders of an ecological movement in Mexico City, and he had agreed to drive us all to the city for a meeting with the group. He had told us that it was a good group that had helped other peasants in Mexico win fights over development issues with the state. After waiting almost a half-hour for don Abram to arrive, the Maestro asked me if I would run to his house to remind him. "He has gotten old, and he forgets these things," he explained. Everyone got in the car, and we drove to the foot of the hill where don Abram lived. I ran quickly up the stone street, dodging horse and cattle droppings on the way. When I arrived at his house—now about 7:30 in the morning—don Abram was already up and talking with a man who had brought a problem with communal land to be resolved. I waited, trying not to appear impatient, as he calmly dealt with the matter. After about a half hour, the man left, and don Abram was ready to leave—he had not forgotten the date in Mexico City, but he had to deal with the land problem first, he explained.

By the time we arrived at the bottom of the hill, the others had managed to find another car and driver to transport us to Mexico City. We now divided into two groups to make the journey to the city: one group in Marcos's car, the other in a taxi. I rode with the Maestro, Marcos, and don Abram.

Marcos had a vision for Tepoztlán's future that was at odds with that of the Coordinadora. Although he shared the Coordinadora's disdain for large-scale tourist projects, he envisioned a network of European-style bed-and-breakfast houses run by Tepoztecans themselves. By gathering and recycling rain water and cooking with solar energy, Marcos had constructed his own house to be ecologically self-sustaining. He hoped that the bed-and-breakfast inns he envisioned would draw on some of his own ideas about sustainability.

As the car made its way toward Mexico City, Marcos took advantage of the time to ask questions about land issues and to offer his own suggestions for solutions. He began with questions about the problem of communal land. The Maestro responded with the answer that I had become accustomed to hearing: that peasants with little education and no political consciousness were selling the pueblo's land. At times, they did not even know that the land they were selling was communal. Marcos objected to the Maestro's characterization, telling him that many of these people were selling the land because they really needed the money. He suggested that perhaps the town could buy land from those who needed the money, and that way the land would once again become communal, with the town holding legal title. But where would the money to buy the land come from? the Maestro asked rhetorically. Perhaps there might be a way for the town to get money from an outside source, perhaps an international NGO, Marcos suggested. The Maestro appeared skeptical. The conversation continued, with Marcos sharing his ideas and the Maestro protesting that either they could not be carried out or that Marcos underestimated the complexity of the situation. The Maestro repeatedly reminded him that the Coordinadora represented everyone—not just the people of the district seat—and that solutions, such as the bed-and-breakfast idea, which might work for the district seat, would not be feasible in the surrounding communities.

When we arrived at the offices of the ecological group, a young man ushered us into a conference room where we all took places around the table. Renato, the organization's leader, introduced himself and then suggested that we all introduce ourselves. Don Abram introduced himself as the commissioner of the Oficina de Bienes Comunales and began to lay out his long involvement in struggles to defend communal and ejido land, emphasizing those issues that had ended in the Supreme Court. Renato interrupted him after several minutes, saying that he was honored to have his wisdom and experience, but that we needed to move on so that we could hear from everyone. When I introduced myself as an anthropologist who had known the Comité para la Defensa de Tierra since 1984, Renato counseled that I would have an important role to play because the Mexican government was very sensitive to international pressure.

After everyone introduced themselves, Renato explained the principles by which his organization operated. He assured those gathered around the table that they were not the type of ecological group that fights to keep the environment pristine. The group, he explained, was more interested in supporting struggles like theirs by using the ecological laws and the criteria of sustainable development in conjunction with local communities' desires. The Maestro responded that the Coordinadora would be holding a communitywide assembly early in August. He added that with the confidence the pueblo already had in Renato's organization, it would mean a great deal if the organization could send a representative to show that it was behind the Coordinadora. Renato guaranteed that someone would be present. He then asked for the facts of the case, which the Maestro laid out. The engineering company ICA had begun work on the train line without consulting with the comuneros, that foreign capital was involved in the project, that the area affected had been designated as an ecological zone in 1988, that just one week earlier ICA had begun to construct access roads that had already damaged the region's ecology. Renato said that if all this indeed had happened, the comuneros had grounds for a legal case that would at least result in an order to stop work until proper environmental studies had been carried out. He counseled that we should send a group up to the work site to get license numbers of the machines being used and if possible the workers' names.

After the brief discussion of strategy, Renato introduced the ecological group's methods of organizing. He explained that their group liked to carry out three days of intensive research in a community, examining the region's ecology, the community's social structure, and the people's economic and health problems. Then its members would convene an assembly. After this initial assessment, they would discuss all the different options for development with the whole community so that everyone could participate in forming a plan. The Maestro and the representative from San Andrés cautioned that every pueblo in the district had powerful caciques who organized people to represent their issues. Those who came to the meetings might be speaking for these caciques' interests. Renato admitted that these people would have to be included in the meeting and that in other projects the organization had not been able to stop unwanted development because it had to negotiate with various community factions. But, he added,

> this project [the railway line] is part of a larger regional plan and has effects at the level of the region. . . . We need to develop a plan to manage these resources, an agreement that . . . will bring a better future. We have to see where the problems are and not wait for [the

Secretaría de Agricultura y Recursos Hidráulicos]. It is not enough to say no to the train because when the government puts in a project like that, it is always part of a larger plan. . . . So, instead of saying no to the train, we need to say, "Instead of the train, let's ask for this project."

Those gathered at the table appeared somewhat uneasy. One man explained, "We have seen that these projects are proposed one after the other, but we also know that the government is a very clever negotiator. They are using these projects to transform our pueblo with tourism: from one with beautiful flowers and birds into a desert."

Another member of the delegation seemed to agree with Renato's ideas, saying that we should demand a project that would truly benefit the pueblo. Renato cautioned, "We cannot leave the future in the hands of the government. . . . [T]he only way we can win is if we take the initiative by putting forth a project that the community wants—by raising questions such as, What type of tourism do you want? This is a complete change in mentality." The Maestro intervened, "We will form a committee, but with the idea of stopping the train. Afterward we will select a few people to work toward the long term, but first we need a group in the community that can reach an agreement about the long term."

Renato seemed to back down: "First, we work to stop the train, and afterward we work to plan the maintenance of resources for seven or eight generations into the future—that is what we have to plan, but for now we must work on the issue of the train."

Based on his work with a Philippine squatter settlement, Philip Parnell (1992) has argued that what appears on the surface to be delay caused by incompetent political leaders might better be viewed as strategies to create time to build organizations. He points out that when the goal is to build an organization, success may be costly if it is presided over by state-level bureaucracy. The latter may usurp the local community's power to designate how a project will be carried out and who will be involved in the planning. Parnell's argument echoes de Certeau's (1984) analysis of the way in which time can disrupt the spatial arrangements of power and by extension can be deployed as a mode of resistance.

The differences between Renato and Coordinadora members revolved around how to best use time within the current configuration of power. Renato's arguments that Tepoztecans needed to develop their own plans for the future failed to take into account contemporary internal Tepozte-can conflicts. Coordinadora members wanted to avoid completing any plans for the future until they felt more secure about local power arrange-ments. They were well aware that the insertion of the future in the form of a plan for sustainable development carried with it the possibility of a direct confrontation with the state, a confrontation they wanted to delay until more local unity had been achieved. Undoubtedly, the perceived need for more local unity reflected the desire for community that I have discussed throughout this book as a product of hegemonic forces. This fact cannot be separated from the Coordinadora's keen awareness that any formalized plan for the future would bear the imprint of existing power arrangements, highlighting inequities in power between the dis-trict seat and the surrounding communities. Moreover, contrary to Re-nato's suggestions, the long-standing practice of fighting development projects one by one had served to delay and disrupt the government's long-term development plans for Tepoztlán. From the perspective of those in the Coordinadora, a development plan that could not be imple-mented was as good as no plan at all. Moreover, the global ecological movement's position in this calculation of local power arrangements re-mained ambiguous.

Although the ecological movement represented itself as an ally in the confrontation over the train line, the Coordinadora did not yet consider Renato and his group trustworthy. The ecological movement and, in-deed, the whole idea of using environmentalism as a strategy to protect community control entailed utilizing new structures of power in defense of community. The contrast between the authority of tradition and that of sustainable development may help to illuminate the problems inherent in alliances between the ecological movement and the Coordinadora.

The discourse of sustainable development required a shift in the local imaginary from past to future as well as a restructuring of authority from that of the insider anciano to that of the outsider expert. When the ancianos deployed the discourse of tradition through narratives of the past, they confronted the state's control over representations of the past from a position of authority. Ancianos could boast that they were speaking from their memories or from what their ancestors had shared with them or both (see Martin 1993). The nuances of a history in which the ancianos controlled the locale, which the state's version of the past sacrificed in favor of a more universal history, buttressed their claims to authority.

The discourse of sustainable development, in contrast, entered through outsiders' discourse. Although sharing the ancianos' concerns with preserving the environment, these outsiders had different methods of organizing and boasted a kind of specialized knowledge that seemed out of reach for many Tepoztecans. In order to be useful to the community, the discourse of sustainable development had to be accompanied by experts' reports on the flora and fauna of the region, engineers' calculations of the project's impacts on water flows and land erosion, and assessments of the community's future resource needs. These results needed to be argued in court by lawyers skilled in deciphering the differences between Tepoztlán's ecological impact statements and the state's, which usually supported the project. Renato's interruption of don Abram's stories of the past with the pronouncement "we must move on and hear from everyone" echoes the kind of restructuring of power that had taken place with the shift from the Comité para la Defensa de Tierra to the Coordinadora. Unlike the democracy movement within the Coordinadora in the late 1980s, however, the ecological movement did reserve a special place for the ancianos' knowledge. Ancianos soon found that ecologists' understandings of sustainable development accorded with their own sense of how to nourish the land without the use of chemicals and pesticides. More important, the ancianos' knowledge garnered respect because the ancianos were seen as representatives of the indigenous past, and the link between sustainable development and indigenous identity commanded attention within global NGOs.

Although the ecological movement participated in the August meeting, the Coordinadora made no effort in the weeks that followed to keep in touch with the ecological group. The Coordinadora did eventually take the case to court and won an injunction against ICA, which forced the company to stop work. Months later I received a call from someone in Tepoztlán: the Coordinadora was sending a representative to a preparatory session for the United Nations Conference on Environment and Development (UNCED). They wanted me to meet her in New York City and help to raise the issue of the train project to participants in the conference and to Secretary-General Butros Butros Ghalli if possible.

As we hurried over to the United Nations building for the Nongovernmental Organization Strategy Meeting, Teresa Muñoz, the representative from Tepoztlán, outlined her analysis of the conference. The meeting included legitimate NGOs as well as organizations that claimed to be nongovernmental but that represented the interests of governments and official government organizations. The latter infiltrated the NGO meetings and pushed an agenda amenable to official members of the United Nations. For example, the World Bank was courting groups claiming to represent indigenous people of Latin America with offers of loans and development projects; these offers were welcomed warmly by groups that Teresa was convinced were really working for Latin American governments. U.S. and western European NGOs, failing to understand or unwilling to deal with the complexity of indigenous groups, pushed all indigenous groups to reach agreements and work together.

When we arrived at the United Nations building, Teresa took me to a second-floor dining-room table where friends she had made at the conference were gathered around the table. They were attempting to translate the legal jargon of the Forestry Principles put forth by the NGOs. I joined them. My companions, Teresa, and some friends she had made at the conference balked at provision H of the preamble. After placing blame for deforestation on the developed world, provision H reads: "Developed countries have the main responsibility for restoring and maintaining an adequate level of global forest cover. This responsibility applies both within their territory as well as to compensate efforts by developing countries without any conditionality." My companions found in this provision evidence of the harmony that they imagined prevails between the United States and western European environmental movements and of the North's domination of the South. The northern environmental movement, in their eyes, was engaged in yet another attempt by the developed world to gain control over southern territory, this time in the name of sustainable development. In fact, the U.S. government, unwilling to accept blame or financial responsibility for global ecological problems, resisted this provision at the Rio conference.

When we joined the other groups to discuss the amendments to the Forestry Principles, environmentalists from the Sierra Club who convened the meeting reminded everyone that time pressures prevented us from talking about the whole document. Our attention was directed to those amendments that concerned indigenous peoples: provision H was not among them. Some of the groups representing indigenous people seemed satisfied with the document and participated actively in the meeting. Others, such as Teresa and the friends she had made from Brazil and

Ecuador, sat quietly, observing the proceedings. As we left the meeting, Teresa told me, "I don't think we can sign this document; the Coordinadora will be really angry."

The difficulty associated with reaching agreements at the NGO Strategy Meeting speaks to the temporal dimensions of representation that develop when "newcomers" to global politics arrive to find their interests already defined in relation to issues of identity. U.S. and western European NGOs, convinced that their demands would command greater legitimacy with official delegates if they were the result of global collaboration, anxiously sought indigenous peoples' perspectives. But the terms of inclusion were set long before the UNCED conference.

In contemporary Latin America, the term *indigenous population* can be used broadly to include the descendants of pre-Conquest populations, descendants of slaves brought to the New World from Africa, and all those people who claim some genetic connection to either of these two populations. The indigenous groups at UNCED represented this wide-ranging diversity. For many, however, the label *indigenous person* responded to the promise of political currency embedded in the term, not to a preexisting identity. For example, although the Comité para la Defensa de Tierra originally formed to defend communal land dating back to the pre-Conquest period, its members had never referred to themselves as indigenous people, preferring instead to issue political demands as campesinos. When groups such as the Coordinadora deployed the term *indigenous* to describe themselves, they entered into a world that gave them political capital, but only within categories carefully circumscribed within a tradition of U.S. and western European scholarship on "primitive peoples."

Environmentalists question notions of "progress" by raising issues of sustainability; that is, in order for an economic mode to be considered progressive, it must demonstrate long-term survivability. The argument for sustainability draws on a notion of ecological limits to economic growth that might be captured in the metaphor of the rivet originally used by Paul Ehrlich and Ann Ehrlich in 1981. Pulling one rivet from the wing of an airplane will have no effect, but as rivets are removed, the wing will eventually break off, and the plane will crash. Such metaphors suggest that although we may not notice the day-to-day impacts of environmental degradation, ecological limits will eventually be reached, and when they do, the economy will collapse as well (Davidson 2000:434). Against this dire prediction, many environmentalists are drawn to the image of sustainable production that bears a relation to the aesthetic of communal land shaped by the ancianos. It posits a time before capitalism when human relations with the land were based less on exploitation and profit and more on a relationship of stewardship to the land. Like the Franciscans who found the counterpart of their own vow of poverty among the indigenous population, contemporary environmentalists look to the indigenous population for confirmation of an ethic of sustainability. As Torgovnick notes, despite the divide between modernism and postmodernism, "the real secret of the primitive in this century has often been the same secret as always: the primitive can be—has been, will be (?)—whatever Euro-Americans want it to be" (1990:9). Environmental discourse places indigenous peoples in a privileged position as representatives of survivability, but it is within these terms that environmentalists add the struggle to protect indigenous peoples to their fight to defend the world's flora and fauna. Although these environmentalists see themselves as drawing on local knowledge, they miss the ways in which such knowledge is a "complex cultural construction" that is both historical and relational (Escobar 1995:204). Belying that complexity, the status of indigenous persons is always already circumscribed by what the environmentalist "knows" about their culture. This circumscription was underscored at the NGO Strategy Meeting at UNCED when the Western environmentalists defined the passages that should be of interest to indigenous people. In short, they designated the role of planning universally to themselves while designating indigenous peoples' interests as particular and specific. As Conklin and Graham point out, the symbolic politics surrounding the inclusion of indigenous people in the environmental movement can lead to essentialist definitions of indigenous identity (1995:703).[2] These definitions in turn clash with the goals of self-determination that many indigenous groups see as primary. Moreover, what the environmentalists know can be misleading.

No necessary relationship links the claim of indigenous identity to a given mode of production. As Fisher (1994) has noted for the Kayapó of Brazil, a double standard prevails in that Indians who use environmentalism strategically—as do many politicians—are charged with being inauthentic. Fisher maintains, however, that most claims of environmentalism are made by indigenous people for strategic reasons. This is particularly true when, as occurred in this conference, international lending organizations court indigenous groups, and governments and industry promise financial rewards to people willing to accept activity damaging to the environment (such as the disposal of toxic waste) in their traditional territories. Although issues of sovereignty and notions of rights over land have been elaborated within the tradition of Western law, for groups such as the Coordinadora these issues have become the foundation of the groups' own struggles to defend land. Any claim of shared responsibility for management of resources sounds like a threat to community-level rights to control land.

The tensions experienced by Teresa and others who shared her perspective at the conference had to do with the tensions between a dynamic notion of identity, one that is in constant flux, and the demands of activists in western Europe that indigenous peoples express a continuity of identity in their legal and cultural demands. As Nelson (1999) notes for Guatemalan Mayan movements, although demands of authenticity require continuity with the past, indigenous people must also embrace contemporary modes of communication, styles of clothing, and methods of work to render that identity politically salient. Nelson argues that in the case of Mayan movements, this tension is resolved through the role of Mayan women as guardians of traditional culture and is made manifest in the injunction that Mayan women dress in traditional *traje,* while their male counterparts don the clothing typical of mestizos. In order to legitimate their demands, groups must be seen as authentic representatives of indigenous identity and must emphasize their culture as static in ways that mirror notions of the timeless primitive (Kearney 1991). And yet, in many ways, the contemporary reemergence of indigenous identity has little in common with a notion of timelessness. As Warren notes, Mayan identity is best seen as "the meaningful selective mix of practices and knowledge, drawn on and re-synthesized at this historical juncture by groups who see indigenous identity as highly salient to self-representation and as a vehicle for political change" (1998:12).

The resurgence of Tepoztecan indigenous identity in the 1990s represents the kind of historical juncture to which Warren's definition points. Everyday practices in Tepoztlán in the 1980s pointed to the indigenous past, but without being marked as such. Lewis reported that the religious conquest of Tepoztlán was made easy by the fusion of Aztec concepts with Catholic belief, which rendered "El Tepozteco god of the wind and son of the Virgin Mary" ([1951] 1972:256), creating a seamless cultural mix that highlighted the nationalist ideology of mestizaje. In the 1980s still, winds were sent by El Tepozteco often because he was angry, and children who developed rashes were said to have been affected by *los aires* (winds or spirits that cause illness), especially if they played in streams (see Lewis [1951] 1972:280). Women suffering from nerves sought out *curanderos*, as did men ill with fever, who were cleansed with messages. But these practices were integral to the fabric of everyday life, and it was not until the 1990s, with the general resurgence of indigenous identity in Latin America, that Tepoztecans began to distinguish between indigenous practices and foreign imports. Halloween celebrations, I was told, were an outside imposition.

I point to these practices not to posit some essential link between these practices and identity, but to highlight the way Tepoztecan indigenous identity emerged as the kaleidoscope of possible identities was adjusted in relation to the political landscape. Certainly, there was much in everyday practices to suggest that Tepoztecan claims to indigenous identity could be countered, but to make this case would be to participate in the adjudication of identity in much the same way as do "taxonomic states" (Stoler 2002:206). Stoler uses the term *taxonomic states* to suggest the role of colonial systems in policing the boundaries of racial categories, establishing morality, and regulating subversion and citizenship. As I argued in chapter 2, there may well be a nationalist counterpart to the taxonomic state, and in the case of Mexico this counterpart would be reflected in the geographies of identity produced by historians and anthropologists who contributed to the construction of a postrevolutionary nationalism. It seems, therefore, that the contemporary task should not be to adjudicate claims to identity, but to interrogate categories of identity in relation to structures of power.

Tepoztecans' embrace of indigenous identity overlapped with the planning throughout Latin America for an indigenous response to the five-hundred-year anniversary of Columbus's 1492 voyage. A 1991 conference of indigenous peoples produced the pamphlet *Quinientos años de resistenca indígena*, which opposed, among other things, modernization, privatization, and the imposition of multinational companies (Nash 1995:35). In 1991, as Coordinadora members fought the train line, they announced that they had joined the movement Five Hundred Years of Resistance, and it was under these auspices that they attended the UNCED.

As Nelson (1999) notes for Guatemala, the anniversary became a time for reflections on the fate of the indigenous population in Latin America and their larger place within the nation's fabric. Organizing around the anniversary enabled indigenous groups to demand attention for a different narrative concerning the "discovery" of the Americas, one no doubt legitimized in part by deconstructionists' critiques of Western notions of knowledge that took place in academia in the 1980s. Such critiques provided for more flexible notions of identity and challenged the standard of continuity through time as a determinant of identity claims; at the same time, however, deconstruction created problems for indigenous identity claims. As Warren notes, "North American anthropology is exploring constructionist perspectives on ethnicity at the very moment Mayas were articulating a nationalist essentialism" (1998:77). Warren goes on to ponder the tensions that emerged when Mayan activists wanted her to document cultural continuities as core cultural traits against her own proclivities to see such approaches as consistent with structures of power.

These tensions are even more intractable in the case of Tepoztecan claims to indigenous identity in the 1990s. On the one hand, as chapter 2 stressed, Tepoztlán, located in what has historically been seen as the mestizo center of Mexico, is geographically mislocated to claim an indigenous identity usually associated with southern Mexico. On the other hand, the persistent use of the category of communal land does speak to the town's pre-Conquest land holdings. In the 1940s, Lewis documented a precipitous decline in monolingual Nahuatl speakers in Tepoztlán and pointed out that the young associated the speaking of Nahuatl with shame ([1951] 1972:33–34). Indeed, if any pride was taken in Nahuatl, it was among the middle-class Tepoztecans who had taken refuge in Mexico City during the revolution ([1951] 1972:33–34). Lewis also reported that the term *indio* was used to indicate low sociocultural status ([1951] 1972:53), and it continued to be used in that way in 1984 when I first came to Tepoztlán, although at times with a nod toward resistance, as when don Abram claimed that even though he was an indio, he understood the norms of respect. Yet, by the 1990s, many Tepoztecans were participating in the overall reinvigoration of indigenous identity.

It is clear that Tepoztecans in the Coordinadora embraced indigenous identity at a time when that identity had cultural capital in the global arena, but it is also clear that it remained an identity category subordinated to the norms of cultural intelligibility. As I have argued throughout this book, we cannot understand social movements without examining their deployment of categories that are both normative and potentially disruptive of the normative order. Indigenous identity became an avenue through which Tepoztecans in the Coordinadora made their movement to protect communal control intelligible to a global audience. Similar to their use of democracy discourse and before that their use of the discourse surrounding communal land, their use of indigenous identity entailed new ways of imagining themselves within a global political world, this time stimulated by the resurgence of indigenous identity throughout the Americas. For a time, indigenous identity inspired passionate attachment that came in no small measure from its potential association with rights to autonomy. Tepoztecan activists who deployed indigenous identity might not be satisfied with my kaleidoscope metaphor, however.

How should anthropologists situate their work within a world in which people turn to anthropology to document authentic claims while the anthropologists themselves are interrogating their own participation in a similar project during the colonial period, this time on the side of the colonizers? Anthropology's role in colonialism has inspired a deconstruction of the categories of identity that contemporary Tepoztecans seek to deploy. It is not, as some might suggest, that deconstructionists seek an apolitical space, but that they seek to interrogate the frameworks of "cultural intelligibility" within which social movements take shape. Certainly, part of this project has been the deconstruction of the distinctions that founded colonial adventures, such as the distinction between "hot" and "cold" societies, and it is for this reason that demands to demonstrate cultural continuity sit uneasily with the anthropologists. To refuse entirely the norms of cultural intelligibility, however, would be to render social movements unintelligible, whereas to repeat the terms of cultural intelligibility would be to participate, at least partially, in those structures of power.[3] In short, the political project of deconstruction does not undermine the foundations of indigenous identity as much as it opens the possibility of a space in which the terms of inclusion are not set beforehand.

Different senses of representation were also behind many of the stalemates that hampered NGOs' work at the UNCED Strategy Meeting. Teresa's difficulties in signing the documents reveal the quandaries of representatives whose identity had been forged through the social ties of group membership. Identity in this latter sense is not an easy achievement; rather, it reflects years of work and often internal conflicts over the right decision. The power of these ties to "nag" representatives distinguishes this form of representation from the form of representation that often prevails in NGO politics in the United States. Many of the NGO representatives at UNCED came from groups whose support was reflected in donation records. Although these representatives needed to be mindful of their abilities to raise money over the long term, they enjoyed more freedom than did Teresa to negotiate alliances. Their accountability to members was based on the achievement of long-range goals; Teresa's accountability, in contrast, was based on a commitment to a specific view of the world, one that sometimes impeded coalition building.

All of this is rendered even more complex by the politics of loose connections. The threat of possible gossip that Teresa had betrayed the community weighed heavily on her demeanor at the conference, as did the reality that there was little unity on these issues within Tepoztlán. As a result, she behaved much as peripheral members of the Comité para la Defensa de Tierra had behaved. She said little during discussions, gossiped widely with her friends in the hallways, and questioned the motives of all who spoke at the meetings.

The formal discussion of the Forestry Principles resulted in a series of modifications that made them more acceptable to all involved. Teresa took notes throughout the discussion and even introduced some of her own ideas. The next day she asked if I could help her find a typewriter or computer so that she could type up her notes. We went to the building where the NGOs had been given offices. A woman there kindly helped us log onto one of the computers, but she became suspicious when she saw that Teresa was typing up notes from the discussion of the Forestry Principles. "What is this for?" she asked me in English. I asked Teresa, who replied that the Mexican governmental representative at the conference had asked her about the forestry discussions so that governmental representatives could better work with the NGO representatives. When I explained this to the woman who helped us, she was not at all pleased. "That is exactly what we don't want," she said with exasperation. "The NGOs must be united first; then we will be more powerful when we talk to the government representatives—that's the point of all this," she said, walking away in anger.

Teresa later told me that she "knew" the Mexican governmental representative and that he was a good guy: "On our side," she explained. Her sense of the Mexican state and its representatives contrasted with the attitude of skepticism she had expressed concerning the global environmental movement. As I discussed in chapter 3, beliefs about corruption and abuse of power at the state level are always complicated by the fact that the bureaucrats one encounters are often also friends and relatives. On the one hand, this means that mistrust of the state often translates easily into mistrust of the entire community. On the other, it means that the search for "friends" in the bureaucracy who might help is never futile. The impersonal bureaucracy is mediated by personal ties. Given the PRI's co-optation strategy, one often trusts individuals in the bureaucracy because one has worked in political projects with them previously. The usually one-dimensional image of the state articulated in discourse becomes far more complex in practice, especially when global actors are involved.

When Tepoztecans contemplated the state's abstract structure, they contemplated a pyramid of hierarchy and corruption (see chapter 3), but in everyday political practice they scanned that hierarchy for familiar faces. They then used these people to work their way up the hierarchy ladder. But this model of political practice made little sense within the global environmental movement. The incentive for attending the NGO conference in the first place was not so much to think about participating in a rethinking of the global environment, but rather to take the issue of the train line to what Coordinadora members perceived as a higher level, the secretary-general of the United Nations. They were, in the familiar idiom of Tepoztecan political practice, "putting the thorn in" at the highest level. Thus, they were not conquering "space" as such, but were ascending a ladder, from the bottom to the top. The global environmental movement was part of the context at the top, but I suspect it was not viewed as an avenue to enhance the Coordinadora's bargaining power with the governor of Morelos and the president of Mexico. Moreover, the movement's concerns with writing global environmental principles seemed not only irrelevant to the problems associated with stopping the train line, but also perhaps contrary to Tepoztecans' desire to preserve control over their community.

In the end, global environmental activists did take up Tepoztecans' fight against the train project. As with the many battles that Tepoztecans had fought in the past, the train project was eventually diverted, and

Tepoztecans could once again celebrate a victory. This victory was especially sweet because Tepoztecans saw it as evidence that the world recognized the legitimacy of their struggle to protect their region's unique flora and fauna. No longer would they boast that they had taken their complaints all the way to the president; now they had gone all the way to the United Nations to receive the support of people from all over the world. In their minds, the beauty of their unity and the magic of the place where they lived had endeared their struggles to the world.

This centrality of place in Tepoztecan understandings of the outcome of their fight against the train project speaks to a reconciliation of the conceptual divide between place and space. Although drawing on the universality of environmental laws and principles, Tepoztecans reinterpreted these laws, placing weight on the unique environmental features of their particular place. They envisioned a global environmental movement driven by the discovery of specific places endowed with unique features. In this regard, they willingly donned the role of indigenous people to add to the symbolic capital of their specific place. Thus, they reached out to the universality of law not with a global vision, but with a reenvisioning of their community as a unique constellation of those universal principles. Universal principles, although seeming to draw on abstract notions of space, inspired a reinvigorated vision of place.[4] Just as Tepoztecans had once drawn on revolutionary nationalism to represent themselves as the heirs of Zapata's struggles, they now formed symbolic capital out of the global language of environmentalism.

We should not underestimate the parallels between global environmentalism and revolutionary nationalism as a force that has shaped Tepoztecan understandings. In 1988, the Mexican government promulgated the ecological laws on which Tepoztecans had come to rely, and the state played an active role in promoting the development of environmental groups (Barkin 1990). As with revolutionary nationalism, the state provided the impetus for the development of the ecological discourse and for organizational development, discovering too late that it could not control the environmental movement (Barkin 1990). At the same time, however, the negotiation of environmental issues does seem to reflect the state's broader economic goals. Thus, environmental laws seem more readily upheld in areas designated for tourism, such as Tepoztlán. Paradoxically, Tepoztecans' political successes may have intersected with the state's agenda for establishing the community as a tourist area, the designation that the Maestro and the Coordinadora wanted to contest. Indeed, as demonstrated in the epilogue, when multinationals contemplated putting a large golf resort in Tepoztlán in 1995, they tried unsuccessfully to argue that golf resorts actually protect the environment.

The tale that highlights global responsibility and cooperation within the environmental movement cannot possibly do justice to the complex forces that intervene in the conversation between environmentalists from the United States and western Europe and populations from around the world. The relationship is dynamic and is being worked out in contexts such as the NGO Strategy Meeting at the UNCED.

In 1984, many Tepoztecans viewed the world through the lens of confrontation between the North and the South, leaving no place in this model for a complex array of class and racial injustices in wealthy nations. Indeed, every rise in Mexico's interest rates had been talked about in 1984 as a benefit for citizens of the United States, who would earn more interest on their savings accounts. By 1991, that conception of the world had become more complex. Many people asked me about poverty in the United States, the struggles of Native Americans, and the weakening of unions. Such a view of the world facilitated the formation of relationships with global environmental groups, although day-to-day work with these groups remained problematic.

Those who participated in global environmental movements did so with a high degree of skepticism that was coupled with the recognition that this collaboration was an avenue to power that could not be ignored. Tepoztecans recognized a potential conflict of interest between their own desires to have rights to territory unambiguously acknowledged in law and the environmental movement's desire to promote a set of global principles to govern relations between people and land. Although in practice many in the global environmental movement were willing to support local communities' struggles and eventually did support them, the rhetoric of the NGO Strategy Meeting emphasized abstract principles aimed at universalizing the discourse of environmentalism. Whereas for U.S. and western European environmentalists the call for universal principles represented a forward step, for Coordinadora members it also meant a further movement toward a global vision that lacked the passions for place that motivated so many of them. The task became translating that passion for place into more universal terms.

As I pointed out earlier in this chapter, environmentalism, even while reaching toward the universality of law, reinscribes the magic of place as it documents the delicate balances between flora and fauna that must be sustained in a particular region. This kind of documentation affords a measure of legitimacy to the specificity of place. Moreover, western European and U.S. environmentalists are not immune to the passions of place. Although the preparatory NGO Strategy Meeting itself was dedicated to the search for universal principles, U.S. and western European environmentalists made contacts backstage with people such as Teresa, who successfully obtained their support in specific struggles around places and issues. The formation of these kinds of linkages has proved critical to Tepoztecans' attempts to use environmental discourse for their own purposes. Furthermore, as I pointed out in chapter 3, groups such as the Comité para la Defensa de Tierra and the Coordinadora have long drawn on the promise of universal laws to wage their own struggles. The point, then, is that the distinction between the specific and the general, between the passions of the local and the abstraction of the global, should not be overdrawn.

In this book, I have argued repeatedly that passionately held political identities need to be located as a product of hegemonic practices that unfold beyond the local level. These identities include the specific place of Morelos in Mexico's revolutionary nationalism, the privileged position of community in agrarian reform laws, and the struggles of traditional male elders to maintain positions of power in the community. Such identities unfold in relation to the kind of productive power that Foucault points to in *The History of Sexuality* (1990). They enable opposition, often serving as points of resistance that inspire restructuring of the forces of power.

themselves and occasionally to outsiders while escaping the taxes paid on private property. If one is willing to forego the niceties of legal documents, communal land is even more valuable than private property because of the tax savings. It is no wonder that Tepoztecans find themselves pondering what kind of people they have become and how they have drifted so far from their ancestors, who, at least in lore, defended land with their lives.[4]

The market in communal land raises questions about its importance to community identity and gives rise to conflicts over Tepoztlán's future. A significant portion of Tepoztlán's youth from the district seat believes that the future lies with the promotion of education and development that will lead to jobs.

The availability of alternatives to communal land as an economic resource and source of identity for the youth of the district seat is not lost on those who come from the surrounding communities and is part of their tensions with the district seat. For many residents of these communities, protection of communal land is synonymous with defense of an agriculturally based economy that, although failing to provide adequately for families, meets a component of their needs for cash and for subsistence. They are unwilling to let the district seat take control of a possession that they feel residents of the district seat do not appreciate.

During my research in 1984, the most intractable tension facing the committee was the set of administrative and political practices associated with the Mexican state, which I described in chapter 3. These practices formed what Bourdieu (1990) terms a habitus. Grounded in a history of practices, a habitus sets up actors' expectations and so informs the seemingly spontaneous moves they make. As Bourdieu notes, the habitus is thus "embodied history, internalized as second nature and so forgotten as history" (1990:56). In the case of the Oficina de Bienes Comunales, peripheral members anticipated reciprocity and expected authorities to display their power in conflicts, thereby balancing the costs of political participation with rewards. When leaders failed to live up to these expectations, peripheral members held back on their own participation and instead spread gossip, suggesting that officials in the Oficina de Bienes Comunales were monopolizing the rewards of political engagement. The more that leaders in the Oficina de Bienes Comunales tried to mold their own behavior to insulate themselves from charges of corruption—for example, by refusing to distribute land to members of the Comité para la

Defensa de Tierra—the more readily peripheral members engaged in corruption gossip.

These tensions do not suggest that the Oficina de Bienes Comunales is an example of the failure of politics in Tepoztlán in the face of disunity. It would be so only if one were to read these tensions against the expectations of unity that I contend are not only unrealistic, but also productive of faulty notions of how social movements take shape and how they manage to achieve favorable outcomes despite tensions. The committee did manage to take back land from those who had extended their boundaries, redistributed land to single women with children, and generated a number of local, colonia-level organizations that used collective labor to build roads, churches, and schools. As shown later, many of these organizations resurfaced in 1988 to support the expansion of the Comité para la Defensa de Tierra into the Coordinadora Democrática. But the committee failed in its goal to rectify the boundaries so as to leave the community with a clear sense of how much land it controlled.

Although I use the concept of loose connections to describe Tepoztecans' approaches to politics more generally, this chapter suggests that loose connections emerged not out of leaders' strategies, but out of peripheral members' practices. Despite the rhetoric of unity and community so eloquently espoused by leaders in various groups, it was the tenacious skepticism that peripheral members managed to combine with a deep commitment to political participation that gave rise to a politics of loose connections. Where did this deep commitment come from? Certainly many of the peripheral committee members entered the political arena with a desire to get a little land for themselves. They imagined the politics of patronage, assuming that their participation would be rewarded. And, as in any exchange, they "held back" that which they had to offer, awaiting indications that their partners in the exchange, the authorities in the Oficina de Bienes Comunales, would be willing to reciprocate. But these "interests" in land were cast in the idiom of Tepoztlán's history of defense of communal land. Even if, following Bourdieu, we take the idiom of the defense of land as a disguise of material interests in land, the analysis must retain "together what holds together in the object, namely the double reality of intrinsically equivocal, ambiguous practices" (1990:118).

In contrast to the image of peripheral members as tontos, this chapter has suggested that those on the margins of political groups are able to transform their positions into symbolic capital by drawing on the discourse of defense of the patrimony. They do so not just as a strategy, but because they are as caught in the passions of the discourse as are the ancianos and leaders who helped to craft a traditional aesthetic. Fantasies of meeting death in a fight over communal land or images of walking the same path as deceased relatives intermingle with interests in land. Images of past unity, which in chapter 4 I called an aesthetic of tradition, weigh heavily on Tepoztecans' conceptions of themselves as a brave community, making it difficult for them to withdraw altogether from the fight to defend communal land. The same people who expressed skepticism about the political arena repeatedly told me stories about past victories when the united community had emerged victorious in confrontations with the state.

The image of tontos also fails to capture the practical knowledge peripheral members of Tepoztecan social movements bring to their positions. Indeed, to avoid a reputation as a tonto, one must skillfully navigate the space between desires for unity and skepticism of the political arena. Gossip about leaders of social movements is the primary way that peripheral members communicate that they "know" what is going on and that they are engaged in politics in order to defend their community. But such gossip must be well timed to shape larger community sentiment. To gossip when the fervor for a social movement is fresh is to appear merely contrary or, worse, merely interested in one's own political power, but to gossip too late is to be judged a tonto. Knowing when to gossip and with whom is rendered all the more complex when one realizes that community sentiment does not change from one day to the next, but does so in a gradual and piecemeal fashion. Thus, one needs to know when and with whom to gossip at various stages in order to transform a possible reputation as a tonto into a reputation as a defender of the community. Finally, one needs to judge when to exit a group and how to reenter it at a later date.

The politics of loose connections emerges, then, at the intersection of this vision of community unity and the tenacious mistrust held for the political arena. Indeed, gossip about corruption and tales of past deceits weigh as heavily on Tepoztecans' subjectivity as do the visions of unity. As I have tried to show in this chapter, that mistrust, even when not warranted, is nurtured by tensions whose roots lie in the history of interactions with the state. Accordingly with their gossip, peripheral members police the boundaries of the community and the state, gossiping vehemently about the leaders' desires for jobs in the state and their susceptibility to corruption. To the extent that Tepoztecans have succeeded in keeping state power at bay even as they reside in the midst of its power, it is probably owing to peripheral members' resilience. Under PRI rule of the Mexican state, it may well have been peripheral members' willingness to shift their allegiance when necessary that kept political groups from being co-opted by the more subtle mechanisms of state power that resided in things such as maps and the delivery of social services.[5]

Viewed through the lens of events relayed in this chapter, the politics of loose connections provides an account of how communities in Mexico have succeeded in retaining an identity and a set of practices that have eluded state control. First, by attending to the loose quality of Tepoztecans' political participation, I have implied that Mexican cultural hegemony is not nearly as strong as conventionally depicted by many theorists of the Mexican state. For example, although the state has demanded political participation, as I pointed out in chapter 3, Tepoztecans, in the district as a whole, have developed styles of participation that garner benefits from the state while withholding loyalty to the state. Second, I have represented the politics of loose connections as consisting of political strategies that take into account the way techniques of state power have affected local communities. This does not mean that peripheral members consciously try to limit the state's power, but rather that out of the multiple forces that give rise to their political practices emerges a strategy that does limit state power.

Peripheral members do not merely drag their feet in the absence of alternatives, nor do they exit the political arena altogether to resort to an individualized resistance; rather, they create a space between resistance and political engagement. Similar to resistance, peripheral members' strategies emanate from a set of practices that are neither conscious nor explicitly coordinated, but are patterned in relation to strategies and knowledge that have been fostered by intimate acquaintance with the structures of the Mexican state. Unlike resistance, however, the politics of loose connections is the product of collective labor and is worked out in the public arena of visible social movements. In short, peripheral members' engagement is not an alternative that expresses dissatisfaction while rejecting the political arena altogether, but an active attempt to make politics work.

Although my own research focused primarily on the Comité para la Defensa de Tierra in 1984, other groups were forming that would provide the foundation for the transformation of Tepoztecan politics. The local priest, a supporter of the committee and a liberation theologist, worked hard to engage young people in a more activist form of religion. In the community of San Andrés, a young professor from UNAM and a local campesino organized an ecology group. And one day in October when I arrived for a committee meeting, the office was filled with high school students. When I asked one of the committee members what was going on, he told me that they were all students and that the Maestro Jorge had organized them to campaign for lower bus fares. Little did I know at the time that these groups would construct a new political aesthetic around an image of democracy that would guide the transformation of the Comité para la Defensa de Tierra into the Coordinadora Democrática, an umbrella organization that included the fight to defend communal land, but in a subordinate manner.

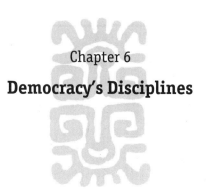

Chapter 6
Democracy's Disciplines

I would simply like to say that we have won an important struggle and are now passing into a different stage. . . . We are changing society, and the changes in society depend on us. We are uprooting a tree . . . and we will have to cut it down one branch at a time. . . . In short, we must work together. . . . This is a new stage in the development of a democratic process that we will use to solve every one of our problems. We ask that you continue participating in a civilized and organized form. . . . For me, that would be the greatest achievement of my life.

—The Maestro Jorge in a speech delivered on June 9, 1988, after the candidate backed by the Comité para la Defensa de Tierra, renamed the Coordinadora Democrática, won the local mayoral election in Tepoztlán

By 1988, the impact of the austerity measures of the 1980s on the Mexican state were clearly visible. The Mexican government had sold nine hundred state and parastatal companies, reduced the government deficit from 17 to 2 percent by cutting state subsidies, and reduced the government share of the GDP from 25 to 17 percent (Knight 1994:31). Miguel de la Madrid's presidency was drawing to a close, and his handpicked successor, Carlos Salinas de Gortari, a Harvard-trained economist, was committed to modernizing Mexico through a neoliberal economic system. Salinas de Gortari campaigned as a technocrat with a político's agenda, making the cornerstone of his campaign a targeted social service program that became known as Solidaridad, which I discuss more fully in the next chapter. Even as Salinas de Gortari touted his social safety net, however, inside the PRI the struggle for power between políticos and technocrats became uncharacteristically vicious. Concerned about relations with foreign creditors, Miguel de la Madrid tightened his technocratic inner circle, leaving políticos increasingly marginalized within the party (Bruhn 1997:17). Unlike other years, when competing factions agreed to disagree, knowing that their time would come, the políticos were now told to get in line with an agenda they found abhorrent or leave the party altogether (Bruhn 1997:96). Lázaro Cárdenas's son, Cuauhtémoc, did the latter on October 12, announcing that he would run as a candidate of one of Mexico's long-standing opposition parties. His candidacy created one of the first truly contested elections since the PRI had taken power.

When I arrived in Tepoztlán in the summer of 1988, the nation was in the throes of an atypical, for Mexico, election campaign. Cuauhtémoc Cárdenas, had managed to draw together a loose coalition of left opposition parties known as the Frente Democrático Nacional (FDN, Democratic National Front) and was campaigning effectively in central Mexico on a program of opposition to the neoliberal economic agenda of the now technocrat-dominated PRI. Despite Cárdenas's rhetoric of peasant and indigenous rights, his strongest support came from communities such as Tepoztlán that were close to urban centers and had fairly educated populations. In the North, the conservative PAN also showed signs of strength. Its candidate, Manuel Clouthier, had the backing of the Catholic Church, business, and the popular sectors in a region that had always been wary of the Mexican state. Together, the two parties provided a steady barrage of charges of corruption even before the elections were held. More important, they elaborated a discourse of democracy that would be seized by political activists in communities such as Tepoztlán and reworked in accordance with more localized political agendas. Local political leaders acted as accomplished *bricoleurs,* creatively knitting together the resources at their disposal to fashion unique forms of political participation.

The emphasis on the need for "electoral democracy" and its association with modernization proved to be an unexpected challenge to PRI party politics. Although the PRI had long staged elections and at times even allowed opposition parties to win governor races, it had never "lost" a presidential election, nor was it ready to relinquish power in 1988. Nonetheless, Salinas de Gortari campaigned as the president who would modernize Mexico, and the international and the national community alike boasted that under his leadership Mexico would make the transition to a system of democratic election even at the level of the presidency. The claim invigorated opposition to the PRI in the name of democracy: Why not begin the democratic process by allowing the 1988 election to be free and fair? These demands for democracy were issued by individuals and groups with very different agendas, but in the highly politicized context of the late 1980s the term *democracy* was used loosely. Many analysts termed any transition from military regimes, no matter how it was brought about, democratic. The notion of democracy thus invited considerable free play at every level of society and provided spaces for local political actors to elaborate their own understandings of democracy.

This chapter focuses on how the politics of loose connections shaped responses to the opportunities presented by the contested national election and to the changes taking place in the Mexican state. As shown in the chapter, to the extent that the Comité para la Defensa de Tierra—now restructured as a loose coalition of groups united under an umbrella organization, the Coordinadora Democrática—succeeded, it did so by using the discourse of democracy as a justification for embracing a form of politics more amenable to the politics of loose connections. The Coordinadora departed significantly from the aesthetic of tradition and by extension from the authority of the ancianos. Indeed, the latter became peripheral members who were replaced by a group of young people nurtured on notions of liberation theology and emboldened by a number of successful struggles that had little to do with land. Although the embrace of democracy refocused the demands for unity in the Coordinadora, I argue that a different kind of unity was nurtured around the creation of rational democratic subjects. Leaders encouraged members of the group to pursue projects specific to their structural interests, and public disagreement became viewed as an expression of democracy. Public disagreement was much more than an expression of democracy, however; it was also a way of disciplining peripheral members' gossip. The specter of the rational subject who took disagreement in stride justified the expectation that gossip was unnecessary and destructive, at least within the group.

When I returned to Tepoztlán in 1988, the Mujeres Tepoztecanas and the Coordinadora Democrática were engaged in a battle to control the Tepoztlán mayoralty. With the support the Coordinadora had gained by aiding surrounding communities in battles over development projects and by pressuring the ejido commissioner to distribute ejidal land to Tepoztecans, it had launched a successful campaign for local mayor. Its candidate, Humberto Robles, a professor at UNAM, had run as a PRI candidate, although the Mujeres Tepoztecanas complained that Robles and the Coordinadora were not truly PRIistas. Pointing to the graffiti that adorned the bandstand in the central plaza, a member of the Mujeres Tepoztecanas asked rhetorically, "How can they be PRIistas and run a no-vote campaign in the national election?" For days, the women occupied the steps of the municipal building, refusing to allow Robles to enter the office, but finally after a negotiated settlement they agreed to allow him to be mayor if other positions were allocated to members of the Mujeres Tepoztecanas. A typical PRI strategy for dealing with contested elections, the arrangement would weaken the Robles mayoral term, finally resulting in his having to relinquish his post. Nonetheless, his term as mayor would usher in a new independence for the town.

From one perspective, the turn of events between 1984 and 1988 bore the stamp of typical PRI politics. One could argue that the Comité para la Defensa de Tierra, as part of the Coordinadora Democrática, had finally been co-opted by the PRI. After all, it was distributing land in return for votes, running candidates for local office, and delivering new members to the PRI. As this chapter suggests, however, the picture was far more complex than a simple co-optation. The decision to join the PRI emerged from one of the surrounding communities as a strategy to protect the lives of those running for office and their supporters. Indeed, one of the community leaders complained that it was difficult to get the Coordinadora to go along with the strategy, and shortly after the decision had been made, Coordinadora members began distributing a "no-vote" pamphlet. The "no-vote" graffiti on the bandstand was signed Asociación Civica Nacional Revolucionaria (ACNR, Civic Association for National Revolution), a group with ties to guerrilla movements of the 1970s in Guerrero.[1] The Mujeres Tepoztecanas believed that the graffiti had come from the Maestro Jorge and his friends; they noted that the Maestro's brother had been an ACNR member.

The support the Coordinadora now enjoyed in 1988 reflected a style that accorded with, rather than countered, peripheral members' expectations as to how politics should operate, expectations that had been set up by Mexico's corporatist state structure, but that the committee had formerly tried to contest. Those who had received land were expected to form a collective identity and to become a governing body of the community in a manner reminiscent of the state-mandated Agrarian Reform Law (see chapter 3). And, as stipulated in the Agrarian Reform Law, the foundations of the collective body were to be found in the notion of "need." It is no wonder, then, that those who received land came to view the redistribution as symbolic of the needs of the poor and to view those who carried out the redistribution as good leaders for the pueblo.

This cultural constitution of interests shaped experiences of the world while serving a political strategy. The Tepoztecans who received land from the Coordinadora did not just "pose" as members of a collective: they passionately experienced themselves as a collective brought together on the basis of common needs. As one woman, doña Carmela, explained, contrasting the Coordinadora with the Mujeres Tepoztecan, "[When negotiating with officials], the people on the other side go with their *refrescos* [soft drinks], but we bring only ourselves because we are all poor and have nothing [to exchange]." In fact, the land redistribution created a "class" of people—defined in Tepoztecan discourse as those who had need—from the sons and daughters of professionals, those who had jobs, and those who had few sources of income and no land. Thus, the demand for land gave birth to the imaginary that might loosely be termed "class" politics.[2]

Although the form of Coordinadora politics mirrored that of the postrevolutionary state, the Coordinadora emphasized the independence of Tepoztlán from the state and located the dangers of corruption and abuse of power among those outside of the community, especially among state- and national-level bureaucrats. As the Mujeres Tepoztecans argued, it is doubtful that the Coordinadora would have won the election without distributing the land, but these contests over the meaning of the distribution did not weaken its impact on those who received land. Indeed, assertions that the land had been improperly distributed fueled the elaboration of an identity based on need as those who received land defended the distribution.

As I suggested in my discussion of Agrarian Reform Law in chapter 2, the use of need to shape a collective identity clearly leaned on the powers of the Mexican state to produce subject positions and therefore reiterated, at least partially, the equations of power established by the state (see Brown 1995:52–76). As such, the notion of need calls to mind the dependency of the poor on the state and the kind of impotence that encouraged one informant to claim that the president was like the family's father: if he was a good father, the community would grow and prosper, but if he was a bad father, the people could do nothing. Viewed through the lens of the history of the Mexican state, then, the notion of need emerged in tandem with the practices of the state administration of land that included the incorporation of opposition in a subordinate position. As an administrative category, need was in a sense depoliticized, rendered part of the natural landscape to be managed by the state.

The Coordinadora's attempt to rescue the notion of need from its depoliticized location within the state calls to mind the proliferation of political identities around terms of derision or categories that are set by the governmental administration and that have become a common source of identity in contemporary political participation. By invoking identities already embedded in extant structures of power, movements resort to "a standard internal to existing society against which to pitch their claims" (Brown 1995:61). Using the example of U.S.–based movements, Brown worries that a decisive critique of capitalism has been forsaken for clamors for inclusion in what she terms the "White, middle-class, masculine ideal" (1995:65). Brown grounds her analysis in the historical specificity of what she terms "late-modern liberalism," in which politics becomes centered around the deeply contradictory desires of those who clamor for inclusion even while remaining attached to an identity shaped around exclusion. Nonetheless, the more general problem of the waging of politics on identities at least in part borrowed from the state is applicable not only to the specific situation of the Coordinadora's borrowing of an identity from the state, but also to the more general situation of contemporary identities.

By emphasizing the origins of contemporary political identities in structures of state power, we risk overlooking the fact that the administrative categories of state power are themselves constantly in flux, and opportunities for the reworking of identity categories emerge from that flux. Indeed, in the case of the Mexican state, when the Coordinadora undertook its land redistribution, large-scale "need"-based distributions of land had not taken place in years, and the whole discourse of need was being replaced by a discourse of social development that highlighted individual and communal participation, efficiency, and the decentralization of power (González Tiburcio 1994). Although not completely apparent in 1988, the new recipients of social development monies would not be individuals who had need, but rather municipalities, and the monies would be allocated to all municipalities (González Tiburcio 1994:67–68). In this way, the vision that the state was endorsing departed significantly from the notion of need that constituted a collective category loosely related to a political-economic position. Instead, municipalities were conceptualized as distinct units with local identities and traditions (González Tiburcio 1994:77), but seemingly without the differences in need that had previously shaped state policy.

Placed in the context of the changing structure of state policy, the redeployment of the notion of need" and the corresponding land redistribution carried out by the Coordinadora suggests the creativity of the bricoleur confronted with the state's garbage dump. With the election of Salinas de Gortari in 1988, the Mexican state would turn away from a politics structured around sectoral participation—that is, peasants, workers, women, and so on—to an emphasis on the municipality as the political unit with claims on the state's resources. In Tepoztlán, however, the discourses of democracy surrounding the 1988 election buttressed the Coordinadora's attempts to disentangle the notion of need from its roots in a paternalistic state structure. A concrete manifestation of this disentanglement was the fact that the Coordinadora collected small sums of money from those who had received land and then returned the money to the collective for social service projects. And under Robles's administration, Tepoztecans would turn to international NGOs for financial and political assistance. In short, in place of the image of those with need begging from the state, the Coordinadora sought to substitute the justice of demands.

That which on a theoretical level appears as an intractable problem— Can one dismantle the "master's house with the master's tools"? (see Lorde 1994)—appears in a very different light when examined against the various forms of bricolage that shape social movements. The seemingly necessary implication of need—that those who have nothing must exchange personal loyalty for something they need—can be rewritten as those with nothing must discover their power in just causes, which is the implication of doña Carmela's description of the differences between the Coordinadora and the Mujeres. In the end, an identity that reiterates the categories produced by the state may do so with an accent that challenges the status quo, all the while drawing on the aura of authenticity and legitimacy that those categories have accumulated from the state.

Coalition Politics in the Coordinadora

Several different forces contributed to the Coordinadora's success in the 1988 mayoral election, including a women's sewing cooperative, Bible study groups set up by a liberation theologist, the group of young people the Maestro organized to lower bus fares, a transportation cooperative, and a health-care clinic. With the exception of the health-care clinic and the cooperative of transportation workers, most of these groups had existed in embryonic form in 1984, but it was not until the late 1980s that they became united in the Coordinadora. Despite their participation with the Coordinadora, each maintained a distinctive profile even in the late 1980s.

As shown later when I discuss Coordinadora meetings, the style shaped by liberation theology came to dominate those meetings, much as the style of a traditional aesthetic had ruled the committee previously. When Father Cristóbal García, a young liberation theologist came to Tepoztlán in the early 1980s, he organized Bible study groups: a group of young people, a group of older women, a group of people who were about to get married, and a group of men. He organized similar groups in the barrios of the district seat and in the surrounding communities. Convinced that gossip was destroying the community's political power, he insisted that members of these groups refrain from gossip. Of course, in practice those in the groups gossiped about their political enemies, even if they refrained from gossiping about one another. At first, most of the groups' work was related to the church. Father Cristóbal organized work projects, and under his tutelage the church floor was repaired with collective labor. In 1984, even the Mujeres Tepoztecans pointed to such examples as evidence that if the town residents worked together, Tepoztlán could deal with its own problems, with or without state resources. Members of the Comité para la Defensa de Tierra sometimes noted the good work that Father Cristóbal was doing, but they kept their distance from any religious organizations, in part because of don Abram's prominent role in the Seventh Day Adventist Church. By 1988, however, many liberation theology participants had joined the Coordinadora.

Another source of support for the Coordinadora was a women's group that had formed originally in the 1980s to teach women in Tepoztlán to sew. The group, which had been organized by women from a nearby city, began to hold sewing classes to help women learn a marketable skill at a time when many women were trying to cope with the economic crises. The organizers hoped that the women would form a cooperative to produce "traditional" clothing to be sold in the United States and western Europe. Although many women participated with the group only long enough to learn a skill that they could market independently, by 1988 the cooperative had approximately thirty members who produced clothing for export.

Unlike the followers of liberation theology who swelled the ranks of the Coordinadora and provided many of its leaders for the group, the sewing cooperative maintained considerable independence from the Coordinadora. Their members participated in the battle over the municipality and agreed to vote for the Coordinadora candidate, but stressed their independent history and their loose ties with the Coordinadora.

Young people who had learned their activism in the campaign to lower bus fares also played a highly visible role in the Coordinadora. Some had been members of the Comité para la Defensa de Tierra in 1984 and had been pulled by the Maestro Jorge into the fight to lower bus fares because they attended high school in a nearby city and used the buses daily. One young man who had been active in that struggle told me that he had always thought of himself as a powerless kid, but when they succeeded in getting the bus fares lowered, he knew he really could do something for his community. Although in 1984 the Maestro had attended the young people's meetings and helped them shape strategy, by 1988 they were an independent group with their own leaders. Nonetheless, of all the groups that now made up the Coordinadora, this group kept the closest ties with the Maestro and with the original members of the committee.

The original struggle to defend communal land had receded in importance as the Coordinadora came to incorporate its members' diverse agendas. The groups that made up the Coordinadora shared a common understanding that organizing should be based on a notion of community empowerment and self-help. In the context of the economic crises of the 1980s, they sought to provide clear solutions to the problems confronting their members. This was also true of the health center that the Coordinadora helped to establish. There, a doctor, using homeopathic medicine, treated patients at very low costs and cured ailments that according to his patients other doctors had been unable to treat. Thus, when the doctor requested a plot of communal land on which to build a new clinic, the Coordinadora gladly agreed.

In the face of the successes that came from this kind of self-help approach, the struggle to defend communal land became the province of a group of ancianos who attended Coordinadora meetings but carried out their work outside of the meetings. Don Tomás, who, according to Coordinadora members, had proved to be corrupt, had been replaced as commissioner of the Oficina de Bienes Comunales. His replacement was a former peripheral member who had left the committee, charging that the leaders were engaged in corruption. This man's reputation for honesty and integrity had helped restore confidence in the struggle to defend communal land, although organizing around communal land, as a resource at the center of so many tensions, continued to inspire division.

With the ancianos now relegated to a segment of a larger struggle, the aesthetics of tradition, at least for the time being, received little attention. Although the ancianos were still treated with great respect, they would never presume to "take the floor" as they had done so frequently in the committee. One anciano told me that when he went to the meetings, he felt embarrassed because he did not know anyone there, so he did not want to talk. Although the young people who ran the meetings valued the ancianos' opinions, those opinions were treated as few among many that deserved to be heard. The notion that the young must learn values from the ancianos, so prominent in the Comité para la Defensa de Tierra, played only a minor role in the Coordinadora. In its place, the Coordinadora's organization diminished the importance of cross-generational affiliation, as it did the notion of self-help, for the members of each group were supposed to look into their own lives and their own circumstances as a basis for their political organizing. In the face of the new ethos of democracy, the idea of unity around values promoted by the ancianos seemed archaic and authoritarian.

The new young leaders of the Coordinadora who had learned from Father Cristóbal's liberation theology groups introduced new concepts of leadership into the Coordinadora. They defined meetings as "little schools," requested observations from Coordinadora members, and talked of politics as a kind of awakening, all in an attempt to create a new political subject in Tepoztlán, one adapted to the demands of a kind of deliberative democracy.[3]

In order to use democracy to solve problems, Tepoztecans had to adapt styles of political participation at odds with the long-standing political practices I described in chapter 5. Asking people to share observations challenged the division between those with words and those without words. In the Comité para la Defensa de Tierra, the ancianos had spoken frequently and freely, admonishing participants for bad behavior and using stories of the past to instruct participants in the resolution of contemporary problems. However problematic their claims to authority, their monopolization of discussions in the committee had reflected a conviction that not all points of view are equal. For the ancianos, the powers of observation increased with the passage of time and, perhaps, with the kind of book learning that the Maestro and others enjoyed. Untutored observation, however, could result only in naive understandings and, worse, might lead the whole group in the wrong direction. To have their "eyes opened," people needed exposure to the insights of those who had won their trust over years of hard work in defense of el pueblo—that is, to the kind of people who had led the committee.

The observations that the young Coordinadora leaders solicited, in contrast, were not designed to display wisdom. They solicited observations in part to equalize the contributions to the discussion. The question frequently asked of those who attended meetings—"What did you observe?"—seemed to disburse authority by evading the more authoritative question "What should be done?"[4] Although answers to the latter question surfaced as part of the observations speakers offered, leaders evaded engaging in dialogue about solutions. Moreover, the carefully laid out agenda of the meeting left little time for the kind of extended sharing of narratives and joking that had characterized committee meetings.

In the Coordinadora, public speaking became a kind of obligation of political participation; to fail to do so was to threaten the group's unity. This demand to speak and to do so reasonably challenged accepted understandings of expressions of dissent. As mentioned previously, the Comité para la Defensa de Tierra had taken power when the former Bienes Comunales commissioner had appeared before the governor's representative in a state of intoxication. Intoxication seemed, at least in the eyes of the former commissioner, to discredit his authority. And in 1984 drunks would often hurl insults into the office as committee members held meetings. However, in these meetings, drunken tirades were readily dismissed as the ravings of un loco (madman) whose charges, the product of alcohol, lacked merit. By 1988, however, even drunken tirades were considered to be grounded in reason. Thus, when a drunk, shouting threats and lobbing rocks, stumbled into the compound while the Coordinadora held a meeting in July, women admonished the newly elected Mayor Robles to call the drunk to his office the next day to "find out what is bothering him."

The women's insistence that the drunk be brought to the mayor's office indicated that the drunk, however inappropriate his actions, had rational reasons for being upset. That he chose to express those reasons under the influence of alcohol did not make him any less responsible for communicating the latent causes of his outburst to the mayor. Moreover, there was the expectation that the mayor would be able to deal with whatever was "bothering" him once it was brought out in an open dialogue. Indeed, the drunk was compelled to confess the causes of his anger and could not disavow his belligerence as an effect of alcohol.

One might look at the demands to speak, therefore, as akin to the confessional practices that Foucault discusses in his *History of Sexuality* (1990). Foucault describes the shift in the confessional practices beginning in the seventeenth century as a kind of compulsion to tell, which shaped a new subjectivity under the sign of sex. Here, I am suggesting that deliberative democracy extends that compulsion to tell in new directions shaped around taking rational control of politics. In the case of Tepoztlán, the desire to rationalize politics came from a conviction that groundless gossip undermined political groups. Group leaders were convinced that if the "norm" became the public airing of discontent, private gossip would give way to processes that enabled groups to deal more effectively with that discontent.

Although many Tepoztecans who participated in the Coordinadora experienced opportunities to speak publicly as a source of power, others were more skeptical. Burdick (1993), who compares devotees of liberation theology with members of the Pentecostal Church in Brazil, notes that the methods of liberation theology worked best among the better off of the poor. These people found it easier to speak in public meetings and were willing to hold meetings in their homes to show off their material possessions. His observations resonate with my own in Tepoztlán, where many poor women felt embarrassed when anyone commented on their observations. Don Pedro's daughter, who had boasted of her respect for her father, complained about the changes Father Cristóbal was making in the church: "We go to learn from the priest what the Bible means, but he tries to make you talk, and everyone realizes you know nothing." She experienced the demand to speak as a test of her knowledge and not as a confirmation of the importance of her perspective. In some ways, she was correct even with respect to the Coordinadora.

For Coordinadora leaders, the eye became the organ of consciousness raising. In 1984, don Abram and others in the committee had spoken of the problem of people who were "blind," were "sleeping," or had their "eyes closed" and therefore could not see the committee's value. In contrast, to be politically conscious was to be "awake," to have one's eyes fully opened. But "seeing" was mediated by already existing expectations. People could easily "see" evidence of corruption even when no evidence existed, or, as the Maestro Jorge expressed in a meeting, observation could lead to misplaced criticisms: blaming oneself or one's leaders, rather than the structures of the state, for failures. For people in positions of power, both in the committee and in the Coordinadora, consciousness raising entailed opening people's eyes with systematic coaching in a way of seeing the world that required transforming the lens through which they normally observed the world.

With the change from the committee to the Coordinadora, however, consciousness raising replaced the authority of the past with the promise of the thoroughly transformed citizen fully equipped to engage in the contemporary tasks of democracy. The ancianos' role in politics, the structure of gender relations, and Mexico's revolutionary nationalism were about to change, and with these changes the idea of the past as a template for the future was also being displaced, at least for a time. Indeed, the Coordinadora was participating in a transformation of Mexican politics that reached far beyond the still contested boundaries of Tepoztlán's communal land. The reverberations of these processes of transformation would be felt in the years to come when Carlos Salinas de Gortari, the new president of Mexico, would preside over an administration that declared all ejido and communal land to be eligible for sale as private property, rewrote history textbooks to diminish the role of the Mexican Revolution in the development of Mexico, made peace with the Catholic Church by allowing the church tax-exempt status, and initiated a new era of relations with the United States through NAFTA. But Salinas de Gortari's road to power would not be easy, for, unbeknownst to him at that time, the support that the PRI enjoyed in places such as Tepoztlán was largely a facade.

Mayor Robles stood and announced that the PRI had asked the Coordinadora to send six buses of people to the closing rally of the 1988 presidential campaign in Mexico City on July 6. The PRI was providing the buses, which would leave at 5:00 a.m. on Saturday, and all who wished to go were invited to attend. The Maestro Jorge added that the Coordinadora was not asking people to vote for the PRI candidate and that anyone who went on Saturday should view their participation as a support for Robles and not for the PRI. He continued,

> We are with Robles because we know him and are trying to help him get things for the pueblo. Some people are saying that we are now pawns of the PRI, but we are not because no one is telling us who to vote for. . . . Does anyone here know Salinas de Gortari? Does anyone know [Cuauhtémoc] Cárdenas? How could we support either of them? We know that elections are not going to resolve our problems. The only thing that will ever help us is a pueblo that is united and organized, that does not have any obligations to any party. . . . No matter who wins, that is not going to change what we are doing. I am not telling you to vote for Salinas de Gortari. If you want to vote for him— fine. If you want to vote for Cárdenas—fine. If you don't want to vote, that's even better still. Everyone knows that if a large number of people vote, that will legitimize the election and make it look like people are looking for change through elections.

The emphasis placed on the community as the primary site of political loyalty was accompanied by a confusing but beneficial array of alliances. The Coordinadora included strategic alliances with the PRI, members who worked in the Cárdenas campaign, as well as the Maestro and his allies, whose left politics envisioned revolutionary, structural changes that could not be brought about through electoral change. In the face of such a confusing array of strategic alliances, one did indeed need to "know" someone to understand his or her political position. Even in those circumstances, one could be easily deceived. Thus, the discourse of "knowing" reflected not a myopic focus on the local, but an attempt to find one's footing on shaky political terrain. Tepoztecans frequently expressed empathy for other communities engaged in struggles to stop unwanted projects, but their empathy was tempered by the conviction that one can never know the intricacies of PRI power in Mexico. To form concrete alliances in this political setting was dangerous. Thus, the notion of community-based struggles enabled the imagination of allies in different places without requiring concrete commitment to specific, named allies. It spoke both to the recognition that people in other places may be in structurally similar positions to one's own community—that is, similarly victimized by the state—but also to the very real possibility that those who appear structurally similar may in fact sustain lucrative alliances with the ruling party. In this sense, the discourse of community needed to be viewed as a location, but not as a limit. One could always move out from communities to form political ties with outsiders as long as one's principles reflected a grounding in the local community. These types of shifting alliances will be clearer in the next chapter when I discuss the Coordinadora's adventures in global politics.

In 1988, feigned support for the PRI was a collective and publicly debated strategy for participating in the electoral process. Indeed, the fact that the number of votes cast for Cárdenas took the PRI by surprise might well be because of the large number of campesinos who dutifully turned out at rallies for Salinas de Gortari while voting for his opponents in the ballot box. I accompanied Coordinadora members to the rally for Salinas de Gortari. The buses arrived in plenty of time to practice a carefully scripted response to Salinas de Gortari's presence, fashioned around cheers proclaiming, "We are all Mexicans, we are all PRIistas, we are all for Salinas de Gortari." When the contingent of campesinos failed to display the requisite enthusiasm while throwing their hats in the air, they practiced again. Protected by the privacy of the ballot box, the people, through their feigned support, were able to garner the personal benefits of associating with those in power, while ultimately betraying them in the ballot box.

Suspecting the coercive power of the social world, electoral democracy constructs the fiction of an individual who, standing alone, makes his or her decision, presumably in relation to privately derived interests and morality. The ballot box thus figures as an extension of the sovereign subject, whose decisions must be protected from public coercion, especially at the moment of voting. In the Coordinadora in 1988, however, the "secret ballot" was democratic not so much because citizens could enter the ballot box as private individuals with a collection of rights, but because the ballot box enabled collective strategies of deception. Faced with a corrupt and dishonest Mexican state, the ballot box was envisioned as a place of collective payback so that behind the symbolism of the individual confronting the ballot box stood a collective imaginary. With a "secret ballot," citizens could invert the commonly understood practice by which the PRI deceived and cheated its supporters; now the pueblo could deceive the PRI. Coordinadora members reminded one another that when the PRI gave you sandwiches at a rally, it was only giving you back what it had already robbed from you. The patronage/clientage system that had sustained the PRI's power for almost seventy years could be overturned by a ballot box that became a kind of guerrilla warfare at the electoral level. Far from serving as the voice of the individual, the ballot box became the voice of the collective community speaking out against corruption and abuse of power.

If Coordinadora members were supposed to refrain from gossip within the group, the ballot box became the site for the displaced power of gossip. Similar to that gossip, the ballot box was a space in which authority could be evaded and even deceived, although, as with gossip, the formal secrecy of the ballot box stood in tense relationships with the collective and public nature of politics. Just as gossip relied on secrecy, but a secrecy that could be betrayed and therefore was dangerous, so too did the ballot box. That so many people righteously reminded each other in 1988 that the ballot box was secret spoke to many people's fears that somehow their vote could indeed be known. In point of fact, regardless of how secret any individual ballot may have been, what mattered for one's standing in the community was not which box one checked, but how people guessed one's vote, often on the basis of somewhat flimsy evidence. Indeed, on election day, I sat with the Maestro as he "guessed" how each person would vote as he or she approached the ballot box. Such guesses were based on the fact that social ties and not just political ideology shaped people's votes. Thus, on the day after the election, don Pedro announced that he had taken his whole family to vote for Cárdenas, or at least he had told them to vote for Cárdenas. In the end, to the PRI's surprise, Tepoztecans voted nearly five to one for Cárdenas.

The Cárdenas campaign introduced the specter of electoral democracy into the nation's political imaginary. In Tepoztlán, the possibility of a PRI defeat at the polls incited the emergence of new forms of political activism. Small groups met in private homes to view videotapes provided by the Cárdenas campaign, and PRI propaganda posters were modified to show ballots being cast for Cárdenas's FDN. Cárdenas organizers held rallies in Tepoztlán, and Tepoztecans, including the Maestro Jorge, traveled to surrounding cities to hear the candidate speak. The excitement generated by the prospect of change was compounded by a widespread sense that to engage in campaigning for Cárdenas violated the tenets of

Mexican politics. People who worked with the campaign for Cárdenas feared for their lives or their livelihoods. Rumors abounded that those who showed Cárdenas campaign tapes would lose their jobs or pensions or both. One woman told me that she had seen a PRI campaign commercial on television that showed pictures of the wars in Central America: it could only be understood, she explained, as a PRI threat that it would not stand for the election of Cárdenas.

Set against the backdrop of this fear, Coordinadora meetings became a kind of public performance of reasoned discourse. If the PRI was using fear to intimate, the Coordinadora appeared to be the place where a reasonable discourse could prevail and disagreements could be aired without jeopardizing political unity.

Paradoxically, the PRI itself introduced the discourse of democracy that proliferated around the 1988 elections in order to deal with its own legitimacy problems and to reshape the state to fit the demands of a neoliberal economy. Under Miguel de la Madrid, the government had undertaken a series of austerity measures that resulted in cuts of government spending, sharp declines in real wages, and soaring unemployment rates (Collier 1992:74; Lustig 1992:61–95). Many analysts concur that the drastic austerity measures made it increasingly difficult for the PRI to represent itself as a partner of its revolutionary allies. Indeed, the various sectors that made up the PRI depended on government spending both to quell members' demands and to grease the relationships between political leaders (Bartra 1989; Collier 1992:75). As revolutionary nationalism became, in the context of economic restructuring, an increasingly difficult ideology to maintain, the PRI turned to the rhetoric of democracy and modernization. Democracy portended the replacement of what had become a cumbersome coalition of peasants, workers, and the popular sector with individual citizens exercising choices at the ballot box. Collier notes: "The state alliance with labor and the peasantry became too costly in the context of the commitment to economic restructuring. . . . The modernizers were no longer willing to protect groups from the market in the same way . . . and the demographic changes that had made Mexico a more urban and middle class society came to be seen as making obsolete the PRI's traditional constituency and its 'over reliance' on labor and peasant support" (1992:120).

Democracy emerged then as the PRI attempted to disentangle its long-standing commitments to labor and peasants while finding new allies among the urban middle classes and within the private sector. Although the labor and peasant sectors could be weakened by the slow withdrawal of PRI support, they remained an active force at the local level, creating a power vacuum. The Cárdenas campaign represented one attempt to fill this vacuum; groups such as the Coordinadora represented another.

In July 1988, the PRI suffered what many believe was its first electoral defeat in a presidential election. Cuauhtémoc Cárdenas, son of Lázaro Cárdenas, had been working within the PRI since the mid-1980s to oppose the power of the technocrats and their economic policies. The president of the PRI, Jorge de la Vega Domínguez, issued a stern warning to followers of the Cárdenas-led Corriente Democrática (Democratic Current) at the party's National Assembly in March 1987: they should respect the party's will or associate themselves with other parties (Bruhn 1997:96). Cuauhtémoc Cárdenas responded with a letter of protest delivered not only to the party, but also to the national press. He began to travel around the country in what seemed an unofficial campaign. In October, he accepted an offer to run as a candidate of the Partido Auténtico de la Revolución Mexicana (PARM, Authentic Party of the Mexican Revolution), one of the long-standing "loyal opposition" parties in Mexico. PARM was unhappy with the way the PRI had managed its standing as an officially recognized party, and the Cárdenas candidacy gave its members a way of expressing their dissatisfaction (Bruhn 1997:84–107).

By election day, July 6, 1988, Cárdenas had managed to bring together a loose coalition of four political parties under the rubric of the FDN. His candidacy seemed to attract support, although few in the PRI believed that this support could turn into a near electoral victory. Indeed, the PRI had not prepared for carrying out a fraudulent election, believing Cárdenas did not present a threat. As a result, the fraud that it did carry out proved embarrassingly obvious. Burned ballots, many marked in favor of Cárdenas, were found in rivers and alleys; the government announced that its new computer system to tabulate the vote had crashed, creating a six-day delay in results; absenteeism was reported as more than 50 percent in urban areas where Cárdenas was strong; and vote counts that appeared to be derived by adding zeros onto the actual vote for the PRI candidate convinced many Mexicans that Cárdenas had indeed won the election (Bruhn 1997:140–44). As mentioned earlier, Tepoztecans voted five to one for Cuauhtémoc Cárdenas, and Mayor Robles posted the results for several days until the PRI made him take them down.

Despite what seemed an obvious victory, the loose coalition of parties joined together in the FDN lacked the organizational unity to carry out a full-scale challenge to the fraudulent election results. Although many who voted for Cárdenas professed a willingness to take up arms to defend their vote, Cárdenas rejected that approach (Bruhn 1997:156–60). On September 10, Salinas de Gortari was declared president-elect by the new Congress in a decree signed only by the PRI members. The fight to secure the presidency for Cárdenas was hampered by the fact that many of the parties in the FDN coalition had won more seats in Congress than ever before. To have continued to challenge the vote would have meant giving up these victories in the interests of winning the presidency, something few believed possible (Bruhn 1997:140–64).

Humberto Robles's tenure as mayor in Tepoztlán would soon show that it was not easy to invert the patterns of PRI politics. He would be removed from office and a new election held before he finished his term because of complaints lodged against him by the Mujeres Tepoztecans. But he managed to introduced new forms of organizing that linked the community to global NGOs and new ideas about the political process.

Mayor Robles and his wife had international connections with various funding agencies and a strong commitment to using these connections in Tepoztlán. His job as a university professor kept him busy, but his wife's willingness to step in when he had to be away enabled him to manage his competing obligations. Unfortunately, the active role that she assumed cost him the mayoralty.

In the first year of his tenure, the Robleses were able to secure several grants from international NGOs that provided the resources to carry out projects in Tepoztlán. The control of the state over municipal-level budgets ordinarily enabled the PRI to exert a heavy hand on internal politics: if a community did not support the PRI, it did not receive the funds needed for local projects (see chapter 3). Yet residents considered a local mayor successful only if he or she managed to build schools, supply water and electricity to barrios, pave roads, and so on—again, activities that normally required PRI support. Robles, however, through his international connections, escaped some of this control, and in the short time he controlled the mayor's office, he presided over the refinishing of roads and began construction on new schools.

Although many Tepoztecans fondly recalled Robles's accomplishments, the Mujeres Tepoztecans complained that he had not been good for el pueblo. One woman explained to me, "The most important thing, Juanita, is that we work for the poor, the *humilde*, of the pueblo, and that is what the Mujeres Tepoztecans are doing. Robles's ideas would not have been good for the poor." She went on to explain that Robles was against progress and that it was only if the whole pueblo progressed that the poor would be helped. In addition, she complained that Robles's wife, not he, was running the district; the pueblo had elected him—not his wife.

The characterization of Robles as antiprogress was a euphemism for a discussion of the place of tourism in the Tepoztecan economy. The women who remained in the Mujeres Tepoztecans owned small businesses in the center of town and profited from a steady influx of tourists to the community. Although they united with other groups to fight against large hotels and restaurant chains that might threaten their businesses, they saw the future of Tepoztlán as depending on small, locally owned establishments similar to those they ran. But these establishments, in turn, depended on a steady flow of tourist income to the area. In contrast, many in the Coordinadora, representing the whole district, believed that tourism benefited only the incomes of those in the district seat and not those of the surrounding communities.

The Mujeres Tepoztecans' conviction that Robles was not good for the town was never debated. Instead, the Mujeres focused their attack on the Robles administration around charges of corruption; they demanded repeatedly that the district books be audited. And when the books finally were audited by a state-level appointed committee, the audit revealed that señora Robles had written the checks for several local projects. As a woman from the Mujeres Tepoztecans explained, "With this we got him—we had elected him, not his wife, yet she was making out the checks." The checks provided the justification for removing Robles from office before the completion of his term, but no doubt the PRI had realized that his commitment to the party was rather shallow. A new election was held. Not surprisingly, a candidate supported by the Mujeres won.

Many Tepoztecans with whom I spoke in 1991 believed that the Mujeres' complaints against Mayor Robles amounted to a not so subtle disguise of the interests of small business owners in the center of town. Albeit with the normal level of reluctance to speak strongly on behalf of anyone who enters the political process, one woman explained, "They say he was not good, but from what I can see he was accomplishing a lot of things for the town." The Robles experiment seemed to have failed, but it had proved the value of working with the international community—a lesson that would be important in 1991.

As I have stressed throughout this chapter, the discourse of democracy emerged in Mexico as part of the contested 1988 election. Nonetheless, its significance at the local level needs to be understood in terms of the meaning it accumulated as it was deployed in local hegemonic struggles. For example, insofar as democracy became aligned with a project of breaking down the distinction between those with words and those without words, it challenged a mechanism that peripheral members had used to resist political leaders' power. The insistence that everyone speak publicly during meetings was at the same time an imposition of silence in private conversations. It compelled people to exhibit public loyalties, but rendered difficult the disavowing of these loyalties in private gossip.

Although the desire to encourage more vocal participation in meetings was not directed against the ancianos, it did weaken the ancianos' power and displaced the authority of tradition. Like hegemonic processes everywhere, the weakening of the ancianos' power did not happen as a result of a conspiracy among the young to displace that power. Indeed, many young people spoke fondly of older committee leaders and of the history of community organizing. But the young people's motivation came from a conception of knowledge as grounded in day-to-day experiences rather than in the accumulation of wisdom over time. This "democratic" notion of knowledge militated against allocating to anyone, not just to the ancianos, the kind of time required for ancianos to express their wisdom. The young wanted the ancianos to participate like everyone else, but for the ancianos their own value lay in what made them distinctive: the fact that they could bring to the conversation wisdom from another time. Everyone could observe and comment, but only they could bring a sense of how the passage of time had transformed what could be observed.

In addition to the prominent place allocated to the young, the Coordinadora created a more prominent role for women than they had ever enjoyed in the committee. Although women continued to participate in groups dedicated to women's issues in the Coordinadora, gender and sex identities gave way to the notion of communal opposition to the PRI.

Coordinadora leaders frequently singled out women for their disciplined participation in the Coordinadora and for their bravery in defending the town's autonomy, but women who participated in the Coordinadora did not construct a discourse that highlighted gender as politically distinctive in a manner reminiscent of the Mujeres Tepoztecanas' discourse. The following quote from a female Coordinadora member illustrates the quandary this provoked for gendered conceptions of politics: "What we need are real men, men willing to shed their blood. Excuse me, we need men / women willing to die for Tepoztlán."

According to the semiotics of gender and power that reigned within the Mujeres Tepoztecanas, female power was located deep within the recesses of their bodies and was reflected in tales of women using their vaginas to hide things from men and their breasts to feed men deprived of food by prison authorities. Women's power rested in their ability to simulate compliance with gender norms while subverting their powerlessness. Men's power, in contrast, resided in their willingness to shed blood, their own and others', in direct and open confrontation, as they did in the Mexican Revolution. Of course, women frequently pointed to the fact that women did fight in the revolution, but these women fighters were singled out because of their violation of the norm, not because they were the norm. It remained to be seen what kinds of roles women could exercise in a group where they shared power with men.

The PRI had turned to the discourses of democracy as part of its overall shift to a modern, neoliberal state in the 1988 elections. This was not the first time the Mexican state had used the language of modernization, but talk of modernization at this time became shorthand for a neoliberal economic agenda defined by the privatization of state-owned industries, the dismantling of trade barriers, and cutbacks in state subsidies to the economy. Alongside the image of a privatized economy, the privacy of the ballot box figured prominently in this latest incarnation of Mexican modernization. Yet, as I have suggested in this chapter, the privatized ballot box became transformed for many Mexicans into the site of a collective response to what at the time was seen as the state's corrupt and abusive power.

Although the national-level focus on democracy in 1988 came mainly from the election campaign, in Tepoztlán talk of democracy was not in the least bit limited to the election. There, the sense of democracy expanded to deal with the problems of internal conflicts within the Coordinadora. The origins of this notion of democracy as a vehicle for solving problems lay in the ancianos' crafting of an aesthetic of tradition in which respect is figured in the image of an anciano carefully listening to his subordinates to work out problems. This image occurs as well in Laura Nader's depictions of legal authorities among the Zapotec in Oaxaca and in don Pedro's explanation of how he came to the decision that his daughter should leave her male children behind when she divorced her husband. The idea that a particular kind of talk—one punctuated by long silences, careful questions, and respectful and reasoned replies—might lead to the resolution of problems resonated with Tepoztecans' desires for ways of working together that would maintain community strength. More important, such an image of respectful listening stood in sharp contrast to the ways of state- and national-level bureaucrats, whose notoriously rude behavior had made them the butt of jokes in the committee. In an aesthetic of tradition, however, the ability to engage in this kind of respectful problem solving is the province of those in positions of power, who gain their power and respect by demonstrating their ability to reach agreements through this kind of talk. Indeed, in this aesthetic, it is this facility to treat others with respect that distinguishes authorities from lesser persons who are likely to speak without listening and to deploy anger and passion in their language. In short, the nonreciprocity of such behavior is fundamental to anciano authority, whereas democratic deliberation demands such reciprocity of everyone.

The invocation of democracy in 1988 was an attempt to decentralize this special form of "talk," rendering it a normative demand of all communication. Although ancianos had often preached the virtues of such talk in the committee as though it were a universal norm, they did so recognizing full well that their command of such talk rendered them superior and provided evidence for their right to rule. Once democratic talk was divorced from its basis in the legitimation of an aesthetic of tradition, the norms associated with it took on a different sense. Democratic talk was to foster the emergence of new kinds of subjectivity that would enable people to participate in collective organizations without demanding the unity previously deemed necessary and desirable. Democracy, as a form of dealing with disagreements, could flourish only when subjects agreed to air their disagreements and to submit them to others' public scrutiny. The promise of democracy was meant to compel peripheral members to forsake the kind of "holding back" that had been so common in the committee and that had authorized the ability to gossip about leaders without having one's gossip subject to scrutiny.

Democratic talk thus promised to discipline disagreements, rendering them organizationally harmless. The traditional aesthetic of respect lacked the disciplinary potential of democracy, for it confined the demands of respectful listening to a small elite, leaving others free to engage in forms of dissent that had proved pernicious to the committee. In order for the Coordinadora not to fall victim to a similar fate, the subjectivity previously understood as a product of the wisdom associated with the age and status of men had to be democratized as a more general ethos.

By and large, the story of democracy, like that of modernization, highlights its European origins in the French Revolution or its association with the American Revolution, rendering all other senses of democracy derivative of these original forms. Discourses of democracy that arise in other places are represented as the impoverished cousins of these original forms, adapted by peoples who are not quite ready for the full spirit of democracy. Authors differ on what is required for the spirit of democracy. For some, it is institutional structures such as constitutions, rules of law, checks on power, and so forth. For others, it is a transformation of the populace through education and reason. In a more generous light, Laclau and Mouffe, although tracing the origins of democracy to the French Revolution and the Declaration of the Rights of Man, emphasize the universal appeal of democracy (1985:154–55). For them, the significance of democracy lies not in the institutional frameworks it establishes or in an associated set of practices, but rather in the way it creates a horizon, the imagination of future possibilities that can never really be reached. Laclau and Mouffe judge democracy to be an inherently subversive power that renders "different forms of inequality . . . illegitimate and anti-natural" (1985:155)

Against these lofty readings of democracy are those who insist on situating democracy within the full scope of power relations that involve what Mallon terms the knot of democracy, nationalism, and colonialism (1994, 1995:9). Read within the framework of power relations, democracy becomes the partner of the expansion of global capitalism and the twin of colonialism and imperialism. Democracy thus takes its place in hegemonic struggles for power, provoking challenges to power but also reasserting dominance. Calls for democracy are never innocent, but rather are deeply intertwined with these other struggles for power and control. Most important, this framework challenges the "impoverished second cousin" reading of democracy in the periphery, asserting for modernity more generally, as Coronil does, that we need to read democracy as a kind of "decentered universality" (1997:394). In short, we need to tell this history of democracy globally, attending to its different manifestations in different contexts and at different historical moments, something I have endeavored to do in this chapter.

Although democracy discourses in Mexico's elections in 1988 were nurtured and encouraged by global economic changes, Mexico already had a deep history of engagement with democracy. As Mallon notes, after the 1855 Liberal Revolution, liberal guerrilla forces in the Puebla highlands used democratic visions to challenge ancianos' hegemonic control (1995:73). At this time, younger males, peasant guerrilla fighters who fought on behalf of liberalism, used appeals to democracy to wrest power from older males while excluding women from their vision of democracy. Mallon eloquently relays the spirit of this democratic fervor and the need to understand its specific manifestations:

> They struggled to bridge the gap between their own dynamic and contested concepts of mutuality and justice and the ideas of individual freedom and equality contained within nineteenth-century liberalism. Situating these ideas in a context of indigenous communalism and reciprocity, highland villagers tempered the individualism and strengthened the promises of equality they contained. *In so doing, they fashioned a Liberal vision quite distinct, in class and ethnic terms, from that held by many citified intellectuals.* (1995:76, emphasis added)

Mallon's description suggests that even if the drafters of the liberal reforms in Mexico drew inspiration from the French and American revolutions, they thoroughly repatriated democracy and rendered it autochthonous through such local struggles.

If democracy occupies a role in struggles for power, it seems reasonable to inquire into its discursive force, recognizing that the discourse of democracy in Tepoztlán, despite its strategic appeal, was not merely strategic. Rather, Tepoztecans became "caught" in the discourse of democracy much as Jean Favret-Saada (1980) describes how western French peasants come to speak of witchcraft. Favret-Saada's analysis

Chapter 8

Theorizing Politics from the Margins

The "right" to signify from the periphery of authorized power and privilege does not depend on the persistence of tradition; it is resourced by the power of tradition to be reinscribed through the conditions of contingency and contradictoriness that attend upon the lives of those who are "in the minority."
—Homi K. Bhabha, *The Location of Culture*

One of the key strengths of Tepoztecan political practice is its adaptability to situations in which mistrust is rampant owing to a history of unequal and abusive use of power, the state of affairs that prevails in much coalition building today. Tepoztecans have entered coalitions in order to garner media attention for their political struggles, to win freedom for political prisoners, and to bypass the state's monopoly of resources, but in doing so they have had to work with those whom they do not trust and whose visions of the future they may not share. Indeed, a shared vision would be difficult to achieve given Tepoztlán's internal divisions. The coalitions that bring together educated urban elites with peasants and first-world activists with indigenous people resemble Tepoztecans' history with the Mexican state. They entail both desires for unity and a history of unmet promises coupled with the specter of betrayal. Although for many this political terrain may not be ideal, it is familiar to Tepoztecans. It is also terrain to which their knowledge of how to participate politically is peculiarly adaptive.

I want to explore a possible paradox: Tepoztecan social movements have been able to form coalitions with a range of political actors over the years not because they have become more open and trusting, but because their history with the state—a history that has inspired mistrust of opposition movements—has left them well prepared to navigate the complex terrain of contemporary coalitions. Navigating this terrain requires knowing how to keep connections alive and viable without becoming so fully absorbed in coalition politics that one's connection to a locale—understood as the place from which one's politics emerges—is forsaken. Properly speaking, the locale is not a geographic space, but an array of competing connections that, although invisible when Tepoztecan political actors participate in national or global coalitions, weigh on their decisions. It is also the context from which one's sense of the political is formed. Thus, when Tepoztecan political actors worry about what "they" will say if the political actors join in this or that proposition or coalition, it is to the locale that they are referring. In short, they participate with an eye toward connections that are never concretely present in coalitions, but whose weight prompts Tepoztecan activists to "withhold" even as they participate. As I suggested in chapter 5, we cannot understand the weight of this connection without attending to the ways silence becomes wedded to gossip. The refusal to speak can be easily interpreted as disagreement. Again, this "holding back" has not impoverished Tepoztecan politics, but rather has rendered it strategically flexible.

If we view social movements as an investment in an uncertain future, flexibility and loose connections have a special place. For example, Tepoztecans' shifting of the defense of communal land from Mexico's Agrarian Reform Law to Mexico's ecological laws even before Salinas de Gortari dismantled agrarian reform left them well positioned to fight the train project in terms intelligible to a global audience. In part, the shift to ecological laws speaks to Tepoztecans' flare for the ironic: when Salinas de Gortari was awarded a global prize for his environmental policies, Tepoztecans demanded he demonstrate that he warranted such a prize by supporting their fight against the rail line.

This is not to suggest that Tepoztecans, or anyone else for that matter, should be viewed as rational sovereign subjects scanning the political field for opportunities, fully cognizant of the costs and benefits of different kinds of participation. Social movements are instrumental, but they are not merely instrumental. They come into being not just to achieve certain ends, but as ends in themselves. The specter of a potential unity shaped the political practices not only of Tepoztecan leaders, but also of peripheral participants. Although the desire for unity was clearly present in its absence in Tepoztlán, this absent presence shaped social movements. Peripheral participants' gossip was fueled not only by a desire to impede the careers of those who would betray the community, but also by a sense of indignation inspired by the failed promise of unity. The posture of righteous indignation that so many Tepoztecan peripheral participants assumed spoke both in the language of cynicism and in the conviction that unity was both necessary and possible: one reason why Tepoztecans peripheral participants understood their own politics as protecting the community from unscrupulous political leaders. Indeed, the politics of loose connections can be properly understood only with attention to both this desire for unity and the undermining of unity by the forces of mistrust and cynicism.

This book has highlighted the structure of the Mexican state to make sense of the politics of loose connections, but contemporary writings on social movements suggest that this style of political participation is pervasive. In a study of peasant movements in Costa Rica, Marc Edelman notes, "while many social movement organizations fall into oblivion their demands and tactics are often taken up by new groups" (1999:118). He goes on to suggest that even these "failed" social movements contribute to further efforts by providing a "reservoir of experience" on which activists can draw (118). Nonetheless, the accent in Edelman's work is on unity, for he posits that the impetus for social movements comes from a reaction against globalization and its impacts on farming. Thus, although his book provides numerous examples of the breakup of social movements, his conviction that these movements were grounded in a commonality of economic interests leads him to overlook the practices that give rise to the fragmentation of social movements.

Taking a very different approach to social movements, Nelson's (1999) study of Mayan movements in Guatemala draws on a concept of fluidarity. Her work seeks to capture the impossibility of stable identities by attending to the ways in which all identities, including that of the anthropologist who seeks relations of solidarity with her informants, come about through a process of articulation. The view of identity that emerges from this notion of articulation suggests that all identities fit badly, a notion that Nelson captures with her metaphors: identity as a prosthetic, identity as an ill-fitted camel-hair coat, the Mayas as hackers. Her point is to write in such a way as to capture the spaces in between, with the effect that her work resists closure. In contrast to Edelman, Nelson suggests that the fragmentation in a post–Fordist economy questions the world as divided into interest blocs, creating anxiety for those who envision liberation struggle (1999:353). Yet demands for unity that issue from those who continue to insist that the world is still divided into blocs of distinct interest groups threaten to cover the very wounds that her analysis seeks to leave open and bleeding (352). Indeed, she seems to suggest that demands for unity are an attempt to silence Mayan activists who are becoming increasingly articulate in questioning either a left model of liberation or the construction of the nation around *ladino* superiority.

This book has tried to shed light on questions other than those concerning unity to highlight how politics takes place in the contemporary world. In taking this approach, I have tried to reposition theory, making its task in relation to social movements less prescriptive and more translational. Thus, my aim has been to use theory to capture the significance of the politics of loose connections and to shed light on the practices of this politics in a way that celebrates that which remains background in studies more focused on the question of unity. As Butler notes, "there is a new venue for theory, necessarily impure where it emerges in and as the very event of cultural translation . . . where the demand for translation is acute and its promise of success uncertain" (1999:ix).

Although both examples given here, Edelman's and Nelson's, are drawn from Latin America, evidence of the politics of loose connections can also be found in the antiglobalization movement. Naomi Klein (2000) views the recent protest movements around World Trade Organization meetings as the Internet come to life. She suggests that the use these movements make of the Internet is significant when considering their form—these movements do not coalesce into a single movement. She concludes, "Thanks to the net, mobilisations unfold with sparse bureaucracy and minimal hierarchy; forced consensus and laboured manifestos are fading into the background, replaced by a culture of constant, loosely structured and sometimes compulsive information swapping" (2000:19). The effectiveness of such loose connections was captured in a report in the *San Francisco Chronicle* on March 21, 2003 (Garofoli and Zamora 2003). Demonstrators protesting the war in Iraq managed to "cripple downtown San Francisco" with hit-and-run tactics. The report noted that demonstrators relied on "organized chaos," blocking intersections and splitting off to move to the next intersection as soon as police officers moved in. One of the "organizers" of the movement explained,

"We don't really know how many people are out there or where they're going next. People make that decision on their own."

The forces that generate such tactics in the United States and western Europe may be different from those that have shaped political practices in Mexico. The former forces' origins may lie in the antidisciplinary movements that Stephens (1998) describes for the 1960s in the United States. Similar to those movements, these new forces are suspicious of plans, documents, and forms of decision making that suggest disciplinary practices, especially those that prevail in the corporate world. My sense is that Tepoztlán's politics of loose connections, in contrast, is founded less on a suspicion of disciplinary practices in general and more on a wary attitude toward the political arena. In this, Tepoztecans' attitude more resembles the attitude that Moses and Cobb describe for many black activists involved in the civil rights movement when confronted by the specter of white volunteers in the summer of 1964: "They had only reluctantly agreed to white volunteers coming in for the freedom vote, and they agreed mainly because it was short term, just two weeks and they would be gone. . . . But the idea of hundreds of such folks generated concern that local leadership just emerging from the grassroots would be drowned in a tidal wave of white volunteers" (2001:74). Although Moses and Cobb's work generally highlights developing unity within the civil rights movement and a turn away from segregation, their observations are reminiscent of the kind of mistrust that prevailed as Tepoztecans entered the global political arena. The notion of making important connections in this case while elaborating limits to those connections seems similar to the history of mistrust between whites and blacks in the United States.

Clearly, my point is not to argue that unity is always pernicious, whereas mistrust is always protective and beneficial, but rather that both are present in social movements, and we err when we privilege one over the other. What we should never presume is that more unity is better than less or that forces that seem to conspire against unity are necessarily pernicious. More important, scholars of social movements need to guard against lending unity a position of theoretical privilege not accorded to its impoverished cousins, mistrust and political gossip. I am suggesting that in order to do this we must pursue political practice at the margins, recognizing that a margin is always a moving target.

In her book *Deadly Words: Witchcraft in the Bocage* (1980), Jeanne Favret-Saada lays out a distinction between her approach to witchcraft and that of classical anthropology. She maintains that those who have viewed witchcraft as form of knowledge or a system of belief miss the point: witchcraft is a way of waging war with words, and in order to understand it one must allow oneself to become caught up in the words. To catch the sense of witchcraft, one must find oneself speculating as to who did what to whom and so on. In her focus on being caught in order to catch, Favret-Saada highlights her difference not only from classical anthropology, but also from poststructuralism: "I wish to suggest that what is needed is a second 'catching' and not a 'getting uncaught.' . . . I suggest that this marks unequivocally the distance that separates me from both classical anthropology and post-structuralist thinking in France in their shared ideal of 'a totally a-topical theorizing subject' " (1980:14).

Leaving aside the question of whether or not witchcraft might also be seen as a form of knowledge and not just a discursive practice, I take the key insight of Favret-Saada's text to be its focus on the way anthropological insights, similar to those of our informants, involve getting caught in conversations. The writing of any ethnographic text, then, is a map of the conversations in which the ethnographer became caught and not a "bird's-eye view" of a place that transcends all location. Indeed, Favret-Saada's critique of the omnipotent observer is echoed in a number of feminist works, but it is her approach to this problem through the lens of fieldwork conversation that interests me. Fieldwork presents opportunities to learn from different locations, but it is not inevitable in the fieldwork process that one will do so, as Favret-Saada's critiques of classical anthropology illustrate. A great deal depends on the conversations in which the fieldworker gets caught as well as on those she or he avoids.

Clearly, getting caught in conversations is not the same as living someone else's life, and Bourdieu's caution that the anthropologist who plays the game as a game while waiting to leave it in order to tell it (1990:34) cannot be lightly dismissed. But if the target of Bourdieu's critique is the naive anthropologist who harbors fantasies of "primitivist participation," Favret-Saada inverts Bourdieu. She notes, in witchcraft "words wage war," and "Anyone talking about it is a belligerent, the ethnographer like everyone else. There is no room for uninvolved observers" (1980:10). In short, whereas Bourdieu is concerned with the epistemological problems associated with the fantasy of participation, Favret-Saada points to an equally compelling drama: one can never really be in a field site without being absorbed into its universe of practice.

Favret-Saada's insights into witchcraft apply as well to the various discourses of politics I have described in this book. In the case of social movements, "words wage war." Calls for unity and charges of abuse of power and corruption both reinforce and undermine each other at every moment, and to interview someone either about unity or corruption is to become caught in a conversation that has consequences. Yet this fact often eludes the anthropologist for precisely the reasons that Bourdieu explains. Not born into the game of politics (at least the game in which we participate during fieldwork), having little stake in its outcome, and lacking the sense of urgency, the anthropologist pursues knowledge for knowledge's sake, treating as spectacle what has real-life consequences for those he or she studies. In fact, the anthropologist is unwittingly drawn into these games as he or she, too, becomes a subject of gossip.

What does this all mean for an anthropology of social movements? For one thing, it matters in which conversations the anthropologist becomes caught. If the anthropologist gets caught in conversations about unity—speculating how it might come about, what obstacles it might face, and what might be achieved were unity to prevail—then he or she is participating in a game in which those who gossip about abuses of power are placed in the position of bewitchers and naysayers. Likewise, if the anthropologist gets caught in the conversations of those who "watch" for signs of betrayal and abuse of power, he or she is participating in a game in which those calling for unity are discredited. Even to inquire into how one might know that so-and-so is engaged in corruption is to become a part of the game of discrediting those who would be leaders.

Although much writing about social movements appears to take a position distant from the scene of squabbles over unity and mistrust as marked by its apparent distance from any specific conversations, what de Certeau notes of the historian is true of ethnographic writing as well. Writing anything involves not only an actual location, but also a fantasy location, and that fantasy is often on the side of those in power. Regarding the work of the historian, de Certeau notes, "he plays to the role of the prince that he is not; he analyzes what the prince ought to do . . . [but] never will; the 'virtual prince,' a construct of discourse, will never be the 'prince in fact'" (1988:8). Those who write about social movements, including myself, may not imagine themselves wielding the power of the prince, but they often do fantasize themselves as bringing about unity. In short, one's sense of the problem is shaped around concerns with unity in a way that all too often renders the gossip of those on the periphery an obstacle to unity. To be sure, such gossip can be reinterpreted as the frustrations of those who have not benefited equally from political engagement. But constituting gossip as an expression of frustration leaves in place the sense that it is a pernicious political practice destined to disappear when times are better. Normatively denigrated, it remains marginal to the real work of politics, which is to bring about unity.

Although scholars of social movements have been drawn to marginalized social movements—such as peasant movements; women's movements; animal rights movements; and gay, bisexual, and transgender movements—it is more difficult to deal with those who find themselves marginalized by movements already deemed to represent the margin. The history and ethnography of social movements looks different when written from the perspective of those who covet a place on the margins of marginalized social movements. Indeed, the actions of those on the periphery of social movements can shape the form and style of political movements more effectively than can those who take up positions as leaders and fully dedicated activists.

A clear case for the richness of the margin has been made for marginalized ethnic, racial, and sex/gender identities and geographic boundaries, but the same cannot be said for those who linger on the margins of such social movements—despite the fact that such margins are often the place that spawn the emergence of new movements. In part, this neglect has to do with the fact that although the margin seems to gesture toward antiessentialism, in practice it has been essentialized as endowed with its own kind of unity. The possibility of a margin within the margin so conceived becomes difficult to conceptualize.

The richness of margins and boundaries comes from the way they place in relief the limits of knowledge by revealing its positionality. Writers such as Gloria Anzaldúa (1987), V. Y. Mudimbe (1988), and José Limón (1998), to mention just a few, have revealed that writing from the borders and margins produces perspectives that challenge hegemonic ways of viewing the world. My argument is that taking up a position in the periphery of political movements, by which I mean allowing oneself to be caught in the conversations on the periphery, enables a reassessment of the strategic and theoretical value of unity. Moreover, from the vantage point of those on the periphery of social movements, one can see the talk of unity as a battle waged with words in which those who would contest unity are erased as political actors. In short, calls for unity are never innocent. But how did unity come to be so privileged, and how is that privilege repeated in scholarly reflections on social movements?

Theorizing Loose Connections in the Domain of Political Practice

A persistent tension that runs throughout this book is how to think of the never-ending calls for unity while holding onto the obvious failures of unity that develop from the politics of loose connections. I include in this sense of tension my own struggles with this dilemma, which is both personal and political. In the case of Mexico, there are cultural and historical reasons why calls to unity seem always to inspire actions that undermine unity, but a broader question needs to addressed: Is there some inevitable link between unity and the suspicion that reads any such calls for unity as a pernicious exercise of power? More precisely, is there anything inherent in calls for unity that should cause us to reconsider unity's hallowed place in progressive politics? Alternatively, has unity somehow been tainted by its history, and can it be redeemed?

One might argue that the persistent failure of unity in Tepoztlán is inherent in the predicament of trying to represent the complexity of any social phenomenon. Any attempts to "name" Tepoztecans' situation are bound to fail because naming always takes place in a terrain where something must be excluded, and that which is excluded persistently re-emerges to pester any social movement that purports to be unified. Judith Butler raises this problem when she suggests that the attempt to shape feminist coalitions around the category of "women" fails to deal with the "multiplicity of cultural, social, and political intersections" in which women are constructed (1999:20). What is needed, she argues, is a genealogy of the category itself that reveals its systematic exclusions. Others suggest, however, that calls to unity might be a necessary or merely desirable feature of political life despite the exclusions implicit in such calls.

Clearly, unity is not an absolute, and a measure of unity may be necessary for certain political ends, even if it is only a temporary unity. We cannot easily dismiss the possibility that the desire for unity, when phrased through certain discourses, enables demands for inclusion even as it sets boundaries around who can and cannot be included. This is the position

Chantal Mouffe takes when she claims that discourses of democracy enable a productive antagonistic relationship in which that which is excluded continually emerges to make demands (1995:44). Full inclusion is always impossible, but the fact that inclusion forms the ethical terms on which politics is waged makes a difference.

The latter position suggests a dimension of innocence to calls for unity. To the extent that calls for unity can be separated from the terms on which unity is to be achieved, they may establish the terrain for infinite inclusion. This position, as I understand it, is the one that Laclau takes on the universal when he claims, "the fullness of society is an impossible object which—through its very impossibility—becomes thoroughly ethical" (Laclau 2000:84). For example, democracy may historically be deployed to reinforce a free-market agenda, but it may formally be associated with the proposition that "different forms of inequality" are "illegitimate and anti-natural" and thus constitute inequality as a form of oppression (Laclau and Mouffe 1985:155).

A different position on unity emerges, however, if we presume that calls for unity are themselves historical products associated with threads of exclusion that persist within the very fabric of any call for unity. In such a situation, calls for unity cannot be innocent, for such calls are always embedded in some play for power. What matters, then, is who or what is excluded by any given call for unity. For example, on the one hand, if those excluded by a call for unity are excluded by virtue of their opposition to widespread inclusion, then the promises of full inclusion may persist even as practical unity remains elusive. On the other hand, if the exclusions embedded in calls for unity are based on protecting an already existing distribution of resources, encompassing such intangibles as the legitimacy of a normative order, then the significance of calls for unity is a different matter. But is there really any way of determining which of these two possibilities is prevailing in any given situation? Is not it always the case that calls for unity are issued on the terrain of a habitus that renders some kinds of inclusions permanently unthinkable—in other words, that structural and historical forces conspire to constrain the terms on which unity is imagined? And is the ethic of full inclusion itself innocent of power? Certainly, the discourse of democracy in Tepoztlán in 1988 seemed to confer the status of a speaking subject on everyone, but it also compelled subjects to speak in a way that disciplined their gossip. At the same time, the discourse of democracy as a method for solving problems opened political participation to women and young people to a degree not contemplated previously by the ancianos' aesthetic of tradition. In short, it seems that each repetition of a call for unity is an opportunity for transformation, even if the vision of full inclusion is never achieved.

One problem with these attempts to theorize unity is that they fail to do justice to the ironic stance Tepoztecans have brought to all political engagement. Contemporary calls for unity remain bound up with the ironic performances of unity that I described in chapter 6 in which the PRI bussed in representatives of various sectors to display their loyalty. In a sense, all subsequent calls for unity repeat this demand for an ironic performance. The question, then, emerges, What would it mean to treat such calls for unity as comedic, rather than serious, and how then should one account for peripheral members' gossip?

Irony is generally theorized as an indication of a destabilizing critical distance, akin to the anthropologist's position on social life. There is no doubt that Tepoztecans cultivate a kind of critical distance toward the whole arena of political life. But when we theorize that critical distance, it is also important to hold onto the founding disappointment that informs that critical distance. However faulty Tepoztecans' memories of the past, their conviction that in the past the community was united is a reminder that social life does not have to be the way it is. Tepoztecans' skills in irony speak, therefore, not only to critical distance, but also to an angry investment in a different form of politics. Certainly, that investment is bound up in the desire for unity that draws Tepoztecans to social movements despite all the obstacles they face.

Interrogating that desire requires doing justice to the possibility that Tepoztecans are pulled into social movements for the sheer pleasure of participating in mass mobilizations. Kundera describes the Grand March as that which is left over after the possibility of really believing in Marxist grand narrative has collapsed, but the pleasures of imagining the world united in revolutionary struggle remain (1999:243–78). A form of leftist kitsch that relies on fantasies, images, and archetypes, the Grand March embraces pleasures that are not primarily cognitive or rational. These pleasures come from emotional investments in a pure image of a collective movement that wipes out the unacceptable. These pleasures are not antithetical to an ironic stance. Indeed, one might theorize the ironic stance as a kind of cognitive protection against the seductive pleasures of participating in the promise of the Grand March. I do not mean a functional relation, but rather that both the Grand March and the ironic stance are responses to unfulfilled desires. Indeed, if we want to make sense of Tepoztecans' continued return to the politics of loose connections, we need to attend not only to the weight of promises of unity, but also to the impossibility of believing in unity. In a sense, the weight of both dimensions of political life lends to political participation the kind of light-heartedness that Tepoztecans capture in their political humor. More so than the scholars who attempt to theorize social movements, Tepoztecans embrace the humorous dimensions of politics.

Political gossip and mistrust are as pervasive and as seductive within social movements as are calls for unity; they simply have not been theorized, grappled with, and attended to with nearly the care and concern directed at unity. Gossip and mistrust have been seen primarily as obstacles, not as ways of maintaining flexibility, as protections against unscrupulous leaders, and, most important, as a particular style of political participation. My argument is that, mesmerized by the promise of unity, we have lost sight of the fact that gossip and mistrust travel along the same surface as calls for unity, and they have their own effects on the political process. What Annette Weiner (1992) so wisely noted regarding the anthropological fascination with exchange might also be said of studies of social movements: so fascinated have we become with the promise of unity that we have lost sight of the fact that people spend considerable time strategizing how to hold back from unity.

Political Passion and the Politics of Identity

The politics of loose connections is not only about maintaining organizational flexibility, but also about a willingness to embrace identities that have strategic utility at a particular moment when issues of power and authority are at stake. As I have argued throughout this book, the terms in which Tepoztecans articulated their political visions—as campesinos, democratic citizens, and indigenous sustainable producers—emerged as new subjectivities linked to discourses produced at the national and global level. Even as Tepoztecans repeatedly attempted to represent their politics in opposition to the state, they borrowed the terms of political participation from the state and global levels. Although there certainly was strategic utility in keeping step with emerging political identities, I have suggested throughout this book that strategic utility alone fails to capture the passion with which Tepoztecans rallied around these new subjectivities. The emergence of new political identities enabled Tepoztecans to enliven the political imagination with promises of a transformed political actor: one less beholden to the image of all políticos as corrupt. Indeed, we might look at these emerging identities as a kaleidoscope of possibilities for imagining the political: with the emergence of new discourses, Tepoztecans began to see their political struggles in a new light. This adjustment meant that at any given moment they held onto claims to identity with a passion that suggested the essential importance of those claims, even if they later abandoned them to embrace with equal passion a different vision of identity.

As in the case with unity, identity needs to be understood in this tense interaction between the essentialist adoption of identity politics and the ironic willingness to drop identities that cease to be politically useful. Identity claims can be playful, disruptive, performative, and ironic at the same time that they are the deeply serious, historically sedimented foundation of political struggles. The difficulty emerges in trying to think of identity in both these senses at the same time: How can an identity be deeply meaningful and revealing of foundations for political struggles, but at the same time playful, performative, and ironic? Furthermore, is either of these senses of identity inherently more politically progressive than the other? Contemporary ethnography is replete with examples of anthropologists distancing themselves from the passion with which identity claims are made by asserting the playful nature of those claims. It seems that now that anthropologists appreciate the dilemmas of essentialism, they can better understand why those they study seem to associate themselves with practices and discourses that at first glance seem essentially conservative and perhaps racist, sexist, and homophobic: the people they study are engaged in play. In the figure of the informant, structurally placed to be disruptive, such practices and discourses destabilize the social order.

When it comes to social movements, the stakes are serious, and so too is the play of identity. Tepoztecan identity assertions are better seen as a form of undisciplined play rather than as the unfolding of a deep cultural logic through which we can link the various identity claims under which Tepoztecans have waged political struggles. But to see Tepoztecan identity claims as a form of play requires adopting a perspective on time that

Tepoztecans themselves did not use when they entered the political arena. The playfulness of Tepoztecan identity claims became apparent only when viewed over time. At any given moment in time, identity claims were serious, deeply passionate, and essentialist. In short, what Bourdieu notes for theory more generally is especially true of play: it depends on the notion of social life as a spectacle in which the theorist remains distant from investments in the action itself. This in no way suggests that the perspective gleaned from seeing identity as a form of play is inferior to those perspectives that emphasize identity's essentialist characteristics. Rather, the play of identity is revealed only within a framework that captures its antidisciplinary twists and turns by examining how identity claims play themselves out over time. At any moment in time, however, identity claims are anything but antidisciplinary. Indeed, as I have suggested throughout this book, every identity claim that Tepoztecans asserted was linked to disciplinary practices to which Tepoztecans became passionately attached.

The potency of identity politics lies not in its ability to be either playful or foundational, but rather in its superb sense of timing as reflected in an ability to "play" a moment in time. Kath Weston ends *Gender in Real Time* with the following prescription for those who want to transform gender relations:

> Want to get the jump on gender? Keep your hands up. Move those feet. You can't just trade punches with a fixed and recognizable opponent. You'll have to attend to everything that calls itself time and everything that refuses to call you. You'll have to circle, bend, step up, feint, give a hand, improvise, yield. Go with synchrony, asynchrony. Count, stop counting. Forget space plus time. Try spacetime. Think relations, not things. Think connections, not profits. Gotta dance. (2002:141)

Her prescription captures my sense of Tepoztecan politics as long as one realizes that such a nimble-footed dancer is not a pragmatic, strategic subject, but one whose quick footwork results from years of training that shape the body as much as, if not more than, the mind. What Tepoztecans know without knowing in any real sense is that political identity is always a form of bricolage in which the tools to carry out a political project are borrowed based on the situations at hand. Of course, one can always see such bricolage as a kind of imprisonment, but that view ignores the very real possibility that envisioning beyond bricolage may have to remain merely a desire; it also underestimates the possibilities of bricolage. Bricolage is only a form of imprisonment if we imagine the tools to carry out a project as fundamentally moored to some original utility whose persistent glow barely dims as the tools are redeployed in new contexts. The strategic utility of the politics of loose connections can be found in the space that it creates for nimble-footed bricoleurs who seize on the possibilities of the moment.

Epilogue

I went to protest against the golf course because I wanted to defend my pueblo, but I knew the leaders would be the only ones to benefit when it was over.
—Woman who had worked with the Comité para la Defensa de Tierra in 1984

I left Mexico for the last time before this book's completion on August 2, 2002, the day President Vicente Fox announced cancellation of plans to construct a new airport terminal on ejido land in San Salvador Atenco. For nearly a year, ejidatarios had refused to sell their land to the government, protesting repeatedly that although government negotiators kept raising the prices they offered for the land, the government failed to understand that peasants were unwilling to sell the land that fed their families. There are some things that even money cannot buy, explained the movement spokesperson, and one of them is land that is attached to a history, to a way of life, and to an identity. It took the loss of an ejidatario's life, the results of beatings delivered by the police in an altercation, to cancel the plans for airport expansion.

I knew that many Tepoztecans would be pleased with the outcome of the struggle in San Salvador Atenco. Some had attended marches and demonstrations in solidarity with the ejidatarios fighting the airport. Moreover, the battle against the airport bore an eerie resemblance to Tepoztecans' own struggles against a multi-million-dollar tourist project in 1995. The tourist project, financed in part by GTE, had included a golf course designed by a company owned by Jack Nicholaus. Tepoztecans had fought the project, concerned that the water demanded by the golf course and tourist resort would exacerbate existing water problems, and pesticides and chemical fertilizers used to maintain the course would damage the environment. Similar to the ejidatarios' battle in San Salvador Atenco, Tepoztecans had used the courts to delay the project with demands for further study, and they had gained international support for their battle from groups such as the Sierra Club and other environmental organizations. During the battle against the golf course and tourist complex, Tepoztecans went further than they ever had: they declared the municipality a free municipality (*municipio libre,* free of federal and state control), elected their own officials, and set up barricades to keep the police and military out. Barrios took turns guarding the pueblo, and public assemblies were used to make decisions. When a Tepoztecan in favor of the golf course was killed in an altercation, the government issued warrants for the arrests of several Tepoztecans and eventually imprisoned the Maestro Jorge and two others. The Maestro was charged with murder, despite the fact that there was no evidence that he had even been present the day the shooting took place. He served two years in prison while groups around the world appealed for his release. As in the situation with San Salvador Atenco, it was not until another Tepoztecan was killed during a protest march on April 10, 1996, the anniversary of Emiliano Zapata's birthday, that the multinational companies began to pull out from the project. The project was eventually halted, although a group of Tepoztecans continues to battle for the formal and legal return of the land to the community. In 2002, Tepoztecans had a verbal commitment from the government that the land would be returned to the community, but they were not given the kind of documentation that would enable them to take formal possession of the land. According to the Maestro Jorge, they planned to use the land to develop green spaces through reforestation and a community park.

The seeds for the struggle against the golf course and tourist center were planted through the various political battles I have described in this book. Tepoztecan organizers effectively used the courts, Mexico's ecological laws, and international pressure to increase the costs of development projects. They had done so with the train project, with the state's efforts to develop a prison in San Andrés, and, in the time before my arrival, with a gondola project. Indeed, Tepoztecans were at their best when confronted by these major threats to the community's future, as evidenced by their tenacity even in the face of threats to their own life. When the battle became most difficult, Tepoztecans reminded themselves of the past successes they had managed to achieve with unity. But how much unity had Tepoztecans achieved in the fight against what became known as a megatourist project? In more theoretical terms, had these earlier struggles contributed to an evolving unity whose import was realized in the battle against the golf course?

Even in 2002, Tepoztlán was full of reminders of the battle of 1995. Cartoon characterizations of the struggle against the golf course adorned the walls of the municipal building; one read, "pride is more valuable than a golf course." Tepoztecans have produced books of photographs documenting every stage of the struggle, including the hanging in effigy of those who are said to have betrayed the pueblo, including don Abram, then commissioner of the Oficina de Bienes Comunales. And there are pictures of masses of people in the streets and of the changing of the guard when one barrio replaced another to stand guard. Paradoxically, when in 2002 I asked people about this unity, few Tepoztecans, with the exception of the movement leaders, admitted to being part of the unity. As soon as I raised issues regarding the golf course, many seemed anxious to set the record straight regarding the alleged unity of this period. A man who had been an activist in the 1984 communal land struggle told me, "I went to the center; they even put me in charge of those they had taken hostage, but I went to do no more than watch—to see what was going on.[1] They asked me to go and talk to don Abram [to keep him from signing for the golf course], and I went, but I said nothing. I just watched because I knew he was under a lot of pressure." Another young woman complained that the battle against the golf course had divided families. She explained, "I like to know about these things, and I am very interested in what is happening in my pueblo, but I don't want to get involved because you never know why people are there. Some are there because they truly care about their pueblo and others because they want the land for themselves: that's why I don't get involved in these things."

The challenge for those committed to thinking critically about social movements is how to deal with both the narrative of unity and the narratives that contest that unity. One way to explain disunity is to point to government actions that made unity impossible. As María Rosas points out in her book *Tepoztlán: Crónica de desacatos y resistencia* (1997), the PRI was active in encouraging Tepoztecans to accept the golf course and tourist center, and certainly those close to the PRI within Tepoztlán openly supported the project. The project's financial backers successfully won the support of many in communities such as San Juan, where poverty rendered the prospect of jobs more seductive. The PRI went so far as to suggest that they would reward San Juan's support by switching the district seat from Tepoztlán to San Juan if the project were completed. Moreover, as Rosas also stresses, what began as a simple opposition to the tourist project became more complex with the passage of time and the maneuvering of the state: Should the free municipality be provisional or exist in perpetuity? How much time should the movement dedicate to freeing prisoners such as the Maestro Jorge, or should they continue to focus on the golf course and let the judicial process unfold? At each of these junctures, the PRI tried to make deals with the community that reinforced internal divisions in the movement. Clearly, Tepoztecans' organizing skills were matched by the state's ability to manipulate public opinion, but can the state's maneuvers account for all sources of disunity? Moreover, to attribute all sources of disunity to the state is to participate in the construction of the all-powerful state, an imaginary construction that, as I have suggested throughout this book, has served to dissuade people from joining social movements.

One source of disunity during the "golf wars," as many Tepoztecans refer to the struggle, was the changes in the Mexican state that came about with the shift to neoliberal economic policies. As I discussed in chapter 4, defense of communal land against the market economy was a central feature of Tepoztecan politics in 1984. Although Tepoztecans in the district seat had sold land illegally, often using borrowed names, the rising prices of private property had encouraged many of them to see communal land as central to preserving community. The notion of preserving a type of land tenure not open to the market economy, although slowly withering away, still found formal support in Mexican law. In 1992, President Salinas de Gortari declared an end to agrarian reform and made sales of communal land legal. Holders of communal land and buyers no longer had to disguise market transactions: they could register the sale of land, thereby transforming communal land into private property. In short, what previously had been, technically speaking, under the jurisdiction of the community became the province of individuals. There was, however, an incentive to keep land communal because communal land was not taxed, and many Tepoztecans told me in 1993 that they had no intention of privatizing their land because of the incumbent tax liabilities.

During the battle against the golf course, the issue of the market in communal land resurfaced with particular virulence. The land on which the golf course was to be built had been illegally purchased from individual comuneros in the late 1950s early 1960s. In September 1961, ejidal authorities (at the time in charge of communal land) had written to President López Mateos of their concerns. Asserting that the land was communal in accordance with the presidential resolution of 1929, they had complained that the land was being "invaded" for the purpose of constructing a development, hotel, or sports field. They had claimed the invasion obstructed the passage to the mountains, where campesinos took their animals for grazing and gathered fire wood. The then "owner" of the land had responded that he did not want trouble and that he merely intended to create a project that would benefit the people of Tepoztlán and the whole state of Morelos.[2] By 1973, the matter had reached a kind of resolution that bears an eerie resemblance to the situation today: the owner continued to hold the land but did nothing to build on it. He contracted with a Tepoztecan to take care of the land and for years rented it to campesinos for farming. The issue did not resurface until the golf course plans in 1995.

When Tepoztecans became aware of the plans for the golf course in 1995, the old issue of how to deal with sales of communal land reemerged, now with the added problem that sales of communal land were technically legal. As I discussed in chapter 5, the concept of communal land has, in some respects, been continually under assault. Because the land is distributed to individuals and inherited in families, many lose sight of the fact that they are holding communal land and not private property. In addition, despite the fact that the law allowed communities to refuse to recognize an illegal sale, Tepoztecans have been divided on how sales should be handled once land has been sold. Sales that involve transactions among Tepoztecans go unnoticed, but those that result in land passing into the hands of non-Tepoztecans draw more attention. The matter might be treated differently, especially in cases where the purchaser can provide a benefit for the pueblo in exchange for being able to keep the land.

The failure of unity in the golf wars was grounded partially in this tension between the market value of land and its place in the community. Many Tepoztecans believed that if the golf course were indeed to have pernicious effects on the community, the fault would lie with Tepoztecans who had chosen to sell their land. As one man explained, "It is not those who buy the land who are to blame—it is ourselves who sell the land that have caused these problems." Some Tepoztecans expressed dismay at the prospect that the descendants of those who had sold the land might reclaim their rights to the land, as communal property, and the person who had paid for the land would lose his investment. For many, the community's right to defend its own land above and beyond individual community members' interests was senseless. Speaking the language of individual responsibility, they argued that Tepoztecans could protect their land only through the medium of individual decision making with responsibility to the collective. Of course, these were not new debates, and some even in 1984 had taken a similar perspective on communal land.

This view was not only at odds with Agrarian Reform Law in effect at the time of the purchase of the land, but also seemingly at odds with the government's attempts, however facile, to gain comunero support for the project. Indeed, state and developer arguments in favor of the project centered on the benefits it would provide to the Tepoztlán municipality, in terms of job opportunities, and on the positive impacts of golf courses on the environment. Nonetheless, some Tepoztecans argued that the prior sales of the land were irreversible, thus speaking more directly and honestly to tensions that are a product of the history of the Mexican state.

As I mentioned in chapter 2, the Mexican state has always been structured around a rather uneasy combination of capitalism and communal rights and responsibilities. Although embracing capitalism, the state has also sought to protect certain areas from market forces. The existence of communal land tenure is one manifestation of that protection, but so too are government subsides of food crops, support for education, and so on. Since the 1980s, Mexico, similar to other nations in Latin America, has been adopting a neoliberal agenda that flies in the face of the contradictory form of the Mexican state by making it increasingly difficult to sustain spaces that resist market forces.[3] Within Mexico, there is at present a battle over *hegemony*, if by that term we understand a struggle to capture the practices of everyday life in the web of a market logic. That struggle is countered not by a single language of refusal, but by a variety of challenges to market hegemony, including ecological concerns, the renewal and recovery of indigenous knowledge, democracy, and so on. Indeed, although in 1995 some Tepoztecans adopted the logic of the land market in opposition to those trying to defeat the golf course, those in the movement seemed to focus not on the status of the land as communal, but on the project's ecological impacts on water resources in the area. I return to this point later, but for now I would argue that the shift to an emphasis on ecological impacts, although resisting the tourist project, also suggested that Tepoztecans themselves accepted the land's market value.

If the lack of unity in the golf wars intersected with hegemonic struggles at the national level, it is also true that at the community level these national struggles intersected with kinship relations. As I discussed in chapter 5, Tepoztecans' suspicions of the political arena were reinforced by the fact that individual members of the same family often participated in different political groups. This happened both for strategic reasons and as a result of individual family members' different life trajectories, but the result was that the family became a site where mistrust of the political arena was continually reinforced as gossip about different political leaders came together. In the case of the golf course, stories of unity are contradicted by the reality that many families found themselves internally divided if not over the issue, then over the tactics some people used. One man, a long-time activist in the fight to protect communal land, was dismayed when activists opposed to the golf course destroyed his son's truck and burned his property. The son had been working in the municipal offices when then-mayor Alejandro Morales was said to have supported the golf course. The man explained that when the activists attacked his son, he felt like they showed their lack of gratitude for all the work he had done over the years to protect communal land. "Now," he explained, "I don't even go to these things because I don't know if I am wanted or what people think about the way I have lived my life." Another woman complained that two of her aunts had not talked for three years after the golf wars because they found themselves on opposite sides: one aunt was married to someone who supported the golf course and the other was an activist against the course.

Many families avoided these kinds of divisions by coveting a position on the periphery of political movements. An old friend, once a member of the Comité para la Defensa de Tierra, in response to my question of whether or not she had become involved in the golf course struggle, explained that she went "para apoyar ellos" (to support them), but she kept her distance. Although she did not want the golf course and thought it should be fought, she remained convinced that at the end of the day those who led the movement would benefit from the struggle, and the rest would be left behind. As I have stressed throughout this book, taking a position at the periphery of social movements enables one to protect one's reputation as being disinterested in personal political benefits while demonstrating one's commitment to community.

In the early 1950s, Oscar Lewis noted that in Tepoztlán "Successful persons are popular targets of criticism, envy, and malicious gossip" ([1951] 1972:294). This remains true today, especially as it relates to political figures. In the years after the golf wars, those who served in leadership roles have been monitored with special attention for evidence that they have somehow benefited from their leadership positions. For example, after leaving prison, the Maestro Jorge was given a high position in the teachers' union and managed to add three rooms to his home, with private bathrooms, to be rented out to weekend tourists. The son of another activist was now working in the municipal offices. These examples were pointed to as evidence that political leaders, despite their contentious relationships with the government and private developers, somehow ended up profiting personally from their organizing activities.

Although it certainly may be true that the initial days of the struggle against the golf course reflected a spirit of *communitas*, it also seems clear that the patterns of the politics of loose connections persisted even in the face of apparent unity. Yet the victory against the golf course represented a substantial increase in the community's power in actions against multinational capital, a fact whose import has not been lost on even average Tepoztecans. Today, Tepoztecans take pride that they control their future and that the community is actively involved in shaping that future.

There is more to the story, however. Although Tepoztecans have defeated a number of projects that herald the expansion of global capitalism, the district seat seems to have come to accept its status as a tourist site. Many have embraced the market value of tradition and have refashioned themselves and their lives into tourist commodities. Stores now market the traditional medicine that previously could be obtained only through personal ties with curanderas; houses are being painted in traditional Mexican colors, as designated by the municipal offices, and on my most recent visit Tepoztecan workers were carefully flattening the rough edges of the cobblestone streets to better accommodate cars. Several Tepoztecans have opened bed-and-breakfast establishments, and restaurants throughout the town serve hamburgers, hotdogs, and pizza. These commodities are not just for tourist consumption, for Tepoztecans themselves have come to enjoy the fresh fruit yogurt drinks and the french fries for sale every night in the center of town. On my latest visit, many children begged me to take them for pizza at one of the local pizza restaurants.

Despite the fact that several of the new businesses are owned by individuals not from Tepoztlán, Tepoztecan-owned businesses are not uncommon. Large global chains such as McDonald's and Pizza Hut have not yet tried to open in Tepoztlán, and, with memories of the golf course struggle still fresh, many Tepoztecans are confident they can and will prevent such franchises from entering the town. The argument against such franchises is that they do not fit with the culture of the town, but one also suspects that the issue is who gets to benefit from tourist dollars. Adjusting the kaleidoscope of identity, Tepoztecans are beginning to reflect on their food as "slow food," capturing the movement that originated in France and Italy to fight large American food chains. To place the golf course struggle in a new light, most Tepoztecans would prefer to rent out rooms in their homes to better capture tourist dollars than carry tourist luggage for a multinational hotel.

Although the point may seem obvious, the fight against the golf course was neither antimarket nor anticapitalist. Indeed, one might argue that the market value of the town measured in tourist dollars substantially shapes Tepoztecan subjectivity. Tepoztecans point to the presence of tourists as evidence of the town's beauty, its unique archaeological value, and the worth of its customs and traditions. My own continual returns to the town seem, to Tepoztecans, indications that I, too, have been captivated by the magic of the town's beauty. Although many Tepoztecans complain about the tourists—there are simply too many of them—they also legitimate their experience of their town through the lens of tourist approval.

This attitude places Tepoztecans in a precarious position with regard to the forces of globalization. Jameson points to a kind of fundamental tension or antagonism between the particular and the universal at the heart of globalization, "in which each term struggles to define itself against the binary other" (1998:54). Although Jameson's categories may be useful in thinking about the kinds of tensions and antagonism that exist in globalization, they can also lead to dichotomies that obscure the kinds of processes happening in Tepoztlán. As Appadurai (1996) stresses, the local and particular come into being in and through processes of globalization not only in a philosophical sense, but also in very practical ways. Tepoztecan attempts to position themselves against the homogenizing forces of globalization, at one level, is at another level entirely consistent with globalization. Tepoztecans have become very aware of their place in the larger context of globalization, whether it be in terms of the community's attractiveness for tourism or their persistent enunciation of political struggles in ways that capture global media attention. In short, to read Tepoztecan struggles as fundamentally against globalization is to overlook Tepoztlán's own attractions to the global in its various manifestations: the tourist market, global commodity consumption, and NGOs' political potential. Tepoztecans do not forsake the particular to embrace the universal; rather, they enter the universal arena from the same positions of tense unity I have described throughout this book.

None of this should be taken to suggest Tepoztecan movements have failed. Such a conclusion would imply that which I have resisted throughout this book: namely, that we can define a single origin for Tepoztecan social movements that would provide a space of pure contestation. Tepoztecans have long been quite savvy about power, recognizing full well that its dynamics cannot be captured in either/or propositions. Local/global dichotomies do little to capture the complexity of their political strategies.

Recognizing that Tepoztecan social movements cannot be encompassed in a globalization/localization dichotomy does not put the matter to rest, however. Even the limited ways in which Tepoztecans have embraced the market economy have had expected repercussions for inequality within the community. On my most recent visit, I marveled that my hosts had enough water even in the dry months of the summer that I could take a daily shower. At first, I failed to interrogate their simple, "Ya, no hay problemas de aqua aqui" (there are no water problems now), assuming that something had been done in Tepoztlán to resolve the long-standing problem of water. Much later I learned that the family had installed a cistern on their roof that was large enough to capture enough water for the family to support its needs for several weeks. The town's water problem had not been resolved. Indeed, inequities in water distribution had been magnified by those Tepoztecans who had access to foreign dollars, as is the case with the family I have just described.

One of the ironies of Tepoztlán's class structure is that the offspring of the traditionalists who held onto land, claiming that it was the pueblo's patrimony, now make up the emerging professional class. In many cases, traditionalist parents now hold land that their offspring do not need or want because they have professional jobs in the city. Some continue to hold onto the land, but others have started to sell it. In other cases, traditionalists have sold land to support their children while they were attending the university, thereby converting the market value of their land into a long-term career.

Unfortunately, a large percentage of Tepoztecans have neither land nor education. For these people, migration to the United States has become a central feature of a family's life cycle. For the most part, it is still men who migrate, leaving behind spouses and young children while they attempt to earn the dollars that will enable them to return and build a house. Indeed, for those at the bottom of the economic ladder, the men's migration to the United States, however difficult, is a critical stage in the family's life cycle. It is the mechanism that allows men to reproduce their roles in the family even in difficult economic times. As one woman explained, her husband had gone to the United States to work in a restaurant because, although she had a career as a secretary, he did not want to depend on her income. They wanted to build a house, and they hoped the money he earned in the United States would enable them to do so.

In short, although Tepoztecans have challenged control of the tourist industry by large multinational capital, they continue to embrace forms of capitalism that allow inequalities to flourish and that force them to calculate the value of their town as a commodity. Of course, the kind of capitalism flourishing in Tepoztlán differs from that which would prevail if Tepoztecans were day laborers working in hotels. Labor relations are submerged within kinship systems, and much of the labor that keeps bed-and-breakfast establishments flourishing is unpaid family labor.

In the final analysis, Tepoztecans have never been able to unite in opposition to either capitalism or globalization, but then it is not clear that they have ever sought such a singular moment of refusal. Instead, their attitude toward both mirrors the politics of loose connections: Tepoztecans have embraced aspects of globalization and capitalism, all the while trying to hold back. The town's history of defense of communal land, however invented or imagined, represents such a move, as does its current limited, yet strategic embrace of globalization. As I have argued throughout this book, to suggest that either the politics of loose connections or the response to globalization is strategic is not to suggest that these approaches result from strategic intention. Like the politics of loose connections, Tepoztecans have remained flexible and adaptive in their responses to the forces of global capital.

Notes

Chapter 1. The Politics of Loose Connections

1. In the early 1980s, seemingly "new" forms of protest commanded the attention of the media, scholars, and the general public. Protest groups that operated with a flexible organizational structure based on rotating leaders, a consensus process of decision making, and dispersed chapters that often set their own agendas seemed to dominate the landscape of protest. Media-captivating direct actions around specific and sometimes local issues dominated organizing. Above all else, they aimed to preserve their autonomy from institutionalized modes of political participation (Fals Borda 1987). Moreover, they crafted identities that spoke to the common issues that drew them together, at times across the divisive lines of race, gender, and class. As a result, new categories of persons emerged, such as "mothers," "environmentalists," "gays," "peace activists," and so on.

2. For example, Edelman questions assumptions that "new social movements" are not class based, asserting that Costa Rican peasant movements coalesced in response to the material forces of economic collapse and drew on deeply rooted peasant identities (1999:20). Despite his argument for the continuing importance of "material forces," however, the unity he describes in his ethnography maintains a loose quality (1999:118).

3. Brunk (1996) provides more recent support for Warman's description in his own examination of Zapatista banditry, in which he argues for the need to take multiplicity into account.

4. In his book *Exit, Voice, and Loyalty* (1970), Albert Hirschman examines the role of "exits" and voice in social organizations. He views both exits (leaving an organization to join another or to become a nonmember) and voice (expressing opposition while remaining in an organization) as ways of correcting organizational decline. Although he associates "exits" with the market or economic sphere and "voice" with a nonmarket or political sphere, his point is to show that both mechanisms operate in either sphere and that neither in isolation is sufficient to correct organizational decline. The value of Hirschman's work is that it takes expressions of discontent, whether in terms of exits or voice, as useful correctives to organizational decline.

5. Appadurai (1996:33) initiated the treatment of this type of question by focusing on the disjunctures between what he labels five dimensions of globalization: ethnoscapes, mediascapes, technoscapes, financescapes, and ideoscapes. His argument that these different dimensions of globalization are marked by disjuncture helped to break up the conception of globalization as a phenomenon subordinated to economic concerns.

6. The first Golden Age would be the 1920s and 1930s, which culminated in the election of Lázaro Cárdenas as president (Moguel 1994:169). For an excellent case study of these movements, see Craig 1983.

7. An exception is Juchitán, Oaxaca, where the radical COCEI won the municipal elections in 1981, making it the only leftist government in Mexico; there the state responded by investing heavily in Juchitán (Rubin 1997:180). The government still found exceptional circumstances in which it used social spending to weaken opposition movements.

8. Translations of all quotations from people I talked to in Tepoztlán in the course of my research are mine.

Chapter 2. The Place of the Communal in the Geography of Time

1. Lomnitz-Adler (1992) defines regions as a product of interactions in political economic spaces that can be demarcated. Although his argument outlines the processes whereby regionalism is produced through social interactions, I take regional identities to be imaginative projects shaped by and through images of a diverse nation. My approach emerges from my concern with how changes in the national imagination affect regional identities.

2. The negotiation of tensions between the economic, political, and legal production of mixture and the desire to maintain distinctions between populations on the basis of race made the process of subordinating the colonized far more complex than simple capitalist expansion. Tutino argues, "During the colonial era, Mexican elites were rarely able to use powers of the state in the role of simple and direct agents of class interest against the peasantry" (1987:238). This remained true certainly up until the 1700s, when missionaries and scholars of jurisprudence fought vigorously to defend the indigenous population against the various means the colonists and the Crown used to exploit their labor.

3. It is important to note that "the" colonial project in New Spain was an early one in colonialist history and perhaps reflects the elevated status of religion prior to the Enlightenment. Indeed, as William Taylor argues in *Magistrates of the Sacred* (1996), religion played a very different role in the late colonial period than it did in early colonialism. Among the shifts Taylor notes is the declining role of the mendicant orders and the corresponding increase in the role of secular clergy, whom the Crown found to be more easily controlled. Moreover, the Franciscans' lofty vision for the indigenous population was replaced by a more generalized view of Indians as lazy (Taylor 1996:173). As the Crown became more concerned with production, the clergy's role shifted as well. In the late colonial period, the notion of religious leaders as protectors of the indigenous population was replaced with the idea of priests as

teachers of proper morality, enforcers of rational settlement patterns, and police of sexual mores. Indeed, it was in this era that the colonialists began to distinguish non-Indians as *gente de razón*, reasonable people, from Indians, who were believed to respond more with passions and emotions (Taylor 1996:176). As Taylor notes, "In the pale light of Spain's Enlightenment, especially from the 1770s on, the emphasis [on separation and protection] was reversed: Indians needed to be civilized and incorporated, their rationality nurtured" (176). In the post-Enlightenment world, colonial religion in New Spain perhaps came to serve more as a handmaiden to economic enterprises—congruent with many contemporary works on colonialism—than it did in the early colonial period.

4. Influenced by Boas, Gamio proposed the use of cultural traits rather than biological ones to define Indian identity. His ideas breathed new energy into popular arts in Mexico and especially into textiles—an energy that inspired the famous Mexican muralist Diego Rivera (Brading 1988:273). More important for the present work, Gamio attacked the liberal reforms of 1856, which put an end to communal land tenure, as foreign in "origin, form and essence" (quoted in Brading 1988:274). Drawing on Montesquieu's ideas of the grounding of laws in the nature and needs of the populations, Gamio defended restoration of communal land to the Yaqui in the North and the Maya of Quintana Roo, and found in Zapata's cry for land and liberty an element of legitimacy and "Indianismo" (as summarized in Brading 1988:274).

5. Although Tepoztecan rights to claim communal land can technically be questioned as a result of Salinas de Gortari's dismantling of the Agrarian Reform Law in 1992, Tepoztecans continue to speak of and act as though communal land still exists. The government's actions in the battle against the golf course seems to provide support for this view in that government officials courted the representatives of communal land as part of their strategy to quell opposition to the project.

6. The *repartimiento* system provided a means for distributing Indian labor to the colonialists after 1549. Under the repartimiento system, Indians were required to provide labor purportedly for the public interest, which was often broadly defined to include work on plantations and in mines.

7. Under Carlos Salinas de Gortari, attempts were made to disengage community-development money from politics, but as I discuss in chapter 7, a clear separation was impossible.

Chapter 3. Political Passion and the Troubled Mexican State

1. The Agrarian Reform Law required five years of residence, but many communities tried to deny rights to land to anyone whose family history did not include several generations in the community. In Tepoztlán, if the requested land was in a colonia, one had to demonstrate the support of future neighbors. In Tepoztlán, most colonias are established on what was previously agricultural or ranching land or mountain. The term *colonia* might be roughly translated as "squatter settlement," and the term *squatters* invokes an image of poor and homeless migrants settling illegally on the land. This was the origin of some colonias, but even Tepoztlán's

wealthier residents established colonias when they were unable to purchase private property in the center of town.

2. This emphasis on the state's power to govern the distribution of land so disturbed Emiliano Zapata that he rejected many offers from would-be allies who failed to understand the centrality of community control to the Zapatista agenda (see Brunk 1995 and Womack 1968).

3. Here I use the Spanish term *político* rather than its English translation *politician* to underscore the specific sets of meanings associated with the term in Mexico. In Mexico, a político is one who exploits social demands to garner political position, financial rewards, and the expansion of networks for himself or herself. Políticos' careers usually begin when the politicos emerge as leaders of social movements, but in the process of negotiating with the state they become incorporated into the political system. Políticos come to play a major role both in mobilizing and demobilizing popular discontent in a way that ultimately reinforces the hegemony of the Mexican state (see Friedrich 1986).

4. Collier offers an alternative, less-static framework for understanding the Mexican state, arguing that the history of the state should be seen through the lens of "critical junctures," which is a "model of discontinuous or punctuated political change and emphasizes the importance of historical watershed . . . when new political structures and institutions are established" (1992:2).

5. I once talked with don Abram's employer and was shocked to discover her impression of this man whom I had observed drafting letters to the country's president, processing difficult cases in the Oficina de Bienes Comunales, and explaining the complexities of Mexico's Agrarian Reform Law both to me and to peasants. His employer began by telling me how stupid he was and how much she worried about him because he spent so much time in "that office"; she was sure they were just taking advantage of him. She acknowledged that he had once taken her and her husband to the labor union, but that was the only time they ever had any of those kinds of problems with him. She expressed concern about his vegetarian diet because she thought he was not getting enough protein. "We offer him meals all the time, but he refuses them," she complained. Ironically, during the course of my research, I shared several meals with don Abram because I so enjoyed the variety of beans and fresh vegetables, produced on his own land without pesticides. At the end of our lengthy conversation, she assured me that because don Abram's work was so bad, they would have fired him except for the fact that they knew he was only a poor peasant and totally dependent on their income.

6. Although the tales of the Maestro Jorge's brother are widely known in Tepoztlán and were told to me, this information comes from data I collected in the municipal archives.

Chapter 4. The Crafting of an Aesthetic of Tradition

1. Sierra (1992) finds a similar category of political leaders in indigenous communities in the Mezquital Valley. They are talked about as those who value "como era antes" (how things were).

2. For a discussion of the use of the term *class* to describe relations of inequality in Mexico, see Wasserstrom 1976, Hewett de Alcántara 1984, Bartra 1986:286, Spalding 1988, and Schryer 1990:33. My use of the term *class* in this chapter differs from these researchers' uses because their primary interest is in finding the economic concomitants of class and, by extension, the peasantry's revolutionary potential. As Laclau and Mouffe (1985:94) point out, the problem with this approach is that each class is seen to have a paradigmatic class ideology, and ideological struggles are conceptualized as taking place between two completely closed systems. In an effort to avoid such economic reductionism, I underscore the semiotic dimension of class, emphasizing the discourse of rich and poor as a form of material praxis used by prominent members of the Comité para la Defensa de Tierra to link the history of problematic relations between rich and poor to a larger political project. As Ulin notes, the shaping of culture and human consciousness can be seen as a form of material praxis (1984:76). Such a perspective challenges the conventional material / ideal split, which tends to represent ideology as a superstructure to an economic base.

3. In the early 1950s, Lewis developed a classification scheme to measure differences in wealth among Tepoztecans ([1951] 1972:174). His wealthiest group (4.4 percent of total inhabitants) were people who controlled large amounts of land or cattle or both. These people employed workers but usually worked alongside of their peons. His second wealthiest group (13.9 percent of total inhabitants) included merchants and better-off farmers. His poorest group (81.5 percent of total inhabitants) melded together the landless, who made up 70 percent of the total of this group, with people who owned some land (the remaining 30 percent). Such a survey would have been impossible to conduct in Tepoztlán in the 1980s. Indeed, I observed many attempts to carry out such surveys and tried myself several times, but Tepoztecans are suspicious of surveys and often make up data to get rid of nosy researchers. Nonetheless, Lewis's data accord with the way Tepoztecans seemed to carve up their world in the 1980s. Here I am suggesting that it is the small faction of land-owning poor who emerged as the political elites in battles with the rich and who shaped the discursive categories deployed in these struggles.

4. Schryer notes that in the region of Huejutla, members of the village elite suffered far more serious attacks from poor peasants than did wealthy absentee landlords. In an argument similar to mine, he suggests that these insider elites were no longer viewed as "good" community members (1990:231).

5. It is important to note that the inequalities that inform relations between ancianos and their followers differ from those described by Lagos (1994) for rural Bolivia. In the case studied by Lagos, the ties of fictive kinship link peasant producers to a regional merchant class. Lagos carefully documents the use of these ties to extract surplus labor. Her description—"both merchants and the peasantry make use of cultural idioms of community, fictive kin, and reciprocity; both groups collude in their acceptance of these unequal relations, which, in their disguised forms, may appear as equal and reciprocal" (1994:103)—may well characterize power inequalities between rich and poor in Tepoztlán. We must, however, understand relations between ancianos and their followers through different terms because the former remain marginal to the market economy.

6. This division of members into a core and a periphery speaks to the peculiar nature of power within the committee and within other similar groups. Although which members are core and which are periphery can change over time, Azaola Garrida (1976) and Sierra (1992) note similar divisions in local-level Mexican politics.

Chapter 5. Communal Passions and the Politics of Loose Connections

Sections of this chapter were published previously in "Motherhood and Power: The Production of a Women's Culture of Politics in a Mexican Community," *American Ethnologist* 17 (1990): 400–490. I thank *American Ethnologist* for allowing me to use portions of that article in this chapter.

1. "Poner la aspine encima" has a double meaning that is relevant to Mexican politics. *La espina* literally is a thorn, but figuratively it can also mean a suspicion. In a world in which suspicion is inherent in political practice, to take something to a higher authority is both to try to motivate that person to act and to suspect him or her of corruption. In the case of Colonia Manantial, both aspects of *la espina* were in play.

2. Bartra (1989) describes a system of "matriotismo": thousands of small, rural, conservative communities, where the people make their living from agriculture and crafts. These communities are ruled by a single, powerful cacique. Bartra has borrowed the term *matriotismo* from Luis González (1987), but in distinction to the latter's use of the term Bartra emphasizes the affinity between the authoritarian, centralized state and matriotismo. I did not carry out systematic research in the subject communities that make up the district of Tepoztlán, so it would be presumptuous for me to argue that these communities are characterized by matriotismo. However, such a characterization fits well with the description of many of the less politically active communities that I heard about from informants in the Comité para la Defensa de Tierra.

3. For a discussion of the Western concept of community and its problematic association with similarity, see Young 1990.

4. Lewis suggests that the market in land in Tepoztlán expanded after 1942 ([1951] 1972:125), although it is not clear whether he is speaking of the district seat or the whole municipality.

5. To be sure, the gossip of peripheral members is not effective against leaders who are more concerned with political careers than with forming movements, but it is the latter that concerns me in this book. The dilemma these groups face is that there are a variety of mechanisms for incorporating themselves into the state, including the possibility that they can serve their constituents much better with state resources and support.

Chapter 6. Democracy's Disciplines

1. At the national level, the ACNR eventually joined with the Cárdenas movement (see Bruhn 1997:319), but internal struggles between those who wanted to maintain

a revolutionary posture and those who joined Cárdenas remained vibrant even throughout the election period.

2. I have placed the word *class* in quotation marks to highlight the differences between my semiotic use of the term and the use in Marxist theory.

3. In the late 1990s, scholars began to discuss the utility of forms of democratic speech, termed *deliberative democracy*, for the resolution of contentious issues within a divided polity (see Benhabib 1996; Gutmann and Thompson 1996; Macedo 1999; Smelser and Alexander 1999; Young 2000). Young describes deliberative democracy as "a means of collective problem-solving which depends for its legitimacy and wisdom on the expression and criticism of the diverse opinions of all the members of the society" (2000:6).

4. The methods that the Coordinadora employed in 1988 drew on Paulo Freire's notions of *concienzación*, which he outlines in his book *Pedagogy of the Oppressed* (1993). Friere's work seeks to empower the poor by acknowledging the validity of their insights: "Critical and liberating dialogue, which presupposes action, must be carried on with the oppressed at whatever stage of their struggle for liberation. . . . [T]o substitute monologue, slogans, and communiqués for dialogue is to attempt to liberate the oppressed with the instrument of domestication. Attempting to liberate the oppressed without their reflective participation in the act of liberation is to treat them as objects which must be saved from a burning building; it is to lead them into the populist pitfall and transform them into masses which can be manipulated" (47).

Chapter 7. Transnational Politics and the Imaginary of Sustainable Development

1. These anxieties cannot be disconnected from the preference many foreign capitalists have shown for hiring female workers.

2. Kearney (1991) argues that the focus on ethnicity as a mode of definition reflects a more general process of identity formation in a transnational world. He argues that migrants seize on ethnicity as a way of asserting boundaries in the increasingly unbounded global economy. Likewise, Gupta and Ferguson (1992) assert that multiculturalism reflects cultures that have lost their moorings in place.

3. Nash (1995) points out that the assertion of indigenous identity can have different senses in different places. She finds that in highland Chiapas those with connections to the PRI deploy indigenous identity in an attempt to safeguard their control of dwindling economic resources, in a manner reminiscent of the Mujeres Tepoztecans' use of indigenous identity. She notes that settlers in the Lacandón jungle, in contrast, have deployed indigenous identity in relation to a project of building on a class solidarity emerging out of shared poverty. Although Nash is quite correct in pointing out that indigenous identity does not automatically imply distance from the structures of state power or immunity to its ability to co-opt social movements, class solidarity and poverty also lend themselves to the norms of cultural intelligibility that govern structures of state power in Mexico. As I have suggested throughout this book, the category of "need" has been a double-edged sword in

Mexico, being used by both activists and the paternalistic state to underwrite practices of co-optation.

4. David Harvey notes that the universality of spatial domination has led to a renewed emphasis on place, but he suggests that this emphasis is largely a matter of image (1990:90–98). Thus, he argues, "The projection of a definite image of place blessed with certain qualities, the organization of spectacle and theatricality, have been achieved through an eclectic mix of styles, historical quotation, ornamentation and the diversification of surfaces" (92–93). Although aspects of his argument apply to Tepoztecans' reenvisioning of their place, Harvey seems to overlook the fact that the attention to surface appearance can rest on a long history of unique experiences of place. There may be both a theatrical representation of place presided over by practices of spatial domination and a reinscription of already existing notions of place into a new language of spatial domination. I would argue that Tepoztecans' deployment of the universal languages of environmental protection represented both theatrics and a deep sense of intimacy with a particular place. Both had become central to the workings of global politics.

Epilogue

1. At one point in the struggle, Tepoztecans took hostage two government officials and a local PRI representative, someone I had known well in 1984.

2. Archivo Nacional, Sala 3 Exp. 404.1 7169, Mexico City.

3. I use the term *resist market forces* to stress that communal land has long been tied to a market economy and so cannot be viewed as a space of nonmarket relations. As the fight over the golf course suggests, however, the concept of communal land invites the interrogation of the limits of market forces.

Bibliography

Abu-Lughod, Lila. 1993. *Writing Women's Worlds: Bedouin Stories.* Berkeley: University of California Press.

Agar, Michael. 1980. *The Professional Stranger.* New York: Academic Press.

Alonso, Ana María. 1995. *Thread of Blood: Colonialism, Revolution, and Gender on Mexico's Northern Frontier.* Tucson: University of Arizona Press.

Althusser, Louis. 1970. "Contradiction and Overdetermination." In *For Marx*, translated by Ben Brewster, 87–128. New York: Vintage.

Alvarez, Sonia E., Evelina Dagnino, and Arturo Escobar, eds. 1998. *Cultures of Politics, Politics of Culture: Re-visioning Latin American Social Movements.* Boulder, Colo.: Westview Press.

Anderson, Benedict. 1983. *Imagined Communities: Reflections on the Origin and Spread of Nationalism.* London: Verso and New Left.

Anzaldúa, Gloria. 1987. *Borderlands, La Frontera: The New Mestiza.* San Francisco: aunt lute.

Appadurai, Arjun. 1996. *Modernity at Large: Cultural Dimensions of Globalization.* Minneapolis: University of Minnesota Press.

Arce, Alberto, and Norman Long. 2000. "Reconfiguring Modernity and Development from an Anthropological Perspective." In *Anthropology, Development, and Modernities*, edited by Alberto Arce and Norman Long, 1–31. New York: Routledge.

Azaola Garrida, Elena. 1976. *Política y conflicto.* Tlalpan, Mexico: Centro de Investigaciones Superiores, Instituto Nacional de Antropología y Historia.

Bailey, John. 1994. "Centralism and Political Change in Mexico: The Case of National Solidarity." In *Transforming State-Society Relations in Mexico: The National Solidarity Strategy*, edited by Wayne A. Cornelius, Ann L. Craig, and Jonathan Fox, 97–122. San Diego: Center for U.S.–Mexican Studies, University of California.

Barkin, David. 1990. *Distorted Development: Mexico in the World Economy.* Boulder, Colo.: Westview Press.

Bartra, Roger. 1986. "Capitalism and the Peasantry in Mexico." In *Modern Mexico: State, Economy, and Social Conflict,* edited by Nora Hamilton and Timothy F. Harding, 286–99. London: Sage.

———. 1989. "La crisis del nacionalismo en México." *Revista Mexicana de Sociología* 51, no. 3: 191–220.

———. 1992. *The Imaginary Networks of Political Power*. New Brunswick, N.J.: Rutgers University Press.

Basanez, M. 1981. *La lucha por la hegemonía en México, 1968–1980*. Mexico City: Siglo Veintiuno.

Baudot, Georges. 1995. *Utopia and History in Mexico: The First Chroniclers of Mexican Civilization (1520–1569)*. Niwot: University Press of Colorado.

Bazant, Jan S. 1979. *A Concise History of Mexico from Hidalgo to Córdenas 1805–1940*. Cambridge: Cambridge University Press.

Behar, Ruth. 1987. "Sex and Sin, Witchcraft and the Devil in Late Colonial Mexico." *American Anthropologist* 14:35–55.

———. 1993. *Translated Woman: Crossing the Border with Esperanza's Story*. Boston: Beacon Press.

Beltrán, Gonzalo Aguirre. 1991. *Regiones de refugio: El desarrollo de la comunidad y el proceso dominical en mestizoamérica*. Mexico City: Fondo de Cultural Económico.

Benería, Lourdes, and Martha Roldan. 1987. *The Crossroads of Class and Gender: Industrial Homework, Subcontracting, and Household Dynamics in Mexico City*. Chicago: University of Chicago Press.

Benhabib, Seyla. 1996. *Democracy and Difference: Contesting the Boundaries of the Political*. Princeton, N.J.: Princeton University Press.

Bennett, Vivienne. 1992. "The Evolution of Urban Popular Movements in Mexico Between 1968 and 1988." In *The Making of Social Movements in Latin America: Identity, Strategy, and Democracy*, edited by Arturo Escobar and Sonia E. Alvarez, 240–59. Boulder, Colo.: Westview Press.

Berthold-Bond, Daniel. 1997. "Hegel and Marx on Nature and Ecology." *Journal of Philosophical Research* 22:145–79.

Bhabha, Homi K. 1994. *The Location of Culture*. New York: Routledge.

Bonfil Batalla, Guillermo. [1987] 1996. *México profundo: Reclaiming a Civilization*. Translated by Philip A. Dennis. Austin: University of Texas Press.

Borah, Woodrow. 1983. *Justice by Insurance: The General Indian Court of Colonial Mexico and the Legal Aides of the Half-Real*. Berkeley: University of California Press.

Bottomore, T. B. 1964. *Karl Marx: Early Writings*. New York: McGraw-Hill Edition.

Bourdieu, Pierre. 1984. *Distinction: A Social Critique of the Judgment of Taste*. Translated by Richard Nice. Cambridge, Mass.: Harvard University Press.

———. 1990. *The Logic of Practice*. Stanford, Calif.: Stanford University Press.

Brading, D. A. 1988. "Liberal Patriotism and the Mexican Reforma." *Journal of Latin American Studies* 20, no. 1: 27–48.

Brown, Wendy. 1995. *State of Injury: Power and Freedom in Late Modernity*. Princeton, N.J.: Princeton University Press.

Bruhn, Kathleen. 1997. *Taking on Goliath: The Emergence of a New Left Party and the Struggle for Democracy in Mexico*. University Park: Pennsylvania State University Press.

Brunk, Samuel. 1995. *Emiliano Zapata, Revolution, and Betrayal in Mexico*. Albuquerque: University of New Mexico Press.

———. 1996. "The Sad Situation of Civilians and Soldiers: The Banditry of Zapatismo in the Mexican Revolution." *American Historical Review* 101:331–53.

Burdick, John. 1993. *Looking for God in Brazil: The Progressive Catholic Church in Urban Brazil's Religious Arena.* Berkeley: University of California Press.

Butler, Judith. 1999. *Gender Trouble: Feminism and the Subversion of Identity.* New York: Routledge.

Camus, Albert. 1955. *The Myth of Sisyphus, and Other Essays.* Translated by Justin O'Brien. New York: Vintage.

Casanova, Pablo Gonzalez. 1970. *Democracy in Mexico.* London: Oxford University Press.

Certeau, Michel de. 1984. "Story Time." In *The Practice of Everyday Life*, translated by Steven Randall, 77–90. Berkeley: University of California Press.

———. 1988. *The Writing of History.* Translated by Tom Conley. New York: Columbia University Press.

Chatterjee, Piya. 2001. *A Time for Tea: Women, Labor, and Post-Colonial Politics on an Indian Plantation.* Durham, N.C.: Duke University Press.

Cline, S. L. 1984. "Land Tenure and Land Inheritance in Late Sixteenth Century Culhuacan." In *Explorations in Ethnohistory: Indians in Central Mexico in the Sixteenth Century,* edited by H. R. Harvey and Hanns J. Brem, 277–309. Albuquerque: University of New Mexico Press.

Cockcroft, James D. 1968. *Intellectual Precursors of the Mexican Revolution, 1900–1913.* Austin: University of Texas Press.

———. 1983. *Mexico: Class Formation, Capital Accumulation, and the State.* New York: Monthly Review Press.

Collier, Ruth Berins. 1992. *The Contradictory Alliance: State-Labor Relations and Regime Change in Mexico.* Berkeley: International and Area Studies at the University of California, Berkeley.

Conklin, Beth A., and Laura R. Graham. 1995. "The Shifting Middle Ground: Amazonian Indians and Eco-Politics." *American Anthropologist* 97, no. 4: 695–710.

Cornelius, Wayne A., Ann L. Craig, and Jonathan Fox. 1994. "Mexico's National Solidarity Program: An Overview." In *Transforming State-Society Relations in Mexico: The National Solidarity Strategy,* edited by Wayne A. Cornelius, Ann L. Craig, and Jonathan Fox, 3–26. San Diego: Center for U.S.–Mexican Studies, University of California.

Coronil, Fernando. 1997. *The Magical State: Nature, Money, and Modernity in Venezuela.* Chicago: University of Chicago Press.

Craig, Ann L. 1983. *The First Agraristas.* Berkeley: University of California Press.

Cross, Andrew. 1998. "Neither Either nor Or: The Perils of Reflexive Irony." In *The Cambridge Companion to Kierkegaard,* edited by Alistair Hannay and Gordon D. Marino, 125–53. Cambridge: Cambridge University Press.

DaMatta, Roberto. 1991. *Carnivals, Rogues, and Heroes: An Interpretation of the Brazilian Dilemma.* South Bend, Ind.: University of Notre Dame Press.

Davidson, Carlos. 2000. "Economic Growth and the Environment: Alternatives to the Limits Paradigm." *BioScience* 50, no. 5: 433–40.

De la Peña, Guillermo. 1981. *A Legacy of Promises: Agriculture, Politics, and Ritual in the Morelos Highlands of Mexico.* Austin: University of Texas Press.

Deluze, Gilles, and Félix Guattari. 1983. *Anti-Oedipus: Capitalism and Schizophrenia.* Minneapolis: University of Minnesota Press.

Díaz-Barriga, Miguel. 1996. "*Necesidad* Notes on the Discourses of Urban Politics in the Ajusco Foothills of Mexico City." *American Ethnologist* 23, no. 2: 291–310.

———. 1998. "Beyond the Domestic and the Public: *Colonas* Participation in Urban Movements in Mexico City." In *Cultures of Politics, Politics of Culture: Re-visioning Latin American Social Movements,* edited by Sonia E. Alvarez, Evelina Dagnino, and Arturo Escobar, 252–77. Boulder, Colo.: Westview Press.

Duara, Prasenjit. 1995. *Rescuing History from the Nation: Questioning Narratives of Modern China.* Chicago: University of Chicago Press.

Eckstein, Susan. 1989. *Power and Popular Protest: Latin American Social Movements.* Berkeley: University of California Press.

Edelman, Marc. 1999. *Peasant Against Globalization: Rural Social Movements in Costa Rica.* Stanford, Calif.: Stanford University Press.

Escobar, Arturo. 1995. *Encountering Development: The Making and Unmaking of the Third World.* Princeton, N.J.: Princeton University Press.

Fals-Borda, Orlando. 1987. "The Application of Participatory Action Research in Latin America." *International Sociology* 4:329–47.

Favret-Saada, Jeanne. 1980. *Deadly Words: Witchcraft in the Bocage.* Cambridge: Cambridge University Press.

Fernandez, James W. 1990. "Enclosures: Boundary Maintenance and Its Representations over Time in Asturian Mountain Villages (Spain)." In *Culture Through Time: Anthropological Approaches,* edited by Emiko Ohnuki-Tierney, 94–127. Stanford, Calif.: Stanford University Press.

Fernandez, James W., and Mary Taylor Huber, eds. 2001. *Irony in Action: Anthropology, Practice, and Moral Imagination.* Chicago: University of Chicago Press.

Fisher, William H. 1994. "Megadevelopment, Environmentalism, and Resistance: The Institutional Context of Kayap Indigenous Politics in Central Brazil." *Human Organization* 53, no. 3: 220–32.

Florescano, Enrique. 1994. *Memory, Myth, and Time in Mexico: From the Aztecs to Independence.* Austin: University of Texas Press.

Foster, George. 1965. "Peasant Society and the Image of Limited Good." *American Anthropologist* 67, no. 2: 293–315.

Foucault, Michel. 1979. *Discipline and Punish: The Birth of the Prison.* Translated by Alan Sheridan. New York: Vintage.

———. 1990. *The History of Sexuality.* Vol. 1, *An Introduction.* Translated by Robert Hurley. New York: Vintage.

Foweraker, Joe. 1990. "Popular Movements and Political Change in Mexico." In *Popular Movements and Political Change in Mexico,* edited by Joe Foweraker and Ann L. Craig, 3–20. Boulder, Colo.: Lynne Rienner.

Freire, Paulo. 1993. *Pedagogy of the Oppressed.* New York: Continuum.

Friedlander, Judith. 1975. *Being Indian in Hueyapan: A Study of Forced Identity in Contemporary Mexico.* New York: St. Martin's Press.

Friedrich, Paul. 1986. *The Princes of Naranja: An Essay in Anthrohistorical Method.* Austin: University of Texas Press.

———. 2001. "Ironic Irony." In *Irony in Action: Anthropology, Practice, and Moral Imagination*, edited by James W. Fernandez and Mary Taylor Huber, 224–52. Chicago: University of Chicago Press.

Gamio, Manuel. [1916] 1960. *Forjando patria*. Mexico City: Editorial Porrua, S.A.

García Canclini, Néstor. 1995. *Hybrid Cultures: Strategies for Entering and Leaving Modernity*. Minneapolis: University of Minnesota Press.

Garofoli, Joe, and Jim Herron Zamora. 2003. "S.F. Police Play Catch-Up." *San Francisco Chronicle*, March 21.

Gates, Marilyn. 1988. "Codifying Marginality: The Evolution of Mexican Agricultural Policy and Its Imposition on the Peasantry." *Journal of Latin American Studies* 10:277–311.

Geertz, Clifford. 1973. *The Interpretation of Cultures: Selected Essays by Clifford Geertz*. New York: Basic.

Gershberg, Alec Ian. 1994. "Distributing Resources in the Education Sector: Solidarity's Escuela Digna Program." In *Transforming State-Society Relations in Mexico: The National Solidarity Strategy*, edited by Wayne A. Cornelius, Ann L. Craig, and Jonathan Fox, 233–53. San Diego: Center for U.S.–Mexican Studies, University of California.

Godelier, Maurice. 1999. *The Enigma of the Gift*. Chicago: University of Chicago Press.

González, Luis. 1987. "Suave Matria." *Nexos* 108:51–59.

González Tiburcio, Enrique. 1994. "Social Reform in Mexico: Six Theses on National Solidarity Program." In *Transforming State-Society Relations in Mexico: The National Solidarity Strategy*, edited by Wayne A. Cornelius, Ann L. Craig, and Jonathan Fox, 63–78. San Diego: Center for U.S.–Mexican Studies, University of California.

Goodman, Bryna. 1995. "The Locality as Microcosm of the Nation? Native Place Networks and Early Urban Nationalism in China." *Modern China* 21, no. 4: 387–419.

Gupta, A., and J. Ferguson. 1992. "Regional Cultures: Space, Identity, and the Politics of Difference." *Cultural Anthropology* 7, no. 1: 6–23.

Gutmann, Amy, and Dennis Thompson. 1996. *Democracy and Disagreement: Why Moral Conflict Cannot Be Avoided in Politics and What Should Be Done about It*. Cambridge, Mass.: Harvard University Press.

Haber, Paul Thomas. 1994. "Political Change in Durango: The Role of National Solidarity." In *Transforming State-Society Relations in Mexico: The National Solidarity Strategy*, edited by Wayne A. Cornelius, Ann L. Craig, and Jonathan Fox, 255–80. San Diego: Center for U.S.–Mexican Studies, University of California.

Hamilton, Nora. 1982. *The Limits of State Autonomy: Post-revolutionary Mexico*. Princeton, N.J.: Princeton University Press.

Hardt, Michael, and Antonio Negri. 2000. *Empire*. Cambridge, Mass.: Harvard University Press.

Harvey, David. 1990. *The Condition of Postmodernity: An Enquiry into the Origins of Cultural Change*. Cambridge, Mass.: Blackwell.

Harvey, H. R. 1984. "Aspects of Land Tenure in Ancient Mexico." In *Explorations in Ethnohistory: Indians of Central Mexico in the Sixteenth Century*, edited by H. R. Harvey and Hanns J. Prem, 83–102. Albuquerque: University of New Mexico Press.

Harvey, Neil. 1990. "Peasant Struggles and Corporatism in Chiapas." In *Popular Move-*

ments and Political Change in Mexico, edited by Joe Foweraker and Ann L. Craig, 183–98. Boulder, Colo.: Lynne Rienner.

———. 1999. *The Chiapas Rebellion: The Struggle for Land and Democracy.* Durham, N.C.: Duke University Press.

Hebdige, Dick. 1997. "Subculture: The Meaning of Style." In *The Subcultures Reader*, edited by Ken Gelder and Sarah Thornton, 130–44. New York: Routledge.

Hellman, Judith Adler. 1978. *Mexico in Crisis.* New York: Holmes and Meier.

———. 1992. "The Study of New Social Movements in Latin America and the Question of Autonomy." In *The Making of Social Movements in Latin America: Identity, Strategy, and Democracy*, edited by Arturo Escobar and Sonia E. Alvarez, 52–61. Boulder, Colo.: Westview Press.

Herzfeld, Michael. 2001. "Irony and Power: Toward a Politics of Mockery in Greece." In *Irony in Action: Anthropology, Practice, and Moral Imagination*, edited by James W. Fernandez and Mary Taylor Huber, 63–83. Chicago: University of Chicago Press.

Hewett de Alcántara, Cynthia. 1984. *Anthropological Perspectives on Rural Mexico.* London: Routledge and Kegan Paul.

Hindley, Jane. 1999. "Indigenous Mobilization, Development, and Democratization in Gerrero: The Nahua People vs. the Tetelcingo Dam." In *Subnational Politics and Democratization in Mexico*, edited by Wayne A. Cornelius, Todd A. Eisenstadt, and Jane Hindley, 207–38. San Diego: Center for U.S.–Mexican Studies, University of California.

Hirschman, Albert. 1970. *Exit, Voice, and Loyalty: Responses to Decline in Firms, Organizations, and States.* Cambridge, Mass.: Harvard University Press.

Ingham, John M. 1986. *Mary, Michael, and Lucifer: Folk Catholicism in Central Mexico.* Austin: University of Texas Press.

Ingold, Tim. 1993. "Globes and Spheres: The Topology of Environmentalism." In *Environmentalism: The View from Anthropology*, edited by Kay Milton, 31–42. New York: Routledge.

Jameson, Fredric. 1998. "Notes on Globalization as a Philosophic Issue." In *The Cultures of Globalization*, edited by Fredric Jameson and Masao Miyoshi, 54–80. Durham, N.C.: Duke University Press.

Katz, Friedrich. 1983. *The Secret War in Mexico: Europe, the United States, and the Mexican Revolution.* Chicago: University of Chicago Press.

Kearney, Michael M. 1991. "Borders and Boundaries of State and Self at the End of Empire." *Journal of Historical Sociology* 4, no. 1: 52–74.

———. 1996. *Reconceptualizing the Peasantry: Anthropology in Global Perspective.* Boulder, Colo.: Westview Press.

Klein, Naomi. 2000. "The Vision Thing: Were the DC and Seattle Protests Unfocused, or Are Critics Missing the Point?" *The Nation* 271, no. 2: 18–21.

Knight, Alan. 1990. "Racism, Revolution, and *Indigenismo:* Mexico 1910–1940." In *The Idea of Race in Latin America, 1870–1940*, edited by Richard Graham, 71–114. Austin: University of Texas Press.

———. 1994. "Solidarity: Historical Continuities and Contemporary Implications." In *Transforming State-Society Relations in Mexico: The National Solidarity Strategy*, edited by Wayne A. Cornelius, Ann L. Craig, and Jonathan Fox, 29–46. San Diego: Center for U.S.–Mexican Studies, University of California.

Kundera, Milan. 1999. *The Unbearable Lightness of Being.* New York: Perennial Classics.

Laclau, Ernesto. 2000. "Identity and Hegemony: The Role of Universality in the Constitution of Political Logics." In *Contingency, Hegemony, Universality: Contemporary Dialogues on the Left,* by Judith Butler, Ernesto Laclau, and Slavoj Žižek, 44–89. New York: Verso.

Laclau, Ernesto, and Chantal Mouffe. 1985. *Hegemony and Socialist Strategy: Towards a Radical Democratic Politics.* Translated by Paul Cammack and Winston Moore. London: Verso.

Lafaye, Jacques. 1976. *Quetzalcóatl and Guadalupe: The Formation of Mexican National Consciousness.* Chicago: University of Chicago Press.

Lagos, Maria L. 1994. *Autonomy and Power: The Dynamics of Class and Culture in Rural Bolivia.* Philadelphia: University of Pennsylvania Press.

Lancaster, Roger. 1992. *Life Is Hard: Machismo, Danger, and the Intimacy of Power in Nicaragua.* Berkeley: University of California Press.

Lewis, Oscar. [1951] 1972. *Life in a Mexican Village: Tepoztlán Restudied.* Urbana: University of Illinois Press.

Ley federal de la reforma agraria, reformada. 3rd ed. 1984. Compiled by Lic. José Carlos Guerra Aquilera. Mexico City: Editorial Pac.

Limón, José E. 1998. *American Encounters: Greater Mexico and the United States and the Erotics of Culture.* Boston: Beacon Press.

Lockhart, James. 1992. *The Nahuas after the Conquest: A Social and Cultural History of the Indians of Central Mexico, Sixteenth Through Eighteenth Centuries.* Stanford, Calif.: Stanford University Press.

Lomnitz, Larissa. 1982. "Horizontal and Vertical Relations and the Social Structure of Urban Mexico." *Latin American Research Review* 17, no. 2: 51–74.

Lomnitz, Larissa, and Claudio Lomnitz-Adler. 1988. *El fondo de la forma: Actos publicos de la campaña presidencial del Partido Revolucionario Institucional México, 1988.* Working Paper no. 135. Notre Dame, Ind.: Kellogg Institute for International Relations.

Lomnitz-Adler, Claudio. 1982. *Evolución de una sociedad rural.* Mexico City: Fondo de Cultura Económica.

——. 1992. *Exits from the Labyrinth: Culture and Ideology in the Mexican National Space.* Berkeley: University of California Press.

——. 1996. "Fissures in Contemporary Mexican Nationalism." *Public Culture* 9:55–68.

Lorde, Audre. 1994. "The Master's Tools Will Never Dismantle the Master's House." In *The Woman Question,* edited by Mary Evans, 369–73. Thousand Oaks, Calif.: Sage Press.

Lugones, Maria. 1997. "Playfulness, 'World'-Travelling, and Loving Perception." In *Feminist Social Thought: A Reader,* edited by Diana T. Meyers, 147–59. New York: Routledge.

Lustig, Nora. 1992. *Mexico: The Remaking of an Economy.* Washington, D.C.: Brookings Institute.

——. 1994. "Solidarity as a Strategy of Poverty Alleviation." In *Transforming State-*

Society Relations in Mexico: The National Solidarity Strategy, edited by Wayne A. Cornelius, Ann L. Craig, and Jonathan Fox, 79–96. San Diego: Center for U.S.– Mexican Studies, University of California.

Macedo, Stephen, ed. 1999. *Deliberative Politics: Essays on Democracy and Disagreement.* New York: Oxford University Press.

Mallon, Florencia C. 1994. "Exploring the Origins of Democratic Patriarchy in Mexico: Gender and Popular Resistance in the Puebla Highlands, 1850–1876." In *Women of the Mexican Countryside, 1850–1990,* edited by Heather Fowler-Salamini and Mary Kay Vaughan, 3–26. Tucson: University of Arizona Press.

———. 1995. *Peasant and Nation: The Making of Postcolonial Mexico and Peru.* Berkeley: University of California Press.

Martin, JoAnn. 1987. "Against the State: The Delegitimation of Opposition in Mexico." Ph.D. diss., University of California, Berkeley.

———. 1990. "Motherhood and Power: The Production of a Women's Culture of Politics in a Mexican Community." *American Ethnologist* 17:400–490.

———. 1992. "When the People Were Strong and United: Stories of the Past and the Transformation of Politics in a Mexican Community." In *The Paths to Domination, Resistance, and Terror,* edited by Carolyn Nordstrom and JoAnn Martin, 177–89. Berkeley: University of California Press.

———. 1993. "Contesting Authenticity: Battles over the Representation of History in Morelos, Mexico." *Ethnohistory* 40, no. 3: 438–65.

———. 1995. "From Revolution to Modernization: Discursive Disruptions in State / Peasant Relations in Morelos, Mexico." *Socialist Review* 3–4:83–112.

Melucci, Alberto. 1996. *Challenging Codes: Collective Action in the Information Age.* Cambridge: Cambridge University Press.

Mercer, Kobena. 1997. "Black Hair / Style Politics." In *The Subcultures Reader,* edited by Ken Gelder and Sarah Thornton, 420–35. New York: Routledge.

Middlebrook, Kevin J. 1995. *The Paradox of Revolution: Labor, the State, and Authoritarianism in Mexico.* Baltimore: Johns Hopkins University Press.

Mignolo, Walter D. 2000. *Local Histories / Global Designs: Coloniality, Subaltern Knowledges, and Border Thinking.* Princeton, N.J.: Princeton University Press.

Miller, Robert Ryal. 1985. *Mexico: A History.* Norman: University of Oklahoma Press.

Moguel, Julio. 1994. "The Mexican Left and the Social Program of Salinismo." In *Transforming State-Society Relations in Mexico: The National Solidarity Strategy,* edited by Wayne A. Cornelius, Ann L. Craig, and Jonathan Fox, 167–76. San Diego: Center for U.S.–Mexican Studies, University of California.

Molinar Horcasitas, Juan, and Jeffrey A. Weldon. 1994. "Electoral Determinants and Consequences of National Solidarity." In *Transforming State-Society Relations in Mexico: The National Solidarity Strategy,* edited by Wayne A. Cornelius, Ann L. Craig, and Jonathan Fox, 123–42. San Diego: Center for U.S.–Mexican Studies, University of California.

Moses, Robert, and Charles Cobb Jr. 2001. *Radical Equations: Math Literacy and Civil Rights.* Boston: Beacon Press.

Mouffe, Chantal. 1995. "Democratic Politics and the Question of Identity." In *The Identity in Question,* edited by John Rajchman, 33–45. New York: Routledge.

Mudimbe, V. Y. 1988. *The Invention of Africa: Gnosis, Philosophy, and the Order of Knowledge.* Bloomington: Indiana University Press.

Nader, Laura. 1969. "Styles of Court Procedure: To Make the Balance." In *Law in Culture and Society,* edited by Laura Nader, 69–91. Chicago: Aldine.

———. 1990. *Harmony Ideology: Justice and Control in a Zapotec Mountain Village.* Stanford, Calif.: Stanford University Press.

Nash, June C. 1995. "The Reassertion of Indigenous Identity: Mayan Responses to State Intervention in Chiapas." *Latin American Research Review* 30, no. 3: 7–41.

Nelson, Diane. 1999. *A Finger in the Wound: Body Politics in Quincentennial Guatemala.* Berkeley: University of California Press.

O'Malley, Ilene. 1986. *The Myth of the Revolution: Hero Cults and the Institutionalization of the Mexican State, 1920–1940.* Westport, Conn.: Greenwood Press.

Pagden, Anthony. 1986. *The Fall of Natural Man: The American Indian and the Origins of Comparative Ethnology.* New York: Cambridge University Press.

———. 1998. "Dispossessing the Barbarian: The Language of Spanish Thomism and the Debate over the Property Rights of the American Indians." In *Theories of Empire: 1450–1800,* edited by David Armitage, 159–78. Brookfield, Vt.: Ashgate.

Parkin, D. 1995. "Latticed Knowledge: Eradication and Dispersal of the Unpalatable in Islam, Medicine, and Anthropological Theory." In *Counterworks: Managing the Diversity of Knowledge,* edited by R. Fardon, 143–63. New York: Routledge.

Parnell, Philip C. 1988. *Escalating Disputes: Social Participation and Change in the Oaxacan Highlands.* Tucson: University of Arizona Press.

———. 1992. "Time and Irony in Manila Squatter Movements." In *The Paths to Domination, Resistance, and Terror,* edited by Carolyn Nordstrom and JoAnn Martin, 154–76. Berkeley: University of California Press.

Paz, Octavio. 1961. *The Labyrinth of Solitude: Life and Thought in Mexico.* Translated by Lysander Kemp. New York: Grove Press.

Pérez Arce, Francisco. 1990. "The Enduring Union Struggle for Legality and Democracy." In *Popular Movements and Political Change in Mexico,* edited by Joe Foweraker and Ann L. Craig, 105–20. Boulder, Colo.: Lynne Rienner.

Rabinow, Paul. 1977. *Reflections on Fieldwork in Morocco.* Berkeley: University of California Press.

Ramírez Saiz, Juan Manuel. 1990. "Urban Struggles and Their Political Consequences." In *Popular Movements and Political Change in Mexico,* edited by Joe Foweraker and Ann L. Craig, 234–46. Boulder, Colo.: Lynne Rienner.

Rosas, María. 1997. *Tepoztlán: Crónica de desacatos y resistencia.* Mexico City: Ediciónes Era.

Rubin, Jeffrey W. 1997. *Decentering the Regime: Ethnicity, Radicalism, and Democracy in Juchitán, Mexico.* Durham, N.C.: Duke University Press.

Sanderson, S. R. W. 1984. *Land Reform in Mexico.* New York: Academic Press.

Schryer, Frans. 1990. *Ethnicity and Class Conflict in Rural Mexico.* Princeton, N.J.: Princeton University Press.

Sierra, María Teresa. 1992. *Discurso, cultura y poder: Ejercicio de la autoridad en las pueblos hnahnus del Valle de Mezquital.* Hidalgo, Mexico: Gobierno del Estado, Archivo General del Estado, Centro de Investigaciones y Estudios Superiores en Antropología Social.

Smelser, Neil, and Jeffrey Alexander. 1999. *Diversity and Its Discontents: Cultural Conflict and Common Ground in Contemporary American Society.* Princeton, N.J.: Princeton University Press.

Soja, Edward W. 1989. *Postmodern Geographies: The Reassertion of Space in Critical Social Theory.* London: Verso.

Sotelo Inclán, Jesús. 1943. *Raíz y razón de Zapata.* Mexico City: Editorial Etnos.

Spalding, Rose. 1988. "Peasants, Politics, and Change in Rural Mexico." *Latin American Research Review* 23, no. 1: 207–19.

Stephen, Lynn. 1991. *Zapotec Women.* Austin: University of Texas Press.

———. 1997. *Women and Social Movements in Latin America: Power from Below.* Austin: University of Texas Press.

Stephens, Julie. 1998. *Anti-disciplinary Protest: Sixties Radicalism and Postmodernism.* Cambridge: Cambridge University Press.

Stoler, Ann Laura. 2002. *Carnal Knowledge and Imperial Power: Race and the Intimate in Colonial Rule.* Berkeley: University of California Press.

Tamayo, Jaime. 1990. "'Neoliberalism' Encounters *Neocardenismo.*" In *Popular Movements and Political Change in Mexico,* edited by Joe Foweraker and Ann L. Craig, 121–36. Boulder, Colo.: Lynne Rienner.

Taussig, Michael. 1980. *The Devil and Commodity Fetishism in South America.* Chapel Hill: University of North Carolina Press.

Tavera-Fenollosa, Ligia. 1999. "The Movimiento de Damnificados: Democratic Transformation of Citizenry and Government in Mexico City." In *Subnational Politics and Democratization in Mexico,* edited by Wayne A. Cornelius, Todd A. Eisenstadt, and Jane Hindley, 107–32. San Diego: Center for U.S.–Mexican Studies, University of California.

Taylor, William. 1996. *Magistrates of the Sacred: Priests and Parishioners in Eighteenth-Century Mexico.* Stanford, Calif.: Stanford University Press.

Torgovnick, Marianna. 1990. *Gone Primitive: Savage Intellects, Modern Lives.* Chicago: University of Chicago Press.

Torres, Gabriel. 1999. "The El Barzón Debtors' Movement: From the Local to the National in Protest Politics." In *Subnational Politics and Democratization in Mexico,* edited by Wayne A. Cornelius, Todd A. Eisenstadt, and Jane Hindley, 133–52. San Diego: Center for U.S.–Mexican Studies, University of California.

Touraine, Alaine. 1981. *The Voice and the Eye: An Analysis of Social Movements.* Cambridge: Cambridge University Press.

Trinh, T. Minh-Ha. 1989. *Woman, Native, Other: Writing Postcoloniality and Feminism.* Bloomington: Indiana University Press.

Tutino, John. 1987. "Peasants and Politics in Nineteenth Century Mexico." *Latin American Research Review* 22, no. 3: 237–43.

Ulin, Robert C. 1984. *Understanding Cultures: Perspectives in Anthropology and Social Theory.* Malden, Mass.: Blackwell.

Varela, Roberto. 1984. *Expansión de sistemas y relaciones de poder.* Unidad Iztapalapa, Mexico: Universidad Autónoma Metropolitana.

Vaughan, Mary Kay. 1997. *Cultural Politics in the Revolution: Teachers, Peasants, and Schools in Mexico, 1930–1940.* Tucson: University of Arizona Press.

Vélez-Ibañez, C. G. 1983. *Rituals of Marginality: Politics, Process, and Culture Change in Urban Central Mexico.* Berkeley: University of California Press.

Vigil, Ralph H. 1987. *Alonso de Zorita: Royal Judge and Christian Humanist, 1512–1585.* Norman: University of Oklahoma Press.

Visweswaran, Kamala. 1994. *Fictions of Feminist Ethnography.* Minneapolis: University of Minnesota Press.

Warman, Arturo. 1980. *We Come to Object: The Peasants of Morelos and the National State.* Translated by Stephen K. Ault. Baltimore: Johns Hopkins University Press.

Warren, Kay. 1998. *Indigenous Movements and Their Critics: Pan-Maya Activism in Guatemala.* Princeton, N.J.: Princeton University Press.

Wasserstrom, Robert. 1976. "La investigación regional en ciencias sociales: Una perspectiva chiapaneca." *Historia y Sociedad* 9:58–78.

———. 1983. *Class and Society in Central Chiapas.* Berkeley: University of California Press.

Weiner, Annette B. 1992. *Inalienable Possessions: The Paradox of Keeping While Giving.* Berkeley: University of California Press.

Weismantel, Mary. 2001. *Cholas and Pishtacos: Stories of Race and Sex in the Andes.* Chicago: Chicago University Press.

Weston, Kath. 2002. *Gender in Real Time: Power and Transience in a Visual Age.* New York: Routledge.

Wolf, Eric R. 1959. *Sons of the Shaking Earth: The People of Mexico and Guatemala—Their Land, History, and Culture.* Chicago: University of Chicago Press.

Womack, John, Jr. 1968. *Zapata and the Mexican Revolution.* Boston: Vintage.

Young, Iris Marion. 1990. "The Ideal of Community and the Politics of Difference." In *Feminism/Postmodernism,* edited by Linda J. Nicholson, 300–323. New York: Routledge.

———. 2000. *Inclusion and Democracy.* Oxford: Oxford University Press.

Zorita, Alonso de. 1963. *Breve y sumaria relación de los señores de la Nueva España.* Mexico City: Universidad Nacional Autónoma de México.

Index

Abram, don, 91, 187, 234; battle against housing development project for outsiders, 81–82; boundary disputes and, 146; Colonia Manantial and, 138, 141, 142; communal land and, 199; Coordinadora and, 172; death of daughter, 80–81, 98; at ecological group meeting, 200; family of, 80–82, 193; had no heirs for his land, 193; as *indio*, 210; life history, 79–84; as "outsider," 81; passion for agrarian concerns, 85; positions in Oficina de Bienes Comunales, 81, 84, 113, 115, 123, 192–93, 200; religious beliefs of, 83–84; risking his life, 135; Rolando and, 134–35; Rubino and, 132; stories of the past, 204; work as gardener, 83, 246n. 5
abuse of power, 71, 223; in communities, 89. *See also* corruption; power
ACNR, 248n. 1
activism, 5
activists, 15; in rural areas, 8; student, 7–8
aesthetic(s): of communal land, 207; conflicts between different, 116; of tradition: *see* traditionalist aesthetic
agrarian reform, 235; in Morelos, 33
Agrarian Reform Law, 46, 54–57, 163, 237, 245n. 1; ambiguous place of communal land in, 145; colonial roots of,

57–66; and the committee, 118; and "community," 76; community corruption and, 77, 133; Consejo de Vigilancia and, 134; families, women, and, 74; modifications of, 69; and obligation to *vigilar*, 132; Oficina de Bienes Comunales and, 134; peripheral members and, 133; representations of state-community relations in, and institutionalized practices, 67–74, 76; treated communal and ejido land the same, 145
agrarian reform movement of Zapata, 33
agriculturalistas (farmers) vs. *campesinos* (peasants), 109
alcohol intoxication, 170–71
alterity, geography of, 35
Althusser, Louis, ix
ancianos: in Comité para la Defensa de Tierra, 97, 121, 162, 169–70
ancianos (elders), 26, 103, 111, 117, 118, 180; crafting aesthetic of tradition, 182; in ecological movement, 204; power amassed by lending land, 101–2, 106–8; relations with followers, 247n. 5; wisdom, 180
Anderson, Benedict, 33–34, 96
Anenecuilco, 51, 53
antagonism, 103

colonial project in New Spain, 244–45n. 3

Colonia Manantial, 138–42

colonias, 75, 116, 245–46n. 1. *See also* squatter settlements

Comisiones Agrarias Mixtas (Mixed Agrarian Commissions), 70–71

Comité para la Defensa de Tierra (Committee to Defend Communal Land), 86, 108, 115–17, 170; agrarian reform and, 118, 119; ancianos in, 97, 121, 162, 169–70 (*see also* Pedro); author as *gente de confianza* to, 90; author's participation in, xii, 16–21, 117, 124, 192; Colonia Manantial and, 138–40; conflicts within, 120; confrontations with the state, 69; Consejos de Vigilancia and, 113, 128; corruption and, 69, 117, 125; corruption in, 71, 90; discourse of need and, 150–51; disputes with colonias and, 116; expansion into Coordinadora Democrática, 25, 156, 159, 172, 204; fears in carrying out work of, 136; formation of, 16, 91; functioning of, 115–16, 124; gossip about, 116, 133; Haber's study of, 28; indigenous people and, 206; meetings of, 18–21, 118, 120, 122–24, 169–70; members/participants, 115–17, 122, 123, 128, 132–33, 152–53; name change, 25; Oficina de Bienes Comunales and, 113, 116, 117, 145, 155–56; peripheral members of, 125, 150, 162, 212 (*see also* peripheral members of groups); politics of loose connections within, 154; PRI and, 163; religious organizations and, 167; women and, 76

Comité para la Defensa Popular (CDP, Committee for Popular Defense), 12

commissioners: of communal/ejido resources, 73; ejido, 81, 82; relations between consejos and, 73

"committee," 128. *See also* Comité para la Defensa de Tierra

communal, the: place in the geography of time, 30–49

communal control as insurance policy for indigenous population, 63

communal land, 16–18, 25; boundaries between private property and, 154–55; concepts of self and community interwoven around defending, 63; defense of, 98, 101, 113, 120, 141, 235 (*see also* Comité para la Defensa de Tierra); demands on, 31, 113–15, 154–55; in the discourse of nationalism, 49–57; expanding market in, 235; forces converging around, 113–14; given to outsiders, 31, 53, 113–14; history of, 31–32, 75; and identity, 155 (*see also* group identity; identity); most serious threat to security of, 142; now available only to the rich, 31; rights to claim, 245n. 5; sales of, 232–37; shifting of defense from Agrarian Reform Law to ecological laws, 218; as symbol of community autonomy, 60–61; threats to, posed by wealthy foreigners, 76; as women's issue, 75

communal land struggle of 1984, 234

communal land tenure, 57, 58

communal rights and responsibilities, 235

community, communities (*comunidades*), 16–17; ambiguities in the discourse of, 144; definitions and meanings of, 145; inequality within, 241; involvement with state, 88; lack of boundaries between state and, 92, 94; land given to, 76; members of, 66; rights and privileges of, 70; as subordinate to and dependent on the state, 76

community boundaries. *See* boundaries

community-level relations between different bodies, 72–73

community rights, 93

community unity, 77, 94, 145. *See also* unity

compadrazgo (fictive kin), 83

comuneros, 73, 74, 112–13, 236

concienzación, 249n. 4

Confederación de Trabajadores Mexicanos (CTM, Confederation of Mexican Workers), 79, 83

Confederación Nacional Campesina (CNC, Confederation of Mexican Peasants), 8, 78

confessional practices, 171

confidential friendship, 89–91

conflict resolution, 4

Conquest, 35, 36, 59. *See also* colonialism

consciousness raising, 171–72

Consejos de Vigilancia (Watchdog Committees), 71–73, 112–13, 128, 132, 133; fear in members of, 133–34

conservatives, 39

Constitutional Convention, 55, 56

Constitution of 1917, 87, 93; Article 27, 56

constructionists, 210

consumption patterns, 48–49

co-optation: in politics, 84, 85; of social movements, 10

Coordinadora Democrática, 25, 156, 159, 162, 172, 191, 198, 200; ancianos and, 167–68; and campaign for local mayor, 162–63; coalition politics in, 166–83; communitywide assembly, 201; corruption and, 168; discourse of democracy and, 162; ecological groups and, 191, 201, 203, 204, 206; engaged in struggle for existence of pueblo, 186; gossip and, 167, 175; groups that became united with, 166–67; holistic health center established by, 168; indigenous people and, 206; injunction against ICA, 204; and land redistribution, 164–66; Marcos and, 199; mayoral election of 1988 and, 163–64, 166–67 (*see also* Salinas de Gortari); meetings of, 168–70, 176; members, 168–69, 196; politics, 164; strategic alliances, 173–74; Tepoztecans who

received land from, 163–64; UNCED and, 204, 209; women in, 170–71, 180–81; women's committee, 194; women's groups and, 167–68, 180; youth committee, 193–94

Coronil, Fernando, 184

Corriente Democrática (Democratic Current), 177

corruption, 53–54, 70, 71–72; Agrarian Reform Law and, 77, 133; Comité para la Defensa de Tierra and, 69, 71, 90, 117, 125; communal land and, 75; in community, 88; "community" and, 126; Coordinadora and, 168; gossip about, 72, 93, 94, 137–38, 142, 156, 157; hierarchy and, 213; local *vs.* higher-level, 72, 74; in Oficina de Bienes Comunales, 192; peripheral members and, 127; Rubino and, 131; Secretaría de la Reforma Agraria and, 71; unity and, 142, 223; as universal, 92. *See also* Consejos de Vigilancia; mistrust

corrupt politicians and peripheral members of groups, 127, 147, 154

Cortés, Martin, 38, 42

courage. *See* machismo

courts, 38

crate-making industry, 198

Cristóbal, Father. *See* García, Father Cristóbal

critical distance toward political life, 227

Crown, 38, 244n. 3; Zorita's correspondence with, 57–59

Cuernavaca, 114–15, 122

cultural difference, 35–39

cultural hybridization, 42. *See also* racial mixing

cultural identity, 110. *See also* ethnic identity; identity

cultural relativism, 40

death and political struggle, 136–37

debtors movement, 13

deconstruction and deconstructionists, 210, 211
deforestation, 205
"de-Indianization," 64
Delgación Agraria (Agrarian Delegation), 72, 73
democracy, 103; deliberative, 169, 171, 249n. 3; discourses of, 162, 176, 180, 182–85, 226–27; electoral, 161, 174–75, 177, 181, 182 (*see also* electoral participation); extension of notion of, 65; history of, 183–84; new ethos of, 168; notions of, 162, 182; power relations and, 183–85; PRI and, 176–77; requirements for the spirit of, 183; solving problems using, 169; witchcraft compared with, 184–85
demographics, 61
deterritorialization, 189
development committee, 196–97
development plans/projects, 25, 115, 143, 203. *See also* Colonia Manantial; housing development; Rubino; sustainable development; train line project
Díaz, Porfirio, 105
dichotomies, 24
difference: fracturing of, 38–39; protection of, 60; value and legitimacy of, 38–40
district seat, 155
diversity, 34, 35, 62, 64, 65. *See also* ethnic diversity
domination of space, 188–89, 250n. 4

earthquakes, 7
Echeverría, Luis, 8
ecological group and movement, 199–204
economic crises, 13; and political process, 17–18; of 1980s, 6–9, 17
economic development, 17
Edelman, Marc, 219, 243n. 2
education, 54, 109
egoism, 63
Ejército Zapatista de Liberación Nacional

(EZLN, Zapatista Army of National Liberation), 8
ejidal land, 52, 60–61; plans to construct airport terminal on, 232–33
ejidal resources, 70
ejidatarios, 73–75, 145, 232
ejido commissioners, 81, 82, 108, 142
ejido land, 52, 56, 69, 145
ejidos, 70, 71
elders. *See ancianos*
electoral participation, 9, 10. *See also* democracy, electoral
elites, 247nn. 3–5
emigration, 190–91. *See also* migration
empowerment, 91
Enlightenment, 244–45n. 3
environment, 204–5; damage to, 233; impacts of humans on, 100. *See also* nature
environmentalism and environmentalists, 203–8, 214, 216. *See also* ecological group
environmental movement, global, 213–15
essentialism, 210, 224, 229, 230
ethical behavior, traditionalist: wealth *vs.* poverty and, 104–5
ethnic diversity, 34–39
ethnic identity, 110, 111, 191
ethnicity as mode of definition, 249n. 2
ethnography, 5–6
evil eye (*mal de ojo*), 83
exchange, 129–30, 141; defined, 129
Exit, Voice, and Loyalty (Hirschman), 243n. 4
"exits," 243n. 4

families, reproductive role of, 74
family relations, 74, 76, 108
Favret, Jeanne, 221–23
Favret-Saada, Jean, 184–85
fear, 135–36. *See also* mistrust
fictive kin (*compadrazgo*), 83
Fisher, William H., 207–8
Five Hundred Years of Resistance, 15, 16

habitus, 78, 155; defined, 155
Hamilton, Nora, 79
Harvey, David, 189, 190, 249n. 4
hegemony, 235
Hirschman, Albert, 243n. 4
historians, 223
historicity defined, 3
homogeneity, national political, 34
homology defined, 3
households, survey of, 61
housing development: for outsiders, 81–
    82, 113–14. *See also* development
    plans/projects
Huejutla, 247n. 4

ICA (engineering company), 201, 204
identity, 155, 219, 224, 244n. 1; decon-
    struction of the categories of, 211; play
    of, 229–30; political passion and the
    politics of, 228–31; and the state, 97.
    See also ethnic identity; group identity;
    political identity
imaginary, local, 203
imagination, constraints on, 87
imagining the world, 190
immigration. *See* emigration
inalienable possessions, 97–98; who
    should be guardian of, 148–49
Indian identity, 245n. 4
Indianization of Mexico, 40. *See also* racial
    mixing
Indian lands threatened by liberal land
    reform, 39
Indians, 36–37, 53, 59, 63; nationalism
    and, 39–40
indigenismo, 40
indigenous communities as civil societies,
    59
indigenous identity: meanings of, 249n. 3;
    resurgence of, 208–12. *See also* ethnic
    identity; identity
indigenous land holdings, 59
indigenous populations, 11, 206–8; mobi-
    lization of, 8; movement to assimilate,

45–46; poverty and isolation of, 46–
    47; transformation in 1920s and 1930s,
    46–47; in 1940s, 47–48
indigenous roots, Tepoztecan rediscovery
    of, 10–16
indio, 47, 210
individualism, 53, 65, 93
intercommunity marriages, 144
intermarriage. *See* racial mixing
International Monetary Fund (IMF), 1, 6
Internet, 220
irony, 119–24, 227–28; ambiguity of,
    119–20; of political rhetoric, 122–23;
    political uses of, 119
Isabella, Maestra, 149

Jakubowska, Longina, xiii
"Jorge" ("Maestro"), 18–20, 24, 86–87;
    don Abram and, 193; ACNR and, 163;
    after release from prison, 239; bound-
    ary disputes and, 146; brothers, 87;
    campaign for lower bus fares, 159, 167,
    168, 193; Colonia Manantial and, 140;
    and the committee, 18–20, 122–23,
    146; Consejo de Vigilancia organized
    by, 112; Coordinadora and, 172, 173,
    201; corruption gossip, collective man-
    agement of land, and, 137–38; defense
    of communal land, 115, 120; on democ-
    racy, 160; detained and beaten by Judi-
    cial Police, 87; election of 1988 and,
    175; on government, 187; imprisoned,
    233; moves to distribute land, 153;
    Oficina de Bienes Comunales and, 115,
    141; don Pedro and, 120–21; risking
    his life, 135; Rolando and, 135; Rubino
    and, 131–33; selling communal land to
    outsiders, 152; speech, 160; on struggle
    for existence of pueblo, 186; train line
    project and, 191, 201, 202
Juana, doña, 150, 152–53
Juchitán, Oaxaca, 244n. 5
Julio (Colonia Manantial representative),
    138–39, 141

"Mexican stability," 78
Mexico City, 7, 143
México profundo (Batalla), 64
midwives, 31
migration, 107; to United States, 107, 242. *See also* emigration
Miguel, don (commissioner of Bienes Comunales), 152
millenarian movements, nativist, 36
minimum wage, 83
missionaries, 37, 60
mistrust, 68, 89, 90, 94, 221; connections and, 153–54; between district seat and surrounding communities, 143–44; *gente de confianza* and, 95; of opposition movements, 217–18; pervasiveness and seductiveness of, 228; political, 217–18; of politics, commitment to community and, 92; of state and community, 213; Tepoztlán as racked by, 95. *See also* fear
"mixing of blood." *See* racial mixing
modernity, 45, 47, 107
modernization, 120, 181; tradition *vs.* forces of, 102
money *vs.* land, ambition for, 54
monitoring. *See* Consejos de Vigilancia
Morales, Alejandro, 238
morality, traditionalist: wealth *vs.* poverty and, 104–5
moral values, 110
Morelos, 35, 57; as birthplace of agrarian struggle, 33; communal *vs.* private property in, 50, 54; land grants in, 33; Mexican revolution in, 2–3; politics, 25; Solaridad program, 195–97; and Zapata's call for liberty and revolution, 105; Zapatista revolution in, 51, 55, 62
Moses, Robert, 221
Mouffe, Chantal, 103, 183, 226
Mugica, Francisco, 56
Mujeres Tepoztecanas (Tepoztecan Women), 18, 75, 76, 149–53; Coordinadora and, 162–63, 194; and female

power, 181; leaders, 194; peripheral members, 153
multiculturalism, 249n. 2
Muñoz, Teresa, 204–6, 211–13
murders over land conflicts, 136–37

Nader, Laura, xii, 4, 18, 182
Nahuatl culture and civilization, 35, 210
narrative forms, 22
Nash, June C., 249n. 3
nationalism, 33–35; colonialism and, 59–60; communal land in the discourse of, 49–57; creation of a homogenous, 40–42; Gamio on, 40–45; Indians and, 39–40; Mexican history and, 45; reconstruction of, 37; revolutionary, 93, 214
nationalistic discourses to transform Indian's position, 63
nationalist identities, 34. *See also* identity
nationhood, 45, 46
nativist millenarian movements, 36
"natural" law, 60
"natural," the, 42
nature: interdependence between humans and, 100. *See also* environment
Navarro, Luis T., 56
need: discourse of, 150–52; notion of, 164–67
Nelson, Diane, 23–24, 34, 111, 112, 208, 219–20
neoliberal economic policies, shift to, 160, 161, 181, 198, 235
neoliberal economy, 176
neoliberalism, 30, 33, 50, 198
nerves (*nervios*), 209
New Spain, colonial project in, 244–45n. 3
nomadic populations, 36
nongovernmental organizations (NGOs), 178, 198–99. *See also under* United Nations Conference on Environment and Development
norteño identity, 36

Index / 271

North American Free Trade Agreement (NAFTA), 48–49

objectification, 99–100
Oficina de Bienes Comunales (Office of Communal Resources), 84, 111–13, 115–17, 128–29, 133; commissioners, 192–93; gossip and, 137, 142, 155–56; peripheral members, 128, 138, 155–56; relations among committee and organizational members, 154
O'Malley, Ilene, 109
opposition movements, 1–2, 87
organizations: expressing opposition while remaining in ("voice"), 243n. 4; leaving ("exits"), 243n. 4
outsiders, 105, 192; communal land given to, 31, 53, 113–14; and discourse of sustainable development, 203, 204. See also foreigners; Rubino

Padilla, Gerardo Demesa, xi
Palacio, Antonio Riva, 195–97
paracaidistas (parachuters), 75
Parnell, Philip, 202
Partido Auténtico de la Revolución Mexicana (PARM, Authentic Party of the Mexican Revolution), 177
Partido Revolucionario Institucional (PRI, Institutional Revolutionary Party), 1, 7, 8, 12, 24, 48, 78, 79, 81, 85–87; campaign to regain power in Tepoztlán, 191; candidate for mayor, 162–63; control of, 94; co-optation of leaders, 141; co-optation strategy, 213; Coordinadora and, 172, 173; corporatist structures, 9; discourse of democracy, 176–77; elections and, 161, 163, 173–78; feigned support for, 172, 174; golf course project and, 234–35; gossip and, 92–93; mass mobilizations and, 140, 141; modernization and, 176; opposition parties and, 91, 94, 122, 161, 177, 191, 198; participatory de-

mocracy combined with political patronage under, 141; popular movements challenging loyalty to, 10; power in Mexico, 173; power struggle between políticos and technocrats, 160–61; presidential campaign of 1988 and, 172–77; relations between leaders and followers, 141; Salinas de Gortari and, 194; "secret ballot," 174–75; Solidaridad and, 195. See also charismo
Paz, Octavio, 46
peasant communities, 69, 70; in Morelos, 63
peasants, 62, 74, 79, 84–85, 108; rights, 88, 94. See also campesinos; Confederación Nacional Campesina
Pedro, don, 108–9, 120–21, 123, 152; injury and withdrawal from the committee, 109–10; Rolando and, 134–35; son of, 199; support for Cárdenas, 175
peripheral members of groups, 127, 156–57; colonias and, 128; compared with residents of surrounding communities, 146–48; corrupt politicians and, 127, 147, 154; create a space between resistance and political engagement, 157–58; defined, 128; keeping state power at bay, 157–58; vs. leaders, 125–27; loose connections and, 156; participation of, as exchange, 129–30; silence and holding back, 130, 133, 156, 183 (see also silence); unity and, 130. See also under Comité para la Defensa de Tierra
periphery of social and political movements, 224
Plan de Ayala, 55
political actors, 218
political identity, 165; as form of bricolage, 230–31. See also identity
political imagination, 68–69
political life: critical distance toward, 227
political organizations, 8
political participation, 7, 96, 127, 218,

228; boundary disputes and, 147; loose quality of, 158; politics of loose connections as emergent style of, 5; popular movements and, 13. *See also* electoral participation

political parties, coalitions with, 10

politicians. *See políticos*

políticos, 1, 7, 89, 127, 128, 160–61, 246n. 3; gossip and, 91–93; meanings, 246n. 3

politics: Tepoztecans' approach to, 141; violations of hegemonic understandings of, 151–52

politics of loose connections, 2–6, 158, 212, 228; antiglobalization and, 220; boundary disputes and, 148; capitalism, globalization, and, 242; communal passions and, 125–59; community as providing window on, 16; as compromise between desires for unity and political engagement, 125; defined, 2; *vs.* demand for unity, 142; democracy and, 162; emergence of, 66–68, 130, 156, 157; exchange and, 129, 130; as founded on suspicion and wariness, 221; *gente de confianza* and, 91, 95; nature of, 228; as persisting in face of apparent unity, 239; pervasiveness of, 219; power of state to shape, 91; roots of, 94; silence/withholding as shaping, 133; state power, absence of unity, and, 148; strategic utility of, 231; as style of political participation, 4; and use of competing political leaders, 153; and ways that techniques of state power affect communities, 158

"Poner la aspine encima," 248n. 1

poor (*pobre*): conflicts between rich and, 101–6, 110, 114; inequalities between rich and, 247nn. 3–5; mass organizing of the, 8–10. *See also* poverty

popular movements, 1, 10; cultural impacts, 13–14; Mexican state and, 6–15. *See also* politics of loose connections

possessions. *See* inalienable possessions

poststructuralism, 222

poverty, 110, 179, 198; indicators of, and "tradition," 102. *See also* poor

power: technologies of, 77–95. *See also* abuse of power

power relations, 183–87, 202–3

PRD, 16

president: relationship between pueblo and, 186–87; role and power of, 70–71

presidential resolution of 1929, 32–33

Programa Nacional de Solidaridad (National Solidarity Program), 11–12, 160, 194–98

property: as needing to be continuously cultivated/worked, 57, 107. *See also* land

proprietarios (private-property holders), 55

protest groups, 243n. 1

protest(s), 5, 220; new forms of, 243n. 1

pseudonyms, 23, 24

public/private distinction, 112

Quincentennial, 15, 16

Quinientos años de resistenca indígena, 209

Quintana Roo, Maya of, 44

race relations, 221

Rachel, Maestra, 149, 150, 152

racial categories, 41

racial mixing, 35–43, 46

radicalism, 5, 8

railway line. *See* train line project

rape, 42, 46

Reagan, Ronald, 191

reciprocity, 99–102, 130. *See also* exchange

Redfield, Robert, 95, 125

reformist perspectives, 8

regional identities, 244n. 1. *See also* identity

regionalism, 244n. 1

regions of refuge, 47–48

religion, 37, 83, 84, 167, 171, 172, 209. *See also* liberation theology

religious conquest of Tepoztlán, 207–8

taxation of land, 235
tax demands on Indians, 59
taxonomic states, 209
Taylor, William, 244n. 3
tea plantations, 112
Tenochtitlán, 35
Tepoztlán (district seat), 16, 151; history
    of, 143; identity and, 144; tension
    between other communities and, over
    economic benefits, 143–48
Tepoztlán (Rosas), 234
tequitatos, 53
time-space compression, 190
Tlatelolco, massacre at, 7–8
Tomás, don (commissioner), 125, 131,
    132, 135, 138, 141–42, 152, 188; and
    corruption, 168–69
tontos, 157
Torgovnick, Marianna, 207
Torres, Gabriel, 13
tourist center project, 232–35
tradition: *vs.* forces of "modernization,"
    102; market logic and value of, 100
traditionalist aesthetic, 97, 114, 124;
    ancianos, respect, and, 182; as "collec-
    tive fantasy," 97; crafting of, 97–112;
    role of women in, 103, 110–12. *See
    also* "love for the land"
traditionalists, 110, 241–42
train line project, 186, 191, 196–97, 201–
    3; diverted, 213–14
travel, 190
Triple Alliance, 35
trouble, making, ix
trust. *See* fear; mistrust

unions, 79
United Nations, 191
United Nations Conference on Environ-
    ment and Development (UNCED),
    204, 207–9; NGO Strategy Meeting,
    204–7, 211–12, 215
unity, 11, 45, 49, 64, 234; calls for, 224–27;
    corruption and, 142, 223; democracy

and, 162; desire for, 3, 95, 96, 218–20,
    225, 227; *vs.* disunity, narratives of, 234,
    235; failure of, 225, 234–39; gossip, mis-
    trust, and, 228; impossibility of believ-
    ing in, 95, 228; ironic performances of,
    227; lack of, within social movements,
    24; local, 203; and mistrust in social
    movements, 221; peripheral members
    and, 130; promise of, 228; in revo-
    lutionary ideology, 94; scholars of social
    movements and, 223–24; state power
    and absence of, 148; value of, 224;
    around values, 168. *See also* community
    unity; politics of loose connections
universalism/universality, 34, 35, 37, 40
universal need, discourse of, 150–52

Vasconcelos, José, 46
Vecinos de Tepoztlán (Neighbors of
    Tepoztlán), 191, 199
Vega Domínguez, Jorge de la, 177
Velasco, Luis de, 51–52
Vélez-Ibañez, C. G., 140
vigilance. *See* Consejos de Vigilancia
violence over land conflicts, 135–37
"voice," 243n. 4

Warman, Arturo, 2–3
Warren, Kay, 208, 210
watchdog committees. *See* Consejos de
    Vigilancia
water supply and water shortages, 241
wealth, 110; classification scheme to mea-
    sure, 247n. 3; *vs.* poverty, 103–5, 110.
    See also outsiders; poor
We Come to Object (Warman), 3
Weiner, Annette B., 129, 130, 228
Weismantel, Mary, x
Western civilization, 64
Weston, Kath, 230
"whitening," 36
Wolf, Eric, 36–37
women, 225; communal land and, 75, 149;
    with dependent children, 74; in grass-

About the Author

JoAnn Martin is professor of anthropology at Earlham College. Her research and writing interests include contemporary social thought, gender/sexuality, and representations of history. Her publications include: *Paths to Domination, Resistance, and Terror* (coeditor with Carolyn Nordstrom, 1992); "Contesting Authenticity: Battles over Representation of History in Morelos, Mexico" (*Ethnohistory* 40, no. 3 [1993]); "The Chasm of the Political in Postmodern Theory" (with Cynthia Kaufman, *Rethinking Marxism* 7, no. 4 [1994]); and "The Antagonisms of Class and Community in Women's Politics in Morelos, Mexico," in *Women of the Mexican Countryside, 1850–1990*, edited by Heather Fowler-Salamini and Mary Kay Vaughan (University of Arizona Press, 1994). She is currently working on the constitution of a revolutionary subject in ethnographic texts through the invocation of ephemeral forms such as ghosts and spirits.